Got it!

2nd edition

Got it!

2 Student Book & Workbook

Philippa Bowen
Denis Delaney
Diana Pye

OXFORD
UNIVERSITY PRESS

Contents

Simple present / Present progressive *be*: Simple past Simple past	*some* / *any* with countable / uncountable nouns *a lot of* / *much* / *many* / *a little* / *a few* Present progressive for future	*How long ...? + take* Comparative adjectives Superlative adjectives

Vocabulary

Musical genres and instruments

1 Reorder the letters and write the instruments.

u l t e f ___flute___

1 o p a n i _____

2 d o r c e r r e _____

3 h a s e o n x o p _____

4 r i t a u g _____

5 m e r t u p t _____

6 s d u r m _____

2 🔊 1.02 **Listen and put the types of music in the correct order.**

1 reggae	_a_	4 classical	___
2 heavy metal	___	5 rock	___
3 hip-hop	___	6 pop	___

3 And you? What is your favorite type of music? Who is your favorite singer / band?

Physical descriptions

4 Complete the descriptions of the two friends.

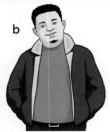

a

b

> beard   black   blue   brown   curly   freckles
> overweight   ~~short~~   shoulder-length
> ~~slim~~   tall   wavy

a She's ___short___ and ___slim___. She has
  ¹_____, ²_____, blond hair,
  and ³_____ eyes. She has ⁴_____ on
  her nose.

b He's ⁵_____ and a little ⁶_____.
  He has short, ⁷_____, ⁸_____ hair, and
  ⁹_____ eyes. He has a ¹⁰_____.

5 And you? Write a short description of yourself and one person in your family.

I'm tall and ...
My brother is short and ...

The weather

6 Match the words with the symbols.

> cloudy   freezing   raining
> ~~snowing~~   sunny   windy

It's ___snowing___.

1

It's _____.

2

It's _____.

3

It's _____.

4

It's _____.

5

It's _____.

7 And you? What is the weather like today? What was it like yesterday?

Movies

8 Match the movies with the definitions.

action movie ___   fantasy movie ___   love story ___

comedy ___   horror movie ___   cartoon _1_

1 a movie with animated characters
2 a very frightening movie with monsters
3 a funny movie
4 a movie about an imaginary world
5 a movie about relationships and romance
6 a movie with a lot of fast and exciting events

9 And you? What's your favorite type of movie? Why?

Food and drink

10 Complete the food and drink words.

<u>c</u> <u>a</u> r r <u>o</u> t s   7 s __ d __
1 c h __ __ s __   8 b __ n __ n __
2 w __ t __ r   9 c h __ c __ l __ t __
3 y __ g __ r t   10 __ p p l __
4 c h __ c k __ n   11 m __ l k
5 h __ m   12 b r __ __ d
6 p __ t __ t __ __ s   13 t __ m __ t __ __ s

11 **And you?** What's your favorite food? What food don't you like?

Transportation

12 Look at the pictures and complete the puzzle. What is the mystery form of transportation?

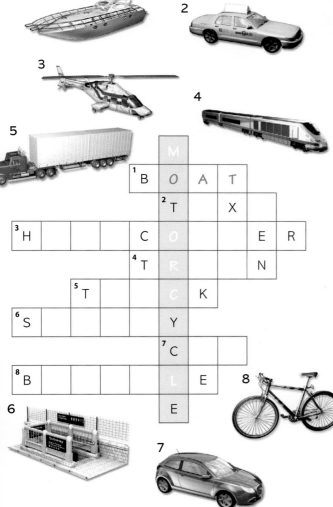

1

2

3

4

5

6

7

8

Mystery word: _____

13 **And you?** What forms of transportation do you often / never use?

Geography

14 Match words 1–6 with the geographical features a–f.

1 desert   <u>d</u>   4 island   ___
2 lake   ___   5 volcano   ___
3 mountain   ___   6 river   ___

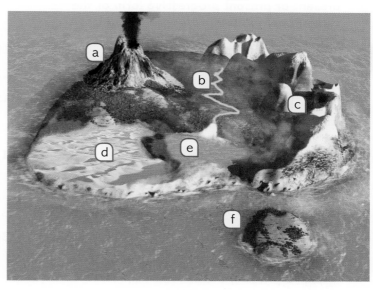

15 **And you?** Can you name an example for each geographical feature?

Feelings and emotions

16 Look at the faces. Choose the correct answers.

(excited) / fed up   1   angry / bored

2   happy / sad   3   embarrassed / annoyed

4   confident / frightened   5   nervous / proud

17 **And you?** How do you feel today?

Grammar

Simple present / Present progressive

1 Complete the sentences with the simple present or present progressive form of the verbs in parentheses.

a Lucas usually _goes_____ (go) to school on Tuesday morning, but today his class ¹_____ (visit) a museum. They ²_____ (study) Inca culture in history this semester, and they ³_____ (look) at ancient Inca objects at the moment.

b Sarah and Lily ⁴_____ (go) to the movies every Saturday. They usually ⁵_____ (watch) action movies, but today they ⁶_____ (watch) a cartoon.

c **A** ⁷_____ (you / play) the guitar?
B No, I don't. But I ⁸_____ (have) piano lessons twice a week.
A ⁹_____ (like) classical music?
B No, I don't. I ¹⁰_____ (prefer) rock music.

d **A** ¹¹_____ (Juan / play) any sports on the weekend?
B Yes, he does. He often ¹²_____ (play) soccer.
A ¹³_____ (he / play) today?
B No, he isn't. It ¹⁴_____ (rain). He ¹⁵_____ (watch) TV at the moment.

2 Write answers to the questions that are true for you.

1 How do you usually travel to school?
2 How often do you go to the movies?
3 Do you like action movies?
4 What sports do you play every week?
5 Are you playing sports now?
6 What are you doing?

be: Simple past

3 Oscar Wide is a sports journalist. Write questions about his day yesterday. Then look at his schedule and answer the questions.

8 a.m.	Breakfast interview with Victoria Azarenka at the Elite Café in New York
10:30 a.m.	JFK Airport – New York
11:30 a.m.	Airplane to New Orleans
1:30 p.m.	Lunch with Terri Ray of *Sports World* (the Stella restaurant)
4 p.m.	Visit Superdome Stadium (American football) with Terri
6 p.m.	Monteleone Hotel
8:30 p.m.	New Orleans Saints vs. Atlanta Falcons football game – Superdome, New Orleans

Oscar / be / in New Orleans / at 8 a.m. yesterday?
Was Oscar in New Orleans at 8 a.m. yesterday?
No, he wasn't. He was in New York.

1 Who / be / Oscar with / at 8 a.m.?
_____
_____

2 Where / be / they?
_____
_____

3 What time / be / Oscar at the airport?
_____
_____

4 Where / be / Oscar and Terri Ray / at 1:30 p.m.?
_____
_____

5 They / be / in the restaurant / at 4:15 p.m.?
_____
_____
_____

6 Where / be / the Saints vs. Falcons game?
_____
_____

Simple past

4 **Complete the text with the affirmative or negative simple past form of the verbs in parentheses.**

A day in my life

Sandra Carroll – Actress, currently performing in *The Lion King*, The Minskoff Theatre, New York

I <u>didn't get up</u> (not get up) late yesterday, for a change. I ¹_____ (get up) at about 9 a.m. After breakfast, I ²_____ (write) e-mails and then I ³_____ (play) my guitar. At lunchtime, I ⁴_____ (meet) my friend, Kate. It was a lovely day, so we ⁵_____ (not eat) lunch in a café. We ⁶_____ (buy) some sandwiches and we ⁷_____ (eat) them in Central Park. After lunch, I ⁸_____ (go) shopping in Greenwich Village. After that, I ⁹_____ (walk) to the theater and I ¹⁰_____ (start) work at 5 p.m. After the show, I ¹¹_____ (not have) dinner with the other actors. I was really tired, so I ¹²_____ (not walk) home; I ¹³_____ (take) a taxi, and then I ¹⁴_____ (watch) my favorite TV show in bed.

5 **Write questions about Sandra using the simple past. Then answer the questions.**

What time / Sandra get up / yesterday?
<u>What time did Sandra get up yesterday?</u>
<u>She got up at about 9 a.m.</u>

1 What / she do / after breakfast?
_____
_____

2 Who / she meet / at lunchtime?
_____
_____

3 What / they buy for lunch?
_____
_____

4 Where / they have lunch?
_____
_____

5 Where / she go shopping?
_____
_____

6 What time / Sandra start work?
_____
_____

7 How / she get home last night?
_____
_____
_____

6 **Complete the text with the simple past form of the verbs in the box.**

appear   become   not become   ~~come~~
go   not have   make   not speak   start

Alfred Hitchcock

Alfred Hitchcock was a great English movie director. He <u>came</u> from London and he ¹_____ making movies in England in the 1920s and 30s. His early movies ²_____ any color – they were black and white. It was "The Silent Era" of movie history and actors ³_____. Hitchcock ⁴_____ to the U.S. in 1939, and he lived there until his death in 1980, but he ⁵_____ a U.S. citizen until 1955. In Hollywood, he ⁶_____ one of the most famous directors of the 20th century and he ⁷_____ 27 movies there, including *Psycho* and *The Birds*. Hitchcock is also well known because he ⁸_____ for a few seconds in most of his movies.

7 **Read the answers. Complete the questions.**

When <u>did Alfred Hitchcock make his first movies</u>?
Alfred Hitchcock made his first movies in the 1920s and 30s.

1 Where _____?
He came from London.

2 When _____?
He went to the U.S. in 1939.

3 When _____?
He became a U.S. citizen in 1955.

4 How many movies _____?
He made 27 movies in Hollywood.

some / any with countable / uncountable nouns

8 **What food and drink is there in the cart? Check (✓) or cross (✗) the food items, then write a sentence about each item.**

| ✗ | chicken | There isn't any chicken. |
| ✓ | carrots | There are some carrots. |

1 ☐ yogurt _____
2 ☐ eggs _____
3 ☐ cheese _____
4 ☐ orange juice _____
5 ☐ tomatoes _____
6 ☐ bread _____

9 **Now write questions and short answers about the food and drink in the cart.**

milk?
"Is there any milk?" "Yes, there is."

1 cookies?
_____

2 eggs?
_____

3 water?
_____

4 potatoes?
_____

5 ham?
_____

6 tomatoes
_____

a lot of / much / many / a little / a few

10 **Choose the correct answers.**

There isn't **many** / **much** sugar in this coffee.
1 These vegetables need **a few** / **a little** salt.
2 **How much** / **How many** people are here?
3 I got **a lot of** / **many** text messages yesterday!
4 My brother spent **a little** / **a few** weeks in Miami last year.
5 Al didn't answer **much** / **many** of the questions.
6 **How much** / **How many** rain was there yesterday?

11 **Choose the correct answers.**

Hi, Jimmy,

How are you? I'm on vacation, but I don't have **much** / **many** free time. I spend ¹**much** / **a lot of** time on the beach. I often go surfing with ²**a few** / **a little** friends. We have ³**a lot of** / **many** beach barbecues. The weather is usually good, but we had ⁴**a few** / **a little** rain yesterday. I don't watch ⁵**much** / **many** TV because there aren't ⁶**a lot of** / **many** good shows on right now. How ⁷**much** / **many** TV do you watch? There are ⁸**a few** / **a little** good concerts. Bruno Mars is coming in August. I'm going with ⁹**a little** / **a few** friends from school. Are there ¹⁰**many** / **much** concerts in your town this summer?

Laura

Present progressive for future

12 **Write questions with the present progressive. Then answer the questions.**

The Allsorts — European Tour

October 25th	London, U.K. @ The O2 Stadium
October 26th	Manchester, U.K. @ The Arena
October 28th	Paris, France @ Palais Omnisports
November 1st	Madrid, Spain @ Palacio Vistalegre
November 2nd	Lisbon, Portugal @ MEO Arena

Where / the tour / start?
Where is the tour starting?
It's starting in London.

1 When / The Allsorts / play / in France?
_____

2 How many / concerts / they / do / in the U.K.?
_____

3 Where / they / play / in Manchester?
_____

4 Where / they / go / after Spain?
_____

5 Where / the tour / finish?
_____

6 How many cities / they / visit / in Europe?
_____

How long ...? + take

13 Write questions. Then answer the questions.

How long / fly from New York City to Los Angeles? (6 hours)

How long does it take to fly from New York City to Los Angeles?

It takes 6 hours.

1 How long / drive from Los Angeles to San Francisco? (6 hours 30 minutes)

2 How long / travel by airplane from Los Angeles to Mexico City? (3 hours 35 minutes)

3 How long / go from Los Angeles to Washington, D.C. by bus? (2 days)

4 How long / travel by train from New York City to Washington, D.C.? (3 hours)

5 How long / travel by taxi from JFK Airport to Manhattan? (30 minutes)

Comparative adjectives

14 Complete the sentences with the comparative form of the adjectives in parentheses.

Florida is _hotter_ (hot) than Chicago.

1 The planet Mars is _____ (small) than the Earth.

2 The weather today is _____ (good) than yesterday.

3 Traveling by train is _____ (relaxing) than traveling by car.

4 Biology is _____ (easy) than physics.

5 Phone calls are _____ (expensive) than text messages.

6 Los Angeles is _____ (far) from New York City than Toronto.

7 Is New York City _____ (big) than Washington, D.C.?

Superlative adjectives

15 Complete the sentences with the superlative form of the adjectives. Then write true answers.

Who is the _youngest_ (young) person in your family?

My sister. She's 6 years old.

1 What is _____ (difficult) subject for you at school?

2 What is _____ (easy) subject for you at school?

3 Who is _____ (good) singer in your country?

4 What was _____ (bad) movie you saw last year?

5 What is _____ (famous) tourist attraction in your country?

6 What is _____ (pretty) area of your town?

7 Who is _____ (tall) person in your family?

8 What is _____ (interesting) show on TV?

16 Complete the quiz with the comparative or superlative form of the adjectives in parentheses. Are the statements true (T) or false (F)? Write a check mark (✓).

General Knowledge Quiz

T F

1 The Earth is _the smallest_ (small) planet in the solar system. ☐ ☐

2 Blue whales are _____ (heavy) than elephants. ☐ ☐

3 Molecules are _____ (big) than atoms. ☐ ☐

4 Usain Bolt is _____ (fast) person in the world. ☐ ☐

5 Australia is _____ (large) island in the world. ☐ ☐

6 Tokyo in Japan is _____ (populated) than Sao Paulo in Brazil. ☐ ☐

7 The River Nile is _____ (long) river in the world. ☐ ☐

8 The Atacama Desert in Africa is _____ (dry) place in the world. ☐ ☐

You must have a ticket

URBAN *Adventures*

HOME   **HOW IT WORKS**   TESTIMONIALS   **TICKET INFORMATION**

Urban Adventures – the coolest way to see a city

Forget those boring sightseeing tours! Get out and have fun!

Urban Adventure games are interactive city tours with a cell phone for your guide. You can play alone, or compete against other teams.

There are games for everyone! Tourists have fun as they visit the main attractions. Local people discover new places and learn fun facts about their hometown. There are games for families and school groups, and special games for birthday parties!

Urban Adventures has something for everyone!

How it works

You need comfortable shoes and a cell phone with a camera. You don't need a map because you receive text messages with directions on your cell phone. Go to the starting point and activate your phone. Then follow the instructions. You must complete challenges. These challenges ask you to find things, solve puzzles, or take crazy pictures. You also receive interesting facts about the places you visit. Games take two to three hours.

Rules

Can anyone play the games? Yes, but there are a few simple rules:

1 You must buy your tickets on our website.
2 Everyone in a group must have a ticket.
3 Children under 13 must be with an adult.
4 You mustn't use a car or a motorcycle.
5 You mustn't enter private buildings.

TESTIMONIALS

"I did the Historic Philadelphia tour with my class. We went everywhere in the Old City, and we visited an old church. Everyone took pictures of the Rocky Statue!"

Stella, 17

"We did a special Sweet Tooth tour in SoHo, New York City for my birthday. Everyone ate lots of cake, cookies, and ice cream, but nobody felt sick!"

Tom, 16

"We went on the Capital tour when we were on vacation in Washington, D.C. The CIA Museum and Congress Library were awesome."

Sofia, 17

Check it out!

Find these words and check their meaning.

guide
hometown
challenges
puzzles

1 🔊 1.03 **Read and listen** Imagine you are playing an Urban Adventure game. Match the cell phones with the cities.

UA: Walk down the street opposite the sports center. Why is this neighborhood called SoHo?

You: It's called SoHo because it's "SOuth of HOuston (Street)."

New York City

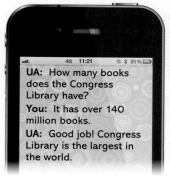

UA: How many books does the Congress Library have?
You: It has over 140 million books.
UA: Good job! Congress Library is the largest in the world.

1 _____

You: Check me out next to the Rocky Statue – so cool!

2 _____

2 Comprehension **Answer the questions.**

Who is the guide on an Urban Adventure tour?
Your cell phone is the guide.

1 What do you need for an Urban Adventure?
2 How do you know where to go?
3 How long do games take?
4 What did Stella see on the Philadelphia tour?
5 Who had a special birthday adventure?

Language focus

3 Complete the rules with *must* or *mustn't*. Then read the web page article again and check your answers.

Each player __must__ have a ticket.
1 You _____ ride a motorcycle or drive a car.
2 You _____ pay for your tickets online.
3 You _____ go into people's houses.
4 Children _____ be over 13 to play the game alone.

4 Look at the web page article again. Complete the sentences with the missing words.

There are games for *everyone* .
1 Urban Adventures has _____ for _____!
2 Can _____ play Urban Adventures?
3 The Philadelphia tour takes people _____ in the Old City.
4 _____ felt sick on Tom's birthday tour!

5 Focus on you **Write what you *must* and *mustn't* do at school. Use the words in the box.**

| be late for school | do your homework | run in the school corridors |
| send text messages in class | study for tests | talk during tests | use your cell phone in class |

We must do our homework.
We mustn't be late for school.

6 Pairwork **List four things you *must* and *mustn't* do at home. Then tell your partner.**
I must get up at seven o'clock.
I mustn't go to bed late.

Places around town

1 🔊 1.04 **Match the words with the places on the map. Listen and check. Then listen and repeat.**

> bank   bus stop   café   church   hospital   library   park   parking lot
> ~~pharmacy~~   police station   post office   shopping mall
> sports center   supermarket   train station

1 _pharmacy_   5 _____   9 _____   13 _____
2 _____   6 _____   10 _____   14 _____
3 _____   7 _____   11 _____   15 _____
4 _____   8 _____   12 _____

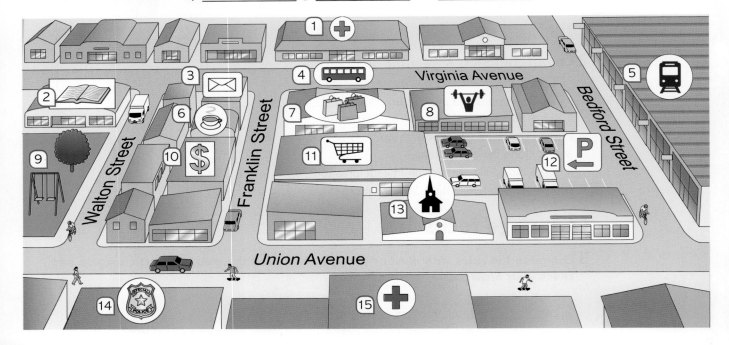

2 🔊 1.05 **Pronunciation** Listen to the pronunciation of the letter *r*. Then listen and repeat.

> church   far   library   park   pharmacy   road   straight   street

3 🔊 1.06 **Look at the map and complete the sentences with the words in the box. Then listen and check.**

> behind   between   in front of   ~~next to~~   opposite

There's a library on Walton Street. It's ___next to___ the park.
1 There's a bus stop on Virginia Avenue. It's _____ the shopping mall.
2 There's a parking lot on Bedford Street. It's _____ the supermarket.
3 There's a church on Union Avenue. It's _____ the hospital.
4 There's a café on Franklin Street. It's _____ the post office and the bank.

4 Pairwork Look at the map in exercise 1. Ask and answer where places are. Use the prepositions in exercise 3 and the places in the box. 🎭

> bank   police station   ~~post office~~   shopping mall   sports center

A Excuse me. Is there a post office near here?
B Yes, there's a post office on Franklin Street. It's next to a café.

(Workbook p.4   (**Extra practice** online

must
Affirmative and negative

> You **must complete** challenges.
> You **mustn't use** a car.

Affirmative	
I / you / he / she / it / we / you / they	must go
Negative	
I / you / he / she / it / we / you / they	mustn't (must not) go

Think!

Choose the correct alternatives.

- We use *must* and *mustn't* to talk about [1]rules / requests.
- *Must* and *mustn't* are [2]the same / different for all persons.
- *Must* and *mustn't* are followed by the [3]infinitive / base form.

Rules p. W2

1 Complete the rules with *must* and *mustn't*.

You __must__ stop.
1 You _____ take photographs.
2 You _____ swim here.
3 You _____ wash your hands.
4 You _____ use your phone here.
5 You _____ eat here.

2 Complete the rules with *must* or *mustn't* and the verbs in the box.

> be ~~come~~ do drink
> use visit wear write

We __must be__ 18 to watch this movie.(✓)
I __mustn't come__ home late. (✗)
1 You _____ this exercise for homework. (✓)
2 The students _____ graffiti on the walls. (✗)

3 Grandma's in the hospital. We _____ her. (✓)
4 You _____ the water in the restroom. (✗)
5 The children _____ calculators in the math test. (✗)
6 It's cold! You _____ a jacket! (✓)

3 Rewrite the orders. Use *must* or *mustn't* and the expressions in the box.

> be quiet   clean your room
> do your homework first   eat a lot of cookies
> ~~go to bed~~   play soccer in class

It's late!
You __must go to bed__!
1 Don't talk, please! This is a library.
You _____!
2 Don't eat all the cookies, Jess!
You _____!
3 Your room is a mess!
You _____!
4 Give me the soccer ball, boys!
You _____!
5 You can't go out now.
You _____!

4 Rewrite the school trip rules. Use *must* or *mustn't*.

School trip to Newport, June 12th
General rules

Be at school at 7:30 a.m.
You must be at school at 7:30 a.m.

1 Bring a sack lunch.
2 Don't stand up on the bus.
3 Don't leave your possessions on the bus.
4 Give your cell phone number to the teachers.
5 Stay with your group in Newport.
6 Don't bring a lot of money.

Finished?

What *must* and *mustn't* you do at your school? Write five sentences.

We must go to all classes.
We mustn't arrive late.

Puzzle p.104

Asking for and giving directions

1 🔊 1.07 **Two people at the train station want to go to different places in the town. Listen and complete the directions with the places in the box. Then listen and check. Listen again and repeat.**

> bank   ~~hospital~~   Pinewood shopping mall   supermarket   sports center

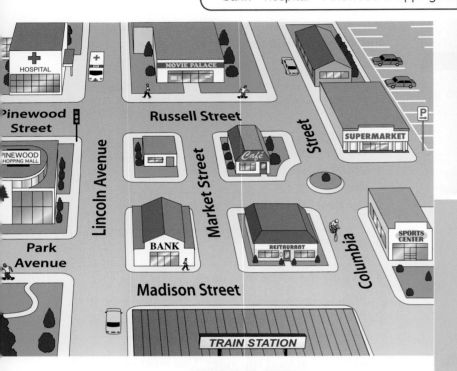

1

A Excuse me. How do I get to the <u>hospital</u>, please?

B Go down Market Street, go past the
1 _____, and then turn left. At the end of the road, turn right, and then take the first turn on the left. The hospital is on the right. It's opposite
2 _____.

A Thanks.

2

A Excuse me. Can you tell me the way to a
3 _____, please?

B Cross Madison Street, go down Market Street, and then take the first turn on the right. Go past the café as far as the traffic circle. Cross Columbia Street and the supermarket is on the left. It's near a
4 _____.

A Thank you.

Learn it, use it!

You ask	You answer
Excuse me. How do I get to …? / Excuse me. Can you tell me the way to …?	Go up / down (Market Street).
	Go past (the bank).
	Go straight as far as (the traffic circle).
	At the end of the road / traffic lights / bank, …
	Turn right / left.
	Take the first / second turn on the right / left.
	Cross the road / street.
	It's on the right / left.
	The … is on the right / left.

Look!

Go up … / Go down …

2 🔊 1.08 **Listen to three people giving directions from Pinewood shopping mall to different places. Follow the directions on the map in exercise 1 and choose the correct destinations.**

the bank / Peppino's restaurant

1 the train station / the parking lot   2 Steps Sports Center / the Movie Palace

3 Pairwork Look at the map in exercise 1 and write two dialogues. Then practice your dialogues. 😊

1 You are at the supermarket. Ask for directions to the park.

2 You are at the sports center. Ask for directions to the hospital.

(Workbook p.6)   **Extra practice** online

Compounds: *some- / any- / no-*

Can **anyone** play the game?
Nobody felt sick!

	Person	Thing	Place
some	**some**one / **some**body	**some**thing	**some**where
any	**any**one / **any**body	**any**thing	**any**where
no	**no** one / **no**body	**no**thing	**no**where

Think!

Read the sentences. Then complete the rules with *affirmative*, *negative*, and *questions*.

The store is **somewhere** on 5th Avenue.
I'm not doing **anything** on Friday.
Is there **anyone** from Canada here?
Nobody wants to play.
We use compounds of:
• *some-* in ¹_____ sentences.
• *any-* in ²_____ sentences and ³_____.
• *no-* with the ⁴_____ form of the verb.

Rules p. W3

1 Choose the correct answers.

There's **anything** / **something** I want to tell you.
1 We don't do **nothing** / **anything** special on Sundays.
2 **Nobody** / **Anybody** in my family speaks Spanish.
3 I can't find my passport **nowhere** / **anywhere**!
4 I met **anyone** / **someone** nice at the party.
5 There's **nothing** / **anything** in the fridge!
6 I don't have **nothing** / **anything** to wear.

2 Complete the sentences with *some-*, *any-*, and *no-* compounds.

I didn't go <u>anywhere</u> yesterday.
1 Are you doing _____ special for your birthday?
2 I think there's _____ at the front door.
3 The test was difficult. _____ got good results.
4 Is _____ using the computer?
5 It's raining! I want to go _____ hot!
6 Mom's cooking _____ nice for dinner.

Compounds: *every-*

Everyone took pictures.
We went **everywhere** in the Old City.

	Person	Thing	Place
every	**every**one / **every**body	**every**thing	**every**where

Think!

Read the sentences. Then check (✓) the correct alternatives.

Is **everything** OK?
We didn't go **everywhere**.
Everyone had a good time.
1 We can use compounds of *every-* in:
   a affirmative sentences ☐
   b negative sentences ☐ c questions ☐
2 We use *everyone* / *everybody* with:
   a singular verbs ☐ b plural verbs ☐

Rules p. W3

3 Complete the sentences with compounds of *every-*.

Jack invited <u>everyone</u> to the party.
1 Are you ready? Do you have _____?
2 _____ in the band plays an instrument.
3 Spring is beautiful. There are flowers _____!
4 Do you know _____ in your school?
5 London was great. We went _____!

4 Game! Find people who did the things below. Write their names in the chart.

Find someone who ...	Name
went somewhere last weekend	_____
did something interesting last night	_____
met someone after school yesterday	_____

A Did you *go anywhere last weekend, Javier?*
B No, I didn't.
A Did you *go anywhere last weekend, Lucia?*
C Yes, I did. I went to the beach.

Finished?

Look at the list in exercise 4. What things did you do? What things didn't you do?

I didn't go anywhere last weekend, but I went to the movies last night.

Puzzle p.104

The Color Run

Sunday, May 19th, Adelaide

Do something different on May 19th this year! Take part in the Color Run in Adelaide, Australia. The Color Run is a 5 km fun run for people of all ages. It's also a way to support important charities. It is a paint race. You start the race in white clothes and you finish it covered in different colors! There are Color Runs in over 200 cities worldwide.

This year, the Adelaide Color Run is supporting Make-A-Wish. This charity makes wishes come true for children with serious illnesses. Everyone can run in the event, so bring your family and friends, too! Make May 19th a date for your diary and be part of something special!

Last year, 10,000 people ran in the race, and everyone has their own story of the day. This is Lucy's story:

"Last year, somebody in our school was in the hospital with a serious illness. Peter's dream was to go on an African safari. We wrote to Make-A-Wish and his wish came true! He visited the Kruger National Park in South Africa. He's well now, and we all wanted to support Make-A-Wish. Thirteen students from our class participated in the Color Run.

Unfortunately, it was cloudy on the day of the run, but nobody cared. Everyone had an awesome time! There were people everywhere in the park and we all had white T-shirts on. The atmosphere was amazing. It isn't really a race, and some people walked from start to finish! Oh, and someone completed the race in a wheelchair. Congratulations, number 1,299!"

Are you interested?

Everyone is welcome to enter, but there are a few simple rules:

1   You must register online before May 3rd.

2   You must pay an entry fee when you register:

    Adults and teenagers: $58, children (under 5): free.

3   You must wear white clothes.

4   You mustn't bring your dog.

Check it out!

Find these words and check their meaning.

wish
come true
illness
nobody cared
entry fee

My reading skills

Completing a chart
Before you read a text for specific information to complete a chart, make sure you know what information you are looking for. Think about the type of answers, for example, are you looking for a place, a date, a price, a number, or a name? Then read the text and find the information. You don't need to read in detail to do this task.

Reading

1 🔊 1.09 **Look at the chart and guess the type of information you need. Then read and listen to the poster and complete the chart.**

Event:	the Color Run	Date:	1
Location:	2	Supports the charity:	3
Entry fee:	4		

2 Read the poster again and answer the questions.

Who can enter the Color Run?
Anyone can enter the Color Run.

1   How many people participated in the Adelaide Color Run last year?
2   What was Peter's wish?
3   How many students from Lucy's class participated in the Color Run?
4   What was the weather like on the day?
5   How did competitor number 1,299 complete the race?
6   Where must you register for the event?
7   Would you like to run in the Color Run? Why? / Why not?

Listening

3 🔊 1.10 **Tom and Jack are participating in the Color Run tomorrow. Listen and choose the correct answers.**

Tom's dad **can / can't** drive him to the park for the Color Run.

1 Jack invites Tom **to go with him and his mom / to meet him at the bus station.**
2 Tom must get the number **14 / 42** bus to Jack's house.
3 It stops at the bus stop in front of the **police station / library.**
4 There's a bus every **30 / 13** minutes.
5 Tom must stay on the bus until it gets to **a shopping mall / an elementary school.**
6 **Tom's house / The school** is on Russell Street.
7 Tom's house is number **80 / 18.**

Speaking

4 Pairwork Imagine that a friend from a different town is coming to your house by bus. Draw a map with the bus stops. Then give directions. Use some of these expressions. 😀

Get the number … bus.

It stops at the bus stop in front of / next to …

Stay on the bus until it gets to …

Get off the bus and turn right / left. Go down … . Take the (first) turn on the right / left. Then …

My house / apartment is on … . It's number … and it's on the right / left. It's near …

Writing

5 Look at the map and complete the message.

Hi, Lucia!

It was great to hear from you. I can't wait to see you! Is everything OK for tomorrow? This is how you get to my house:

Take the number 5 bus. It stops at the bus stop _opposite the_ ¹_____. Get off the bus in ²_____. Turn ³_____ and go down Humbolt Street. Go past a ⁴_____ and then turn ⁵_____. Take the ⁶_____ turn on the ⁷_____. That's Lynne Street. I live at number ⁸____ Lynne Street. It's on the ⁹_____ near a ¹⁰_____.

Don't worry, it's easy! See you at about two o'clock tomorrow. Text me if you have a problem.

Bye for now,

Tina 😊

6 Write an e-mail to a friend giving him / her directions to your house. Include a map. Use the text in exercise 5 as a model.

My Top Five Worst Chores
by Adam Bowen

Nobody enjoys doing chores, but everyone has to clean the house. It's best to start with the worst chores. After that, things can only get better!

1 _c_ _____

This is at the top of my list of chores I hate because dirty dishes never stop! We have a dishwasher, so I don't have to wash the dishes, but I still have to load and unload the dishwasher. I don't have to put away the clean dishes; that's my sister's job. ☺

2 _____

Everyone in my family hates cleaning the bathroom. There are always hairs in the bathtub, especially after my sister with long hair takes a shower. Gross! Why don't self-cleaning bathtubs exist?

3 _____

Taking out the trash is a horrible chore. I hate doing it because the trash bags smell terrible. If there's a hole in the bag, the trash goes everywhere. And then I have to pick it up! Aargh!

4 _____

It's very hard work and it's noisy, too. I have to get the vacuum cleaner out of the cupboard, and push it all over the house. I have to move sofas, chairs, and tables. Why are clean floors so important? We don't have to eat on the floor!

5 _____

I have to do the ironing on Sunday evening to be ready for school on Monday. It's soooo boring! Mom says I mustn't look messy for school! What a joke!

What's your worst chore? Do you have to do a lot of chores?

Comments

Yes, I do! We don't have a dishwasher! I have to put my hands in dirty water with horrible, wet food in it. Gross! I cut my hand on a dirty knife once! Aargh! **Stacey, 14**

I'm lucky. I don't have to clean the bathroom, but my parents always say I must clean my bedroom. I hate doing it. ☺ **Dan, 15**

I have to do chores on weekends. I don't mind vacuuming, but I hate cleaning the toilet. That's disgusting! Eww! **Ana, 16**

I like doing housework. It's relaxing – especially ironing, because I can listen to music. **Marcus, 15**

Check it out!

Find these words and check their meaning.

dishes	push	disgusting
smell	messy	

1 🔊 1.11 **Read and listen** Match the headings a–e with sections 1–5.
- **a** Taking out the trash
- **b** Doing the vacuuming
- **c** Washing the dishes
- **d** Doing the ironing
- **e** Cleaning the bathroom

2 Comprehension Answer the questions.

How often does Adam wash the dishes? *He never has to wash the dishes (he has to load and unload the dishwasher).*

1 Who leaves long hairs in the bathtub?
2 Why does Adam think taking out the trash is horrible?
3 Why does Adam iron his clothes on Sunday evenings?
4 Who cut her hand on a knife?
5 Who does the ironing and listens to music at the same time?

Language focus

3 🔊 1.12 **Listen and complete these blog comments with *have to* or *don't have to*.**

I'm lucky. I *don't have to do* any household chores.

1 I _____ load and unload the dishwasher after every meal. I don't mind because my mom pays me!

2 I _____ make my bed before I go to school. ☹

3 My dad loves housework and he does it all. I _____ do anything! ☺

4 Why do people _____ do housework? What a waste of time!

5 My brothers _____ do anything at home. It isn't fair!

4 Look at the pictures and read the web page again. What chores do Stacey, Dan, Ana, and Marcus like doing and hate doing?

1 Ana hates cleaning the toilet.
2 _____
3 _____
4 _____

5 Focus on you Write dialogues about things you *like* and *hate* doing. Use the words in the box.

clean the bathtub	clean your room cook do housework	get up late
go to the movies	hang out with friends make your bed	play sports

A What do you like doing on the weekend / after school?
B I like *playing sports* , and I like *hanging out with friends* .
A What do you hate doing?
B I hate _____, and I hate
_____.

6 Pairwork Practice the dialogues in exercise 5. 😊

Housework

1 🔊 1.13 **Match the expressions in the box with the pictures. Then listen and repeat.**

> clean my bedroom   clean the bathroom   do the cooking   do the ironing
> do the laundry   do the vacuuming   feed the dog   ~~load / unload the dishwasher~~
> make my bed   set / clear the table   take out the trash   wash the dishes

load / unload the dishwasher

1 _____

2 _____

3 _____

4 _____

5 _____

6 _____

7 _____

8 _____

9 _____

10 _____

11 _____

My listening skills

Collocations
Many verbs and nouns go together naturally, *e.g., do chores, make the bed.* It is useful to note down these word partners or collocations, and learn them together.

2 🔊 1.14 **Listen to Mark talking about who does the housework in his family. Then complete the sentences.**

> Mom usually *does the cooking*.

1 She always _____.
2 Dad often _____.
3 He sometimes _____.
4 I always _____ in the morning.
5 I usually _____ before dinner.
6 Luke sometimes _____ after dinner.
7 He always _____ our dog, Snoopy.

3 Pairwork Ask your partner about who does the housework in his / her family. Use the expressions in exercise 1. 😊

A Who does the housework in your family?
B Well, my mom usually does the cooking, but my dad …
A What housework do you do?
B I always make my bed and I usually …

Workbook p.10   **Extra practice** online

have to

Affirmative and negative

I **have to** wash the dishes.
I **don't have to** clean the bathroom.

	Affirmative	Negative
I / You / We / You / They	**have to** work.	**don't have to** work.
He / She / It	**has to** work.	**doesn't have to** work.

Think!

Read the rules and choose the correct alternative.

- We use *have to* to talk about obligations.
- We use *don't have to* to say that it isn't necessary to do something.
- *Have to* and *don't have to* are followed by the *-ing* form / **base form** of the main verb.

Rules p. W8

1 **Complete the sentences with the affirmative (✓) or negative (✗) form of *have to*.**

On school days, Liam <u>has to</u> get up at 7:45 a.m. (✓)

1 Liam and his sister, Rosie, _____ walk to school. (✓)
2 They _____ walk home after school. Their mom takes them home. (✗)
3 Liam _____ do his homework in the afternoon. He usually watches TV. (✗)
4 In the evening, he _____ set the table for dinner. (✓)
5 He _____ clear the table. That's Rosie's job! (✗)
6 On school days, Liam _____ go to bed at nine thirty. (✓)

2 **Do you have to do these things on school days or on weekends? Write affirmative or negative sentences.**

get up early?

On school days I have to get up early. / I don't have to get up early on weekends.

1 make your bed?
2 do chores?
3 go to bed before 10 p.m.?
4 cook dinner?
5 do your homework?
6 stay home in the evening?

yes / no questions and short answers

Do you have to do a lot of chores?
Yes, I do!

yes / no questions	Short answers	
	Affirmative	**Negative**
Do I / you **have to** work?	Yes, you / I **do**.	No, you / I **don't**.
Do we / you / they **have to** work?	Yes, you / we / they **do**.	No, you / we / they **don't**.
Does he / she / it **have to** work?	Yes, he / she / it **does**.	No, he / she / it **doesn't**.

Rules p. W8

3 **Write questions with the correct form of *have to*. Then write true answers.**

you / wear a uniform to school?

Do you have to wear a uniform to school?
No, I don't.

1 you / go to school on Saturday?
2 your parents / work on the weekend?
3 you / help with the housework at home?
4 your best friend / walk to school?
5 you / do a lot of homework?
6 your best friend / study in the afternoon?

4 **Complete the note with the correct form of *have to* and the verbs in parentheses.**

Hi, Flor!

I can't come to computer club this afternoon. I <u>have to go</u> (go) to the dentist 😞 and then I ¹_____ (help) Mom cook dinner. It's Dad's birthday today!
²_____ (you / do) anything tomorrow? Do you want to come to my house? You can come for lunch because Mom ³_____ (not work).
I ⁴_____ (finish) my geography project in the morning, but I ⁵_____ (not do) any homework in the afternoon, so we can watch a movie or play video games. Please say yes, Flor! You ⁶_____ (come)! ☺

Carola

Finished?

Write five things you *have to* or *don't have to* do at home. Then compare lists with a partner.

I have to take the dog for a walk every evening.

Puzzle p.104

2 Communication

Asking for permission

1 🔊 1.15 **Listen and complete the dialogues with the phrases in the box. Listen and check. Then listen again and repeat.**

> ~~Can I watch~~   Could I borrow   May I go   No, I'm sorry,   Yes, of course,

Lisa	_Can I watch_ the end of this movie, Mom?
Mom	¹_____ you can't, Lisa. You have to go to bed now.
Lisa	Oh … can I watch it on the computer tomorrow?
Mom	Yes, of course you can.

1

Dan	²_____ your cell phone, Mark? I forgot my phone today and I have to call my mom.
Mark	Sorry, Dan, but I don't have any credit on my phone. Ask Tina.

2

Jack	³_____ to the bathroom, please, Mrs. Greene?
Mrs. Greene	⁴_____ Jack, but come back to class immediately. Don't talk to your friends in the hall!
Jack	OK. Thanks.

Look!

May and *could* are more polite than *can*.

Learn it, use it!

You ask	You answer
Can I (watch this movie), please?	Yes, (of course) you can. / No, (I'm sorry,) you can't.
Could I (borrow your cell phone), please?	Yes, of course. / (I'm) sorry, but …
May I (go to the bathroom), please?	Yes, of course. / (I'm) sorry, but …

2 🔊 1.16 **Listen to four teenagers asking for permission to do things. Complete the chart with their requests. Then check (✓) if they get permission or put a cross (X) if they don't get permission.**

Request for permission	Reply
Joe wants to _use the computer_.	✓
1 Olivia wants to _____.	☐
2 Tom wants to _____.	☐
3 Lucia wants to _____.	☐

3 Pairwork Write dialogues for these situations. Then practice your dialogues. 😊

1 You ask your dad if you can go to the sports center. You explain that you have to practice for the basketball game on Saturday. Your dad agrees.

2 You ask your mom if you can go to a friend's house. You explain that you have to study for a math test tomorrow. Your mom says no. You have to clean your room and finish your homework.

Workbook p.12   **Extra practice** online

mustn't / don't have to

> I **mustn't** look messy for school.
> I **don't have to** put away the dishes.

Think!

Choose the correct alternatives.

- We use ¹*mustn't* / *don't have to* to say that something is prohibited.
- We use ²*mustn't* / *don't have to* to say that something isn't necessary or obligatory.

Rules p. W9

1 Complete the sentences with *mustn't* or *don't / doesn't have to*.

> If the movie is boring, we <u>don't have to</u> watch it.

1 School students _____ pay for the museum. It's free.
2 It's a secret! You _____ tell anyone!
3 You _____ eat a lot of candy and chocolate. It isn't healthy.
4 I _____ walk to school. My mom drives me.
5 You _____ copy from other students in a test.
6 Sam has a lot of time before his bus goes. He _____ leave now.

Gerunds

> **Taking** out the trash is a horrible chore.
> **Doing** the ironing is boring.

Think!

Circle the gerunds in the sentences.

1 Doing the vacuuming is hard work.
2 Washing the dishes is gross.
3 Visiting a foreign country is exciting.

Rules p. W9

2 Complete the sentences with the gerund form of the verbs in the box.

| dance | do | eat | learn | ~~listen~~ | play | watch |

> <u>Listening</u> to music is relaxing.

1 _____ housework is boring.
2 _____ is good exercise!
3 _____ a new language is interesting.
4 _____ soccer is more fun than _____ it on TV.
5 _____ a lot of chocolate is bad for you.

Verb + -*ing* form

> I **like doing** housework.
> I **hate cleaning** the toilet.

3 Complete the sentences with the -*ing* form of the verbs in the box.

| chat | clean | cook | ~~listen~~ | make | sing | walk |

> I love <u>listening</u> to pop music.

1 Yuko and Hiro hate _____ their bedroom.
2 We don't like _____ to school.
3 My dad loves _____. He's a great cook!
4 I enjoy _____ to my friends online.
5 My mom likes _____. She's in the choir.
6 Vanessa doesn't mind _____ her bed.

4 Write questions and answers.

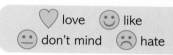

> ♡ love   ☺ like
> 😐 don't mind   ☹ hate

> you / like / play chess? ☹
> *Do you like playing chess?*
> *No, I don't. I hate it.*

1 he / like / read? ♡
2 they / like / listen to rock music? ☺
3 your brother / like / do chores? ☹
4 your friends / like dance? ♡
5 you / like / run? 😐

5 Write true sentences for you.

> I love <u>swimming.</u>

1 I love _____
2 I like _____
3 I enjoy _____
4 I don't mind _____
5 I don't like _____
6 I hate _____

6 Pairwork Ask and answer questions about the sentences in exercise 5.

Do you like swimming?
No, I don't! I hate swimming!

Finished?

Write about your partner's likes and dislikes.

Eva likes cooking, but she hates cleaning.

Puzzle p.104

Caribbean Adventure Bahamas
Sailing and scuba diving
For ages 15 and 16

the ultimate adventure summer camp

If you love sailing and the sea, this adventure is for you. The adventure lasts 23 days, and everybody learns to sail the boat and go scuba diving. We focus on team work and responsibility, but also on having a good time!

Life on the boat | Activities | Itinerary | FAQ

Voyage Blog Entries

Author: Dwayne **Our third night**

We all slept outside last night and the sky was amazing! There are twelve people on the *Neptune* (our boat) – nine students and three adults. There are five cabins, and I share one with Tim and Juan. We have to clean it every day because it's small!

Author: Sally M. **The Work Wheel**

Everyone has to do chores and every day we have a new job. We turn the Work Wheel to find out what our day's work is. Today, I am cabin cleaner, so I have to clean the cabins and bathrooms!

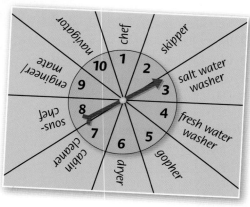

Author: Maria **Day six**

Today was a fantastic day! It was windy and sunny – perfect conditions. We sailed for five hours, so everyone learned a lot. Chloe was "captain for the day" and she was excellent. It's my turn tomorrow! I love sailing! 😊

Author: Lucas **Rules**

There are only a few rules on the boat, for example, we mustn't smoke and we have to wear life jackets when we're sailing. They're very fair, so everybody respects them. The instructors are great and they help us a lot.

Author: Ana **Sea legs!**

I hope I don't have to do the cooking tomorrow. It's very windy and the boat is moving a lot. I hate going inside when the sea's rough. It makes me feel sick! ☹

Check it out!

Find these words and check their meaning.

lasts
focus on
life jackets
respects
rough

Reading

1 🔊 1.17 **Read and listen** to the web page. Decide what type of text it is.

a an educational blog   b an activity vacation website   c a sailing club website

2 Answer the questions.

How long does the Caribbean Adventure last?
It lasts 23 days.

1 Where did Dwayne sleep on the third night?

2 Why does he have to clean his cabin every day?

3 Who has to do the chores on the boat?

4 What do people have to wear on the boat?

5 What does Ana hate doing when the sea is rough?

6 Do you prefer doing water or land sports? Why?

7 What activities do you like doing on vacation?

Listening

3 🔊 **1.18** **Listen to Freya talking about summer camp. Look at the symbols below and the list of activities and complete the boxes.**

(✓) things she has to do   (✗) things she mustn't do   (–) things she doesn't have to do

sleep in tents	–	go to bed at 10:30 p.m.	☐
clean the bedroom	☐	talk after 11 p.m.	☐
eat in the bedroom	☐	get up at 8 a.m.	☐
do the cooking	☐	leave the camp	☐

Speaking

4 Pairwork **Imagine that you are on a school trip at Talkeetna Lodge. Read the rules and check (✓) things you have to do and put a cross (✗) for things you don't have to do. Ask and answer questions.** 😊

make the beds	✓
clean the bathroom	✗
clean the bedrooms	☐
set the table	☐
clear the table	☐
put the trash in the garbage cans	☐
wash the dishes	☐
clean the kitchen	☐
do the laundry	☐

A *Do we have to make the beds in the morning?*
B *Yes, we do.*
B *Do we have to clean the bathroom?*
A *No, we don't.*

5 Ask and answer questions about the chores in exercise 4. Ask your partner if he / she likes doing these chores.

A *Do you like making your bed?*
B *No, I don't. I hate it. What about you?*
A *It's OK. I don't mind it.*

Writing

6 Complete the e-mail from Freya to her parents with information from exercise 3.

7 Imagine that you are with your class at Talkeetna Lodge. Write an e-mail (60–80 words) to your parents or to a friend. Use these ideas and Freya's e-mail to help you.

- Give your opinion of Talkeetna Lodge, and describe your bedroom.
- Say what chores you have to do.
- Say what time you have to go to bed (11 p.m.) and get up (7:30 a.m.).
- Give your opinion about the food and say what your favorite food is.
- Give your general opinion about the trip.

10th grade geography trip to McKinley May 10th–15th

As you know, we are staying at Talkeetna Lodge in the Denali National Park near Mount McKinley. Talkeetna Lodge is an education center, not a hotel. That means you have to do a few jobs to help!

Your rooms
Please make the beds every morning and clean the bedrooms.
Don't leave your clothes on the floor!

Dining room / Kitchen
The meal times:
Breakfast 8–9 a.m.
Lunch 1 p.m.
Dinner 7 p.m.
Please clear the table when you finish your meal.
Put your trash in the garbage cans in the dining room.

Washing
The staff at the center do the laundry on Wednesdays and Fridays.
Please put your dirty clothes in the laundry basket in the bathroom.

Hi, Mom and Dad!

I'm having a great time here! I'm in a room with three girls and they're so nice. The food is good, too – probably because we don't do the cooking! The only problem is that there are a lot of rules! We ¹_____ at 8 a.m. because we ²_____ our bedrooms before breakfast. (I hate cleaning!) We mustn't ³_____ in our bedrooms (so we can't have parties)! We have to go to bed at ⁴_____ ☹, and we ⁵_____ talk after 11 p.m.! I don't mind that because I'm always so tired in the evenings. My days are very busy and I'm learning a lot of new things!

See you soon!
Lots of love,
Freya

Vocabulary

1 Write the names of the places in town.

_c_ _a_ _f_ _é_

1 h __ __ __ __ __ __ __
2 s __ __ __ __ __   __ __ __ __ __ __ __
3 l __ __ __ __ __ __
4 p __ __ __ __ __   __ __ __ __ __ __ __
5 c __ __ __ __ __
6 p __ __ __ __ __ __ __   __ __ __

2 Match A and B to find chores.

A		B	
1	do _b_	a	my bedroom
2	set __	b	the ironing
3	make __	c	the trash
4	take out __	d	my bed
5	clean __	e	the table
6	feed __	f	the dog

Grammar

3 Complete the rules with *must* or *mustn't* and the verbs in the box.

~~drink~~   feed   listen   stop   use   wear

You _mustn't drink_ the water.

1 You _____ here.

2 You _____ your cell phone in the library.

3 You _____ the animals.

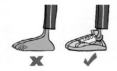

4 You _____ sneakers in the gym.

5 You _____ in class.

4 Complete the sentences with *some-*, *any-*, *no-*, and *every-* compounds.

Did you do _anything_ interesting last night?

1 There's _____ on TV. Let's play video games.
2 I didn't meet _____ in town.
3 There's _____ in the yard! Who is it?
4 Did you go _____ nice at the weekend?
5 Eggs, butter, sugar, and flour … OK, we have _____. Let's make a cake!

5 Complete the sentences with *have to / don't have to* and the verbs in the box.

be   clean   feed   ~~study~~   take   wear

Jason can't go out. He _has to study_ for a test.

1 Sam's bedroom is a mess! He _____ it.
2 You _____ good at tennis. Beginners can join the club.
3 You _____ an umbrella. It isn't going to rain.
4 Dad _____ the dog. Mom feeds him.
5 It isn't fair! We _____ a uniform at our school.

6 Complete the sentences with *mustn't* or *don't / doesn't have to*.

The bus is at 10 a.m. You _mustn't_ be late.
Dad _doesn't have to_ work on Saturdays.

1 I have to load the dishwasher, but I _____ unload it.
2 Friday is Maria's birthday. I _____ forget to call her.
3 Slow down! You _____ run around the swimming pool.
4 Mom _____ wash the dishes – Dad always does it.
5 We _____ go shopping today. There's a lot of food in the fridge.

7 Use the prompts to write sentences.

I / enjoy / read.
I enjoy reading.

1 Listen / to music / be / relaxing.
2 Your sister / like / play / tennis?
3 Mateo / hate / take / out the trash.
4 I / not mind / cook.
5 Learn / Chinese / not be / easy.

Communication

8 🔊 1.19 **Complete the dialogues with sentences a–h. Then listen and check.**

a You have to do your homework.
b Go down this street, go past the post office, and then turn left.
c No, I'm sorry, you can't, Tom.
d Thanks.
e Yes, of course you can.
f But Hugo and Luis are going.
g It's at the end of the road.
h OK. But can I go out tomorrow night?

Dialogue 1

A Excuse me. How do I get to the library, please?
B 1 _____
_____
_____
2 _____
_____
A 3 _____
_____

Dialogue 2

C Can I go to the movies tonight, Mom?
D 4 _____
C 5 _____
D 6 _____
C 7 _____
D 8 _____

Pronunciation

have /hæv/ and *have to* /'hæftə/

9 🔊 1.20 **Listen to the pronunciation of *have* /hæv/ and *have to* /'hæftə/. Then listen and repeat.**

In the words *have to*, the /v/ sound in *have* becomes a /f/ sound.

/hæv/ I have breakfast at seven o'clock.
/'hæftə/ I have to go to school at 7:30.

10 🔊 1.21 **Listen and write a /hæv/ or b /'hæftə/. Then listen and repeat.**

a 1 __ 2 __ 3 __ 4 __ 5 __

11 🔊 1.22 **Listen and repeat the sentences.**

1 I have to set the table, but I don't have to clear it.
2 We have math at 9 a.m., and then we have history and art.

Listening

12 🔊 1.23 **Listen to the five short conversations and check (✓) the correct answers.**

Where are Ana and her friend going?

a ☐   b ✓   c ☐

1 What job does Alice hate?

a ☐   b ☐   c ☐

3 What does Kenji like doing on Saturday mornings?

a ☐   b ☐   c ☐

2 Find Amanda's list of housework.

clean bedroom ✓,
set the table ✓,
wash the dishes ✓,
take out the trash ✗

clean bedroom ✓,
set the table ✓,
wash the dishes ✗,
take out the trash ✓

clean bedroom ✓,
set the table ✓,
wash the dishes ✗,
take out the trash ✗

a ☐   b ☐   c ☐

4 What is forbidden at the beach?

a ☐   b ☐   c ☐

A Culture club

Friendly Visitors

Americans don't have to do military service, but many young people do voluntary community service. In some high schools they have to do 10 to 100 hours of community service if they want to graduate. Many students enjoy the experience and continue as volunteers. Nina Davis is 17 and she is a Friendly Visitor volunteer. She visits Maggie Lewis every week. Maggie is 82 years old and she lives alone. She doesn't have a family, so Nina's visits are very important to her.

66 I joined Friendly Visitors last year as my community service project. Volunteers have to visit an elderly person once a week, but I see Maggie two or three times every week. I enjoy visiting her. We talk about movies and books. She loves watching science fiction movies and she has an amazing collection of DVDs. Her life isn't easy because she has to use a wheelchair. She never asks me to do chores, but I sometimes wash the dishes and clear the table. It's difficult for her to do these things. Maggie likes cooking, and she makes delicious cookies for me to take home. I never think about our age difference. Maggie is a young person inside! 99

66 Before Nina started coming, I was very lonely. It was a lovely surprise when Nina arrived one day. She comes here after school and we talk about different things. She shows me photos of her family and school. She likes playing chess, and we sometimes have a game. I was a teacher when I was younger, and I help her with her homework. Her grades are better these days! She takes me to the park when it's sunny. Volunteers don't have to do housework, but Nina often does the grocery shopping for me. She also takes out the trash. She's kind to me. I am very grateful. 99

To become a Friendly Visitor volunteer, you must complete an application form and give three references. For those under 18, parents have to give their permission.

Check it out!

Find these words and check their meaning.

lonely
grateful
elderly
references

1 🔊 1.24 **Read and listen** **Answer the question before you read. Then read and listen to the article and check your answer.**

Which of these types of service do some American students have to do?

a military service   b community service   c civil service

2 Answer the questions.

Why are Nina's visits very important to Maggie?
Because she doesn't have a family.
1 How often does Nina visit Maggie?
2 Why is life difficult for Maggie?
3 What chores does Nina do for Maggie?
4 What game do Maggie and Nina play?
5 How does Maggie help Nina?
6 Where do Maggie and Nina go on sunny days?
7 What must you do if you want to become a Friendly Visitor?

3 Presentation **Prepare a presentation about a popular charity in your country. Use these questions to help you. Present your charity to the other students.**

• What is the name of the charity and where is it?
• What does it do and who does it help?
• What do volunteers have to do?
• Why is it important?

Vocabulary and speaking

I can identify places in a town. (p.12)   A2

1 Complete the words. Then say true sentences to your partner.

You get money from the b_ank_____.

1 I go to c_____ every Sunday.
2 There's a p_____ with a lake in my town.
3 I buy my clothes at the s_____ m_____.
4 My friends play basketball at the s_____ c_____.
5 My sister borrows books from the l_____.

__ / 5

I can ask for and give directions. (p.14)   B1

2 Complete the dialogues. Then practice.

Ella Excuse me. _How_____ do I get to the bus station, please?

Man Go down Cameron Street as ¹_____ the post office. Then ²_____ left.

Ben Excuse me. Can you tell me the ³_____ to the church, please?

Girl Go straight, and then take the first ⁴_____ on the right. ⁵_____ the road and the church is near the bank.

__ / 5

I can give directions to my house. (p.17)   B1

3 Reorder the words to make sentences.

the / bus / number / take / six .
Take the number six bus.

1 every / a / there / minutes / bus / twenty / is .
2 get / to / your / I / do / house / how ?
3 opposite / off / the / bus / get / library / the .
4 hospital / and / walk / right / the / past / turn .
5 house / to / is / a / next / my / café .

__ / 5

I can identify different types of housework. (p.20)   A2

4 Reorder the letters and write the housework words. Then make questions and answers with your partner.

clear the _table_____ (b l t a e)

1 wash the _____ (s i e h s d)
2 do the _____ (n i r i n o g)
3 take out the _____ (h a s r t)
4 do the _____ (r y n a l d u)
5 clean the _____ (o b r m h a t o)

__ / 5

I can ask for permission and respond. (p.22)   B1

5 Complete the sentences with the words in the box. Then practice the dialogue.

but	~~Can~~	can't	May	of course	sorry

Lola _Can_____ I go to the movies, Mom?

Mom No, I'm ¹_____, you ²_____, Lola. You have school tomorrow.

Lola ³_____ I watch a movie on TV, then?

Mom Yes, ⁴_____, ⁵_____ go to bed after the movie.

__ / 5

I can ask people what housework they have to do. (p.25)   B1

6 Write the questions. Then write true answers.

your brother / make his bed?
Does your brother have to make his bed?
Yes, he does. / No, he doesn't.

1 you / do the laundry?
2 your sister / load the dishwasher?
3 your parents / clean the kitchen?
4 your dad / take out the trash?
5 I / do the cooking?

__ / 5

Reading, listening, and writing

	Got it?		
	Yes	I'm not sure	No
I can read and answer questions about a charity sports event. (p.16) B1	☐	☐	☐
I can understand people talking about a charity sports event. (p.17) B1	☐	☐	☐
I can write an e-mail with directions to my house. (p.17) B1	☐	☐	☐
I can read and answer questions about a summer camp. (p.24) B1	☐	☐	☐
I can understand a person talking about a summer camp. (p.25) B1	☐	☐	☐
I can write an e-mail about the rules on a school trip. (p.25) B1	☐	☐	☐

Follow Your Passion

How are you going to choose your future career? Would you like your passion or hobby to become your work? Read about three teenagers with plans to do exactly that.

Music is my passion, and I want to make it my career and be an audio engineer. I want to work at concerts and music festivals. I think I have the right qualities for the job. I'm a musician, and I'm hard-working and flexible. This is important because the working hours aren't regular in the music world. This summer, I'm not going to go on vacation; I'm going to help at a music festival in July. When I graduate, I hope to study sound engineering at the University of Melbourne. *Brad (16), Australia*

After I graduate, I want to be a wildlife biologist and work for a national park. I hope to study biological sciences at the University of Sao Paulo. It's the perfect profession for me because I am passionate about nature. I'm very patient and I'm hard-working, too. I love being outdoors, and I enjoy taking wildlife photos. This summer, I'm going to spend a month in the Pantanal region of Brazil. I'm going to work as a volunteer on a conservation project. *Elena (15), Brazil*

I'd like to be a movie stunt artist. It's the perfect job for me because I'm a very active person. I love extreme sports. At the moment, I'm learning to ride a motorcycle. I'm going to start a martial arts class soon. This summer, I'm going to spend two weeks at a Stunt Camp in Hollywood. They teach jumping and falling techniques, and hand-to-hand combat. When I finish school, I'm not going to go to college; I want to go to a stuntman school in Florida. *Ethan (16), U.S.*

Check it out!

Find these words and check their meaning.

career   wildlife   stunt

1 🔊 1.25 **Read and listen** Match the people with the activities they enjoy doing.

1 Brad   a   doing extreme sports
2 Elena   b   playing music
3 Ethan   c   taking photos

2 Comprehension Answer the questions.

Why does Brad want to be an audio engineer?

Because music is his passion.

1 Why is it important for an audio engineer to be flexible?
2 Where does Brad want to study?
3 Where does Elena want to work after she graduates?
4 What are her personal qualities?
5 What does she enjoy doing in her free time?
6 What type of person is Ethan?
7 What is he learning at the moment?
8 Where does he want to go when he finishes school?

Language focus

3 Complete the sentences from the article. Then write the name of the person who said them.

I'm going to start a martial arts course soon.   _____

1 I_____ a month in the Pantanal region of Brazil.   _____
2 I_____ on vacation.   _____
3 I_____ at a music festival.   _____
4 I_____ two weeks at a Stunt Camp in Hollywood.   _____
5 I_____ to college.   _____
6 I_____ as a volunteer on a conservation project.   _____

4 Read the article again. Then complete the sentences.

Brad

> I want to make it my career.
> I ¹_____ sound engineering at the University of Melbourne.

Elena

> I ²_____ a wildlife biologist.
> I ³_____ biological sciences at the University of Sao Paulo.

Ethan

> I ⁴_____ a movie stunt artist.
> I ⁵_____ to a stuntman school.

5 Focus on you Write about your plans for the future. Use the ideas in the box.

get a summer job   get married   go to college after school   learn more languages
learn to drive   live in a different country   travel around the world

I'm (not) going to go to college after school.
I'd like to live in Australia.

6 Pairwork Tell your partner about your plans for the future.

Personality adjectives

1 Are the adjectives positive (P) or negative (N)? Use a dictionary.

ambitious	P	5	flexible	___	10	outgoing	___
1 arrogant	___	6	hard-working	___	11	patient	___
2 confident	___	7	honest	___	12	selfish	___
3 creative	___	8	lazy	___	13	shy	___
4 enthusiastic	___	9	organized	___	14	stubborn	___

2 🔊 1.26 Listen and repeat the adjectives in exercise 1.

3 Choose adjectives from exercise 1 to describe these people.

Lucas writes poems and songs.   He's _creative_____.
1 Lee is nervous when she meets new people.   She's _____.
2 Emma doesn't study very hard.   She's _____.
3 Bruno loves parties and meeting new people.   He's _____.
4 Carina never changes her mind.   She's _____.
5 David doesn't think about other people.   He's _____.
6 Rachel thinks she's the best at everything.   She's _____.
7 Ichiro doesn't mind waiting.   He's _____.
8 Nicole spends all her free time studying.   She's _____.

4 🔊 1.27 **Pronunciation** Listen to the /ʃ/ sound in these words. Then listen and repeat.

1 ambi<u>ti</u>ous   3 pa<u>ti</u>ent   5 <u>sh</u>y
2 fa<u>sh</u>ion   4 selfi<u>sh</u>

5 🔊 1.28 Listen to three dialogues and choose the best adjectives to describe the people.

1 Liza is **patient** / **confident**, but she's also **lazy** / **honest**.
2 William is **enthusiastic** / **arrogant**, and he's also **shy** / **flexible**.
3 Camila is **ambitious** / **outgoing**, but she's also **arrogant** / **selfish**.

6 Pairwork Describe and identify the people in the pictures.

A She looks very lazy.
B Number 1?
A Yes, that's right.

1   2   3   4

7 Pairwork Discuss your personality.

A What's a positive thing about your personality?
B I'm enthusiastic.
A What's a negative thing?
B I'm stubborn!

Workbook p.16   Extra practice online

be going to (1)

Affirmative and negative

I'm **going to** get work experience this summer.
I'm **not going to** go on vacation.

Affirmative	Negative
I **am** ('m) **going to** play.	I **am not** ('m not) **going to** play.
You **are** ('re) **going to** play.	You **are not** (**aren't**) **going to** play.
He / She / It **is** ('s) **going to** play	He / She / It **is not** (**isn't**) **going to** play.
We / You / They **are** ('re) **going to** play.	We / You / They **are not** (**aren't**) **going to** play.

Think!

Read the sentences. Then choose the correct alternative.

She**'s going to** be a dentist.
He **isn't going to** study math in college.
• We use *be going to* to talk about **intentions / present activities**.

Rules p.W14

1 Write sentences with *be going to*. Use the short form of *be*.

I / see / the *Iron Man* movie tonight.
I'm going to see the Iron Man movie tonight.

1 Al / not visit / his friend in Canada next summer.
2 You / not study / Chinese next year.
3 We / make / a birthday cake for Melissa.
4 They / do / their homework later.
5 I / not watch / this movie again.
6 Carl and I / get married next month.

2 Complete the text with the correct form of *be going to* and the verbs in parentheses.

Jack: "I want to leave the band!"

Terrible news! Jack Finley *'s going to leave* (leave) Magic Live! He wants to be a solo singer, but he ¹_____ (not start) his solo career immediately.
He ²_____ (have) a vacation, and then he ³_____ (write) some new songs. The other members of the band ⁴_____ (stay) together. They ⁵_____ (not change) the name of the band. They ⁶_____ (look) for a new singer. I'm devastated!
POSTED May 10ᵗʰ 14:30

yes / no questions and short answers

"**Are** you **going to** get work experience?" "Yes, I **am**."
"**Is** he **going to** go to college?" "No, he **isn't**."
How **are** you **going to** go to choose your future career?

yes / no questions		
Am	I	
Is	he / she / it	**going to** play?
Are	we / you / they	

Short Answers					
Affirmative			**Negative**		
	I	**am.**		I	**'m not.**
Yes,	he / she / it	**is.**	**No,**	he / she / it	**isn't.**
	we / you / they	**are.**		we / you / they	**aren't.**

Rules pp.W14–15

3 Write questions with *be going to*. Then write affirmative (✓) or negative (✗) short answers.

Jo and Ed / play tennis tomorrow? (✓)
Are Jo and Ed going to play tennis tomorrow?
Yes, they are.

1 Matt / buy a guitar? (✗)
2 you / send Andy a text message? (✓)
3 Denise and Clara / bike to school? (✗)
4 we / have a test tomorrow? (✓)

4 Complete the questions using a question word in the box, *be going to*, and the verbs in parentheses.

How long   What   When   Where   Why

"*How long are you going to stay* (stay) in Rio?"
"I'm going to stay in Rio for a week."

1 "_____ (buy) at the shopping mall?" "She's going to buy some jeans."
2 "_____ (meet) Sally?" "They're going to meet Sally tomorrow afternoon."
3 "_____ (study) law in college?" "Because I want to be an attorney."
4 "_____ (stay) in New York?" "We're going to stay at the Hilton."

Finished?

Write about your plans for the weekend. Write three things that you're going to do and three things you aren't going to do.
This weekend, I'm (not) going to ...

Puzzle p.105

At the airport

1 🔊 1.29 **Listen and complete the dialogues with the questions in the box. Listen again and check. Then listen and repeat.**

> Are you wearing a watch or a belt?
>
> ~~Can I see your ticket and passport or ID card, please?~~
>
> Do you have any baggage to check in?
>
> Do you have any liquids or a laptop in your hand baggage?
>
> Do you have any metal items in your pockets?
>
> Would you like a window or an aisle seat?

At the check-in desk

A Good morning. <u>Can I see your ticket and passport or ID card, please?</u>
B Yes, here you are.
A Thank you. ¹_____
B I'd like a window seat, please.
A OK. ²_____
B Yes, I have this suitcase.
A OK, here's your boarding pass. You're boarding at gate 7. The gate opens at 11 a.m.

At the security checkpoint

A ³_____
B I don't have any liquids, but I have a laptop.
A Please put it in this tray. ⁴_____ – keys, a cell phone, coins?
B No, I don't.
A ⁵_____
B I'm wearing a belt.
A Please remove it.

Learn it, use it!

You hear	You say
Can I see your ticket and passport, please?	Yes, here you are.
Would you like a window or an aisle seat?	I'd like …
Do you have any baggage to check in / any liquids or a laptop in your hand baggage / anything in your pockets?	No, I don't. / Yes, I do.
Are you wearing a watch or a belt?	Yes, I am. / No, I'm not.

2 🔊 1.30 **Listen to two conversations at the airport and choose the correct options.**

window / (aisle)

1 suitcase / hand baggage
2 gate 13 / gate 30
3 4:15 / 4:50
4 liquids / laptop
5 keys / cell phone
6 watch / belt

3 Pairwork **Choose details from the options below and then write dialogues at the airport check-in and the security checkpoint. Use the dialogues in exercise 1 as a model. Then practice your dialogues.**

> 11:30 / 11:13   gate 12 / gate 20   keys / cell phone in your pocket
> liquids / laptop in your hand baggage   suitcase / hand baggage
> wearing a watch / belt   window / aisle seat

Workbook p.18   **Extra practice** online

be going to (2)

Think!

Look at the sentences. Then choose the correct alternative.

It's sunny and there aren't any clouds. It**'s going to be** a beautiful day.
They aren't playing well. They**'re going to** lose the game.

• We use *be going to* for **a prediction** / **an intention** based on present evidence.

Rules p.W15

1 **Look at the pictures. Complete the sentences with *be going to* and the verbs in the box. Use the short form of *be*.**

be eat fall jump sit win

It**'s going to eat** your sandwich!
1 She_____on the cat!
2 Brazil_____the game.
3 He_____over the truck.
4 It_____a sunny day.
5 He_____off his skateboard!

2 **Complete the dialogues with the correct form of *be going to* and the verbs in parentheses.**

Manchester United is playing very well at the moment. It**'s going to be** (be) a difficult game for Real Madrid.

1 It's very cold and cloudy.
It_____ (snow).
2 Look at this traffic. We_____ (be) late for the concert.
3 Hannah can't drive very well. She _____ (not pass) her driving test.
4 It's starting to rain. We_____ (get) wet!
5 I didn't pass my English test. My parents _____ (not be) happy!

Verb + infinitive / -ing form

I **want to** be a wildlife biologist.
I **love doing** sports.

Verbs + infinitive	Verbs + *-ing* form
I **hope to** write.	I **love** writing.
I **want to** write.	I **enjoy** writing.
I**'d like to** write.	I **like** writing.
	I **don't mind** writing.
	I **prefer** writing.
	I **hate** writing.

Think!

Complete the sentences with *going* or *to go*.

I like ¹_____ to the movies.
I'd like ²_____ to the movies.

Rules p.W15

3 **Complete the sentences with the infinitive or *-ing* form of the verbs in parentheses.**

I hope _to travel_ (travel) around the world one day.
I love _shopping_ (shop).

1 Jason doesn't like _____ (wash) the dishes. He prefers _____ (set) the table.
2 I'd like _____ (study) biology in college.
3 My dog enjoys _____ (play) with a ball.
4 We want _____ (watch) the game at Victor's house.
5 I hate _____ (get up) early.

4 **Complete the text with the infinitive or *-ing* form of the verbs in the box.**

get go ~~learn~~ study travel visit work

My name's Katia, and I'm at high school. I really enjoy _learning_ languages and I want ¹_____ French and Chinese in college. I love ²_____ to different countries, and I'd like ³_____ in the tourist industry one day. This summer, I hope ⁴_____ a job in the U.S. When I finish school, I'd like ⁵_____ around Asia for six months. I especially want ⁶_____ China.

Finished?

Write sentences about you. Then compare your ideas with a partner.

I'd like … I don't want … I hate …
I hope to … I love … I want …

Puzzle p.105

RI InternQuest

Summer Internships | Ages 16–18

Doctor, software developer, mechanic, hairdresser – what job do you want to do in the future? How are you going to choose your career? A summer internship is an opportunity for you to learn about different careers. It gives you a chance to experience a career and find out if it's the right one for you. We offer three- to six-week summer internships in twelve different U.S. cities. Each program gives students the opportunity to get real-life work experience. Our team can also help you choose the best program for you.

Here are the experiences of two students who were interns last summer.

I'm Scott Rankin and I'm 16. I did a three-week internship at a garden center in L.A. last summer. My experience was very useful. I did a lot of different things, including taking care of plants and helping customers. I asked a lot of questions and I learned so much from the people there. When I graduate from high school, I want to be a garden designer. I think it's the perfect career for me because I love gardening, and I'm artistic, creative, and enthusiastic. Also, I don't mind working hard outside in all types of weather. I'm going to take classes in environmental studies and art next year. After school, I'm not going to get a job immediately. I'm going to study landscape design in college.

I'm Clara Svenson and I'm 17. I love being with animals and I'd like to be a vet. I did a veterinary internship in a pet hospital in Dallas for six weeks last summer because I wanted to find out more about the job. I had an amazing experience there, and the internship was a great opportunity because I did a lot of varied work behind the scenes. I looked after the animals – I fed and cleaned them. I also watched operations and helped the vets when they examined animals. I know veterinary medicine is the career for me because I'm hard-working and patient. That's important when you work with animals. I'd like to go to Texas A&M College of Veterinary Medicine, but I need excellent grades!

Check it out!

Find these words and check their meaning.

chance
real-life
behind the scenes
operations

Reading

1 Read the website quickly. What is an internship?

  a a summer job   **b** a way to get work experience

2 🔊 1.31 **Read and listen to the website and answer the questions.**

    How long do the internships last? They last three to six weeks.

  1 Where did Scott do an internship last summer?

  2 What work does he want to do in the future?

  3 What does he plan to do after school?

  4 Where did Clara do her work experience?

  5 Why was it a good opportunity for her?

  6 What would she like to study in college?

  7 What do you think of internships? Are they a good idea for young people? Why? / Why not?

Listening

3 🔊 1.32 **Look at the places a–f and think about the type of jobs and internships people can do in these places. Then listen to Kelly, Emi, and Rafael talking about their plans for the future. Choose the best place for their internships.**

1 Kelly _f_
2 Emi ___
3 Rafael ___

a Massachusetts General Hospital
b Express Transport Company
c Atlanta Recreation and Sports Center
d Styles Beauty and Hair Salon
e Lux Hotel
f CBS Newsroom

4 🔊 1.32 **Listen again to Kelly, Emi, and Rafael and choose the correct answers.**

Kelly wants to be a (journalist) / English teacher.
1 Kelly loves **writing** / **telling** stories.
2 She'd like to work in **radio** / **television** news.
3 Emi enjoys **meeting people** / **buying clothes**.
4 She hopes to have her own hairdressing **salon** / **products** in the future.
5 Rafael wants to be a **professional soccer player** / **fitness coach**.
6 He'd like to work **with a professional soccer team** / **in a sports center**.

Speaking

5 Pairwork Ask and answer the questions about your future plans. Make notes of your partner's answers. 😊

• Are you going to go to college?   *Yes, Sao Paulo University (medicine)*
• What type of work would you like to do?   • Are you going to travel?
• Would you like to do an internship?   • Would you like to live in a foreign country?

6 Pairwork Tell another student about your partner's plans for the future. 😊

Valeria hopes to go to college and study ...

Writing

7 Complete Flavio's e-mail with *the*, *a / an*, or Ø (no article). Then write a reply telling him about your plans for the future (70–100 words). Use Flavio's e-mail as a model and your answers to the questions in exercise 5.

Hi!

Thanks for your e-mail. You asked me about my plans for **the** future! Well, I have ¹____ lot of ideas!

I'm going to stay at ²____ school until I'm 18. I'm not going to go to ³____ college immediately because I'd like to travel around ⁴____ world first. I really want to visit ⁵____ Europe. I'd like to do ⁶____ internship for ⁷____ few months, too.

After that, I hope to go to ⁸____ college. I want to study ⁹____ information technology because I'd like to be ¹⁰____ web designer. This type of work appeals to me because it's creative, but it's also technical. It's also well paid, and I'd like to make a lot of money! What about you? What are your plans? Are you going to get a job or go to college?

Write soon,

Flavio

What will their future be like?

They Will Make the World a Better Place

Our magazine asked high school students about the future. Many students have definite plans for their future life, but others don't know what they're going to do. How about you? Who will you be ten years from now? Where will you live? Do you think the world will be a better place?

Teenager Nathan Rebelo has some strong ideas about his future. "If I get married, I won't have more than one child. Today there are more than seven billion people on the planet, and overpopulation is going to be a big problem." However, Nathan generally feels positive about the future. "Most teenagers know about the world's problems and they want to change things. We're lucky because we have a good education, and this will help us make the world a better place."

Nathan also has career plans. "In five years, I'll be 20, and I hope to be in college. I want to be an architect, and I'll have to study hard if I want to graduate. If I become a successful architect, I'll design sustainable buildings, and I won't live in a big city."

Rachel Barnes is enthusiastic about her future. "In ten years, I'll be 26. I'm not sure where I'll be, but I hope I'll have good qualifications. I'm going to apply to medical school. If I graduate, I'll be a doctor. I won't get married very young; I want to see the world first! I'd like to work on health projects in Africa."

Rachel is worried about the future. "My generation will be in charge of the country in thirty years, and things won't be easy. We'll have to clean up the environment and find new forms of sustainable energy." Rachel hates it when adults criticize teenagers. "Adults are responsible for the world's problems, but today's teenagers will have to solve them."

Check it out!

Find these words and check their meaning.

overpopulation
however
sustainable
in charge of
criticize

1 🔊 1.33 **Read and listen** Check (✓) the topics the readers made predictions about.

1 having children	✓	5 marriage ☐
2 age and health	☐	6 technology ☐
3 the weather	☐	7 environment ☐
4 study and work	☐	8 population ☐

2 Comprehension Answer the questions.

How does Nathan generally feel about the future?
He generally feels positive about the future.
1 Why does Nathan think that most teenagers are lucky?
2 What career does he want to have?
3 Where would Rachel like to work?
4 What does she hate?
5 What does she think adults are responsible for?

Language focus

3 Reorder the words to make sentences from the article. Then read the article again and check.

will / live / where / you ?
Where will you live?
1 five / be / years / in / 20 / I'll .
2 city / won't / a / in / big / live / I .
3 I'll / sure / where / I'm / be / not .
4 I / qualification / I'll / good / hope / have / a .
5 very / get / won't / young / married / I .

4 Complete the sentences with phrases from the article.

1 If I get married, _____.
2 I'll have to study hard if _____.
3 If _____ I'll design sustainable buildings.
4 If I graduate, _____.

5 🔊 1.34 **Listen to two students talking about the future. Choose the correct answers.**

Twenty years from now, our lives (will)/ won't be very similar to our lives today.
1 We **will** / **won't** live on a different planet.
2 We **will** / **won't** go on vacation in space.
3 There **will** / **won't** be more technology.
4 Everyone **will** / **won't** use computers at school.
5 I **will** / **won't** be married.
6 I **will** / **won't** have children.

6 Focus on you What do you think about the predictions in exercise 5? Circle the words that match your opinions.

7 Pairwork Discuss your choices in exercise 5 with a partner. 😊

A *I don't think we will live on a different planet.*
B *I agree. But I think we will go on vacation in space.*

4 Vocabulary

Life events

1 🔊 1.35 **Match the pictures on the timeline with the expressions in the box. Then listen and repeat.**

> apply to college / for a job   be born   die   get a job   get married
> graduate   have a baby / children   pass your driving test   retire   start school

be born _____

1 _____   4 _____   7 _____
2 _____   5 _____   8 _____
3 _____   6 _____   9 _____

2 **Lily's timeline shows some important life events in her family. Complete it with the simple past of the verbs in exercise 1.**

1989 Dad _applied_ to college to study engineering.

1993 Dad _____ from college with an engineering degree.

1996 Mom and Dad _____ married.

1999 I _____ born.

2004 I _____ school.

2006 Mom _____ a new job.

2008 My grandpa _____ from work.

2012 My great-grandma Luisa _____. She was 95.

2013 My brother _____ his driving test.

2014 Aunt Virginia _____ a baby.

3 Pairwork **Draw a timeline and write six important life events in your family. Tell your partner about each event.** 🎭

4 Pairwork **Ask and answer questions about life events.** 😊

What age do people usually …
• start school?
• finish school?
• graduate from college?
• pass their driving test?
• get their first job
• get married?
• retire?

A What age do people usually start school?
B They usually start school at 5 or 6 years old.

Workbook p.22   Extra practice   online

will: future

Affirmative and negative

> In five years, I'll **be** 20.
> I **won't get** married very young.

Affirmative		
Full form		**Short form**
I / you / he / she / it / we / you / they	will go.	'll go.
Negative		
Full form		**Short form**
I / you / he / she / it / we / you / they	will not go.	won't go.

Think!

Read the sentences. Then choose the correct alternative.

I think he'll **get** the job.
It **won't rain** this evening.
- We use *will* or *won't* to **talk about intentions / make predictions.**

Rules p. W20

1 Complete the sentences with *will* or *won't* and the verbs in the box. Use short forms.

> be   buy   go   ~~have~~   retire   win

Nick always celebrates his birthday. I'm sure he <u>'ll have</u> a party.

1 Oh no! There's a history test tomorrow. I think it _____ difficult!
2 Noemi can't sing very well. She _____ the karaoke competition.
3 I think I_____ when I'm about 65.
4 Mark doesn't like classical music. I'm sure he _____ to the concert.
5 My aunt and uncle want to live in Canada. I think they_____ a house there soon.

2 Write predictions with *will* (✓) or *won't* (✗).

> We / win the soccer game tomorrow. (✗)
> *We won't win the soccer game tomorrow.*

1 He / graduate / next year. (✓)
2 It / rain this afternoon. (✗)
3 They / go to the school concert on Friday. (✗)
4 She / be famous one day. (✓)
5 I / see Luis on the weekend. (✗)

yes / no questions and short answers

> Will the world **be** a better place?
> Yes, it **will**. / No, it **won't**.

yes / no questions		
Will	I / you / he / she / it / we / you / they	win?
Short answers		
Yes,	you / I / he / she / it / you / we / they	will.
No,	you / I / he / she / it / you / we / they	won't.

3 Write *yes / no* questions with *will*. Then answer the questions with your opinions.

> it / rain tonight?
> "Will it rain tonight?" "Yes, it will." / "No, it won't."

1 you / go to college?
2 you / leave home before you are 20?
3 Brazil / win the next soccer World Cup?
4 people / live longer in 2050?
5 you and your family / visit the U.S. one day?

will / be going to

Think!

Read the sentences. Then choose the correct alternatives to complete the rules.

Good news! Camila**'s going to** have a baby!
Lucia wants children. I think **she'll** have a baby soon.
1 We use [1]*will / going to* to make predictions based on an opinion.
2 We use [2]*will / going to* to make an opinion based on evidence.

Rules pp. W20–21

4 Complete the sentences with the correct forms of *will* or *be going to*. Then match the sentences with the correct rule from the Think! box.

> I think he <u>'ll</u> do well on his test. <u>1</u>

1 The score is 4–0 to us! We _____ win! ___.
2 I think we _____ travel in space. ___.
3 Look at those black clouds! It _____ rain! ___.
4 I don't think my sister _____ get the job. She arrived late for the interview! ___.

Finished?

Make predictions about your future.

> be famous   learn to cook   live in a big city

Puzzle p.105

At the bus station

1 🔊 1.36 Listen and complete the conversation with the words in the box. Then listen again and repeat.

> change   gate   ~~ticket~~   trip   next   one-way   round-trip

Kyle	Hello. I'd like a _ticket_ to Baltimore, please.
Assistant	Would you like a ¹_____ or a round-trip ticket?
Kyle	A ²_____, please.
Assistant	OK. Are you leaving today?
Kyle	Yes, I am.
Assistant	And when are you coming back?
Kyle	I'm coming back ³_____ Tuesday.
Assistant	OK, so you'll need an open return. That's $28, please.
Kyle	Here you are, here's $30.
Assistant	Thank you. Here's your ticket and $2 ⁴_____ .
Kyle	What time is the next bus?
Assistant	There's a bus for Baltimore every 30 minutes. The next bus leaves at ten thirty.
Kyle	OK, thanks. What ⁵_____ does it leave from?
Assistant	It leaves from gate five.
Kyle	Thanks. Oh … how long does the ⁶_____ take?
Assistant	It takes about three and a half hours.
Kyle	OK. Thanks. Goodbye.
Assistant	Goodbye.

Learn it, use it!

You say	You hear
I'd like a ticket to …, please.	Would you like a one-way ticket or a round-trip? Are you leaving today? / When are you coming back?
What time is the next bus?	It leaves at …
What gate / Where does it leave from?	It leaves from …
How long does the trip take?	It takes about …

2 🔊 1.37 Listen to three more people buying bus tickets. Choose the correct answers.

Destination	Type of ticket	Price	Next bus	Gate	Duration
1 New Haven	¹one-way / round-trip	²$22 / $32	³8:00 / 9:00	⁴8 / 10	⁵2 / 3 hours
2 Boston	⁶one-way / round-trip	⁷$27 / $37	⁸10:15 / 10:50	⁹1 / 11	¹⁰3 / 4 hours
3 Long Island	¹¹one-way / round-trip	¹²$15 / $16	¹³6:45 / 6:55	¹⁴5 / 9	¹⁵40 / 50 minutes

3 Pairwork Look at the bus information below. Choose a destination and take turns to buy a bus ticket. Find out when the next bus is and where it leaves from. 🙂

Transport from Boston, Massachusetts

From	To	Time	Departure	One-way	Round-trip	Duration
Boston	Newport	10:30 AM	Pike Street	$27	$52	1 hour 40 minutes
Boston	Providence	8:00 PM	South Station	$8	$16	1 hour
Boston	New York	10:30 AM	Downtown	$29	$58	4 hours 20 minutes
Boston	Montreal	7:15 AM	South Station	$91	$173	7 hours 30 minutes

Workbook p.24   Extra practice   online

First conditional

If I get married, I **won't have** more than one child.

If clause	Main clause
If I **pass** my test,	my mom will be happy.
If I **don't pass** my test,	my mom won't be happy.
If you **pass** your test,	**will** your mom be happy?

Main clause	if clause
My mom will be happy	if I **pass** my test.
My mom won't be happy	if I **don't pass** my test.
Will your mom be happy	if you **pass** your test?

Think!

Look at the sentences. Then choose the correct alternatives.

I'll **buy** a DVD if I **go** shopping.
If I **go** shopping, I'll **buy** a DVD.

- We use [1]the simple present /
  will + base form of the verb in the *if* clause.
- We use [2]the simple present /
  will + base form of the verb in the main clause.
- There is a comma after the *if* clause when
  it comes at the [3]beginning / end of the
  sentence.

Rules p.W21

1 Choose the correct answers.

If we(get)/ 'll get the next bus, we arrive /
('ll arrive) at 6 p.m.

1 We **miss** / 'll miss the bus if we **don't go** /
  won't go now.
2 **Will** / Do you play soccer if it **rains** / will rain?
3 If I **have** / 'll have children, I **call** / 'll call them
  Mia and David.
4 They **don't win** / won't win the game if they
  don't play / won't play better.
5 If Sylvia **gets** / will get home late, her mom **is** /
  will be angry.
6 I **go** / 'll go to college if I **get** / 'll get straight A's.

2 Complete the sentences with the correct form of the verbs in parentheses.

If Ellie _gets_ (get) a job, she'll leave (leave)
home.

1 If you _____ (not water) these plants,
  they_____(die)!
2 I_____ (visit) you tomorrow if
  I _____ (have) time.
3 You _____ (not be) late for school if
  you _____ (leave) home now.
4 If it _____ (be) sunny tomorrow,
  we _____ (have) a barbecue.

3 Write first conditional sentences. Use short forms.

We / go / to the skate park / if / it / be /
sunny / tomorrow.

*We'll go to the skate park if it's sunny
tomorrow.*

1 If / Lucas / get / good grades / his parents /
  be / pleased.
2 We / buy / some sandwiches / if / we / get /
  hungry.
3 If / he / go / to Canada / he / speak / English.
4 Those children / be / sick / if / they / eat /
  all those cookies.
5 If / you / not come / with me / I / not go.
6 Kate / not come / if / she / have / a lot of
  homework.

4 Game! Make first conditional sentences with the verbs in the box. You get one point for each complete correct sentence.

get   go   have   meet   miss   pass   rain   win

A say the *if* clause of a first conditional sentence.
B Complete the sentence, and start a new
  sentence.
A If I get home early, ...
B If I get home early, I'll go swimming. (1 point)
A If it rains tomorrow, ...

Finished?

Write first conditional sentences. Use the ideas in the box.

it rains on Sunday
you don't feel well tomorrow
you get some money for your birthday
you're bored this afternoon
your mom is tired this evening

If it rains on Sunday, I'll stay home.

Puzzle p.105

Workbook p.23   **Extra practice** online

In the Next One Hundred Years ...

What will the world be like 100 years from now? Will it be possible to manipulate the weather? Will we all speak one language? Will everyone live to be 150 years old? Nobody really knows because the future is very difficult to predict. Nevertheless, more than 100 years ago, an American engineer, John Watkins, made some predictions about life today — and a lot of them were correct!

In 1900, John Watkins wrote an article for an American women's magazine. The title of the article was *What May Happen in the Next Hundred Years* and it started with the words: "These prophecies will seem strange, almost impossible ... ." Today, however, a lot of the things that he predicted are part of our everyday lives. Here are some of the predictions that came true ... and two that didn't!

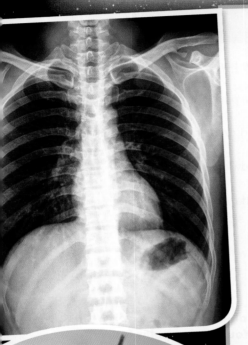

- *People will watch events from all over the world on home screens in their living rooms.*

  ✓ Watching TV is a normal everyday activity today. In the U.S., 97% of houses have a TV.

- *Doctors will use rays of invisible light to see internal parts of a body.*

  ✓ Today X-rays are a common medical procedure in all hospitals.

- *We will use wireless telephone systems to talk to people all over the world.*

  ✓ Six billion people in the world today have a cell phone. That's 86 people in every 100!

- *Americans will be taller by 4–5 centimeters.*

  ✓ In 1900, the average American man was 1.68–1.70 m tall. In 2000, the average American man was 1.75 m tall.

- *There won't be any mosquitoes or flies.*

  ✗ Mosquitoes and flies are still a big problem! Mosquitoes are responsible for more than 650,000 deaths from malaria every year.

- *There will be no C, X, or Q in our everyday alphabet.*

  ✗ The alphabet is the same today, but it may change in the future because of text messaging and other modern methods of communication.

Check it out!

Find these words and check their meaning.

nevertheless
may happen
prophecies
came true
flies
accurate

John Watkins was very optimistic about the future. He only predicted positive changes in the 20th century.

Today, a lot of people are pessimistic about the future of the world in the next 100 years. But who knows? If we're lucky, today's predictions won't be as accurate as Watkins' prophecies were!

Reading

1 🔊 1.38 Read and listen to the magazine article. **Which predictions were not correct?**

2 Answer the questions.

What nationality was John Watkins? *He was American.*

1 What was his job?
2 When did he make his predictions "for the next hundred years"?
3 What magazine published his predictions?
4 Which of these things did he predict?

cell phones ☐   miniskirts ☐
hotter summers ☐   X-rays ☐
TV ☐   the Internet ☐
physical changes to the body ☐   new materials ☐

5 Are you optimistic or pessimistic about the future? Why?

Listening

3 🔊 1.39 **Futurology is the study of how people will live in the future. Read the topics a–g. Then listen to a radio interview with a futurologist. Number the topics in the order they discuss them. There are two extra topics they do not discuss.**

a Languages   ___   e Space travel   ___
b World population   ___   f Money   ___
c Life expectancy   ___   g Cities   ___
d Weather   <u>1</u>

4 🔊 1.39 **Listen again. Does the futurologist think each prediction *will* (✓) or *won't* (✗) come true in the next 100 years?**

It will be possible to control the weather.   ✓
1 We will all speak one language.   ☐
2 Some people will live to be 150 years old.   ☐
3 Space travel will be possible for most people.   ☐
4 We will all use the same money online.   ☐

> **My listening skills**
>
> **Identifying main ideas**
> Some questions ask you to identify and sequence the main ideas in a listening text. Before you listen, read the questions and identify the key words. Then listen and try to recognize these key words. Don't worry if you don't understand every word.

Speaking

5 Pairwork **Ask and answer questions about the future of the world in 50 years. Use these and your own ideas.** 🙂

Will …

- students use computers or books at school?
- the climate be different?
- people still use paper money?
- all cars be electric?
- vacations in space be common?
- hobbies and sports be different?

A *Do you think students will still use books at school?*
B *I think there will still be some books, but all students will have laptops or tablets.*

Writing

6 Write a short paragraph (70–100 words) about the future. Use your ideas from exercise 5 or your own ideas. Start like this:

In my opinion, many things will be different / the same in 50 years.

Vocabulary

1 Complete the sentences with personality adjectives.

Maria designs her own clothes.
She's very c<u>reative</u>.

1 That man thinks he's very important.
He's a_____.

2 Elena is friendly and makes friends easily.
She's o_____.

3 Steve wants to be an astronaut.
He's very a_____.

4 I always plan my study time.
I'm quite o_____.

5 Lily never changes her mind.
She's very s_____.

6 I don't mind changing my plans at the last minute. I'm f_____.

2 Complete the timeline with seven life events. Use the simple past.

1928	1933
1950	1951
1954	1956
1993	2010

1928   Sarah <u>was born</u>.

1933   At the age of 5, she ¹_____ school in Boston.

1950   She ²_____ in engineering from Stanford University.

1951   She ³_____ at Ford Car Company.

1954   She ⁴_____ to her boyfriend Charles in Old South Church, Boston.

1956   Sarah and Charles ⁵_____. They named him Simon.

1993   Sarah ⁶_____ from work. She became a pensioner.

2010   She ⁷_____ when she was 82 years old. She had a good life.

Grammar

3 Complete the sentences with the affirmative (✓), negative (✗), or question (?) forms of *will* or *be going to*.

I <u>'m going to</u> watch the movie at 8 p.m. (✓)

1 I _____ play volleyball today.
I don't have time. (✗)

2 Who do you think _____ win the next soccer World Cup? (?)

3 The weather forecast says that it _____ rain today. (✗)

4 You _____ pass your test.
You don't work hard enough. (✗)

5 What _____ life be like 20 years from now? (?)

4 Choose the correct answers.

I don't mind (playing) / to play hockey at school.

1 I don't want **getting** / **to get** up early tomorrow.

2 Steve enjoys **reading** / **to read** crime stories.

3 The students hate **doing** / **to do** P.E. outside in winter.

4 I hope **seeing** / **to see** you soon!

5 I'd like **buying** / **to buy** some new jeans.

5 Complete the sentences with the correct form of the verbs in parentheses. Use short forms if possible.

If it <u>'s</u> (be) sunny later, we <u>'ll go</u> (go) for a walk.

1 We _____ (wait) for you if you _____ (be) late.

2 If you _____ (be) hungry, I_____ (make) you a sandwich.

3 If Jack _____ (not leave) now, he _____ (miss) the bus.

4 If the band _____ (not practice), it _____ (not play) well.

5 I _____ (help) you with your math if you _____ (not understand) it.

6 If Tina _____ (go) to the movies, she _____ (not be) home until 10 p.m.

Communication

6 🔊 1.40 **Complete the dialogues with the phrases in the box. Then listen and check.**

> A round-trip, please.   I'd like an aisle seat, please.   It leaves at 3 p.m.   It takes about three hours.
> Thank you.   ~~Yes, here you are.~~   Yes, I have this suitcase.

1

A Good morning. Can I see your ticket and passport, please?

B _Yes, here you are._

A Thank you. Would you like a window or an aisle seat?

B ¹ _____

A OK. Have you got any baggage to check in?

B ² _____

A OK, here's your boarding pass. The gate opens at 10:30 a.m.

B ³ _____

2

A I'd like a ticket to Dallas, please.

B Do you want a one-way ticket or a round-trip?

A ⁴ _____

B Here you are.

A What time does the next bus leave?

B ⁵ _____

A How long does the trip take?

B ⁶ _____

Pronunciation

The pronunciation of '*ll*

7 🔊 1.41 **Listen to the pronunciation of '*ll*. Then listen again and repeat.**

1 I'll see you on Friday.
2 You'll have a good time!
3 He'll buy the movie theater tickets.
4 We'll get the bus home.
5 They'll meet us at the bus stop.

8 🔊 1.42 **Listen and choose the correct answers.**

I'll live / (I live) in Newport.

1 **We'll go** / **We go** to high school.
2 **They'll have** / **They have** a long vacation in the summer.
3 **You'll study** / **You study** chemistry in college.
4 **I'll take** / **I take** the dog for a walk.
5 **We'll buy** / **We buy** a lot of souvenirs on vacation.

Listening

9 🔊 1.43 **Listen to five short conversations and check (✓) the correct answers.**

What's Ken going to do on the weekend?
a He's going to go ice skating. ☐
b He's going to go to Nick's party. ☐
c He's going to stay home. ☑

1 Who is Luke?
a He's a boy that goes to Lily's school. ☐
b He's Lily's boyfriend. ☐
c He's Lily's math teacher. ☐

2 What does Katie want to be when she leaves school?
a She wants to be a psychologist. ☐
b She wants to be a nurse. ☐
c She wants to be a teacher. ☐

3 What prediction does Sophie make about her life ten years from now?
a She'll be married. ☐
b She'll be a fashion designer. ☐
c She'll be famous. ☐

4 Ben and Freya are having a baby. If the baby is a boy, what will they call him?
a They'll call him Jack. ☐
b They'll call him Benedict. ☐
c They'll call him Kyle. ☐

What Will Life Be Like in 2100?

Children who are born today will be in their 80s in the year 2100. About 5.3 million Americans will be over 100. What will their lives be like? We asked readers for their predictions about life in the United States in 100 years. Here are six predictions and what the futurologists think of them.

9/10. Very probable.

1 The U.S. coast will be different.

Because of global warming, temperatures will be 6°C higher. If global temperatures rise, polar ice will melt, and sea levels will rise. Scientists predict that parts of nearly 1,700 cities near the ocean will be underwater in 100 years. These will include New York, Boston, and Miami.

9/10. Very probable.

2 Families won't be as big as they are today.

There will also be more families with only one parent. Today, the average American mom has her first child at the age of 23. This will go up to 29. Most moms will only have one child, instead of two today.

5/10. Possible.

3 Spanish will be the first language.

Spanish is already the most common foreign language taught in U.S. schools. It is now the second language in the United States. The Hispanic population is growing very fast. If this trend continues, more people will speak Spanish than English, but it will be difficult for Spanish to become the first language.

6/10. Quite possible.

4 Fewer people will get married. Instead they will sign a contract every year.

Marriage won't disappear, but it will change. Traditional marriage will still exist, but there will be other options. Many people will live more than 100 years, and they won't get married for life. They will get married for ten or twenty years.

7/10. Quite possible.

5 California will become an independent country.

There are already signs that this will happen. California is a very wealthy state, and if this continues, it's possible it'll want to be independent from other poorer states so that it can keep its wealth. If California becomes independent, some states on the East Coast will want to become independent, too.

10/10. Definite.

6 People will live longer. People won't get sick as often as they do now.

If they have an active lifestyle, today's babies will live for 100 years. Most people will stay healthy until they die because of new medical discoveries. This means that there will be more old people than children! And some people will live to 150!

VOTE VOTE VO
VOTE HERE TODAY
VOTE HOY AQUÍ

1 🔊 1.44 **Read and listen** to the article. Which prediction do the specialists think will definitely come true?

2 Answer the questions.

How many people in the United States will be over 100 years old in 2100?
About 5.3 million Americans will be over 100 in 2100.

1 What will happen to many cities near the ocean 100 years from now?
2 How will families be different?
3 What is the most common foreign language taught in U.S. schools?
4 How will marriages be different?
5 What will happen to some states in the U.S.?
6 How will medical discoveries change people's lives?
7 How old will some people live to?

3 Presentation **Prepare a short presentation on the future of your country in 2100. Answer the questions below with your opinions. Present your predictions to the other students.**

• What will the population be? • Where will people live? • What will the biggest cities be?
• What language(s) will people speak? • How long will people live?
• What will families be like? • Will life be better? Why? / Why not?

Check it out!

Find these words and check their meaning.

coast
melt
sea levels
to rise
wealthy (a) / wealth (n)

Vocabulary and speaking

I can describe people's personalities. (p.32) B1

1 Read the descriptions and complete the personality adjectives.

Kate wants to be President. a<u>mbitious</u>
1 Tom studies for school every day. h_____
2 He says he's better than his friends. a_____
3 Pablo designs beautiful clothes. c_____
4 Kelly never does any chores. l_____
5 Al doesn't think of other people. s_____

__ / 5

I can check in at the airport. (p.34) B1

2 Complete the dialogue with the words in the box. Then practice the dialogue.

> baggage   boarding pass   ~~Can~~   here
> I'd like   Would

A <u>Can</u> I see your ticket and passport, please?
B Yes, ¹_____ you are.
A ²_____ you like a window or an aisle seat?
B ³_____ a window seat, please.
A Do you have any ⁴_____ to check in?
B Yes, I have this suitcase.
A OK. Here's your ⁵_____ pass.

__ / 5

I can talk about future plans. (p.37) B1

3 Write the sentences in the correct order.

country / like / live / I'd / in / to / another
I'd like to live in another country.
1 hopes / college / Ana / study / in / art / to
2 is / sister / get / going / my / to / married
3 like / internship / would / do / an / to / you ?
4 to / Arabic / learn / we're / going
5 be / Juan / wants / pilot / to / a

__ / 5

I can talk about life events. (p.40) B1

4 Complete the words.

Ana and Juan got m <u>a r r i e d</u> last July.
1 Tom didn't p __ __ __ his driving test.
2 I am going to a __ __ __ __ for a job in a bank.
3 My brother wants to h __ __ __ children.
4 My dad is going to r __ __ __ __ __ next year. He's 65.
5 Her baby was b __ __ __ last night.

__ / 5

I can ask for information at the bus station. (p.42) B1

5 Complete the dialogue. Then practice.

> How long   ~~I'd like~~   leaves
> takes   What time   Where

A <u>I'd like</u> a ticket to New Haven, please.
B Here you are. That's $15.
A ¹_____ is the next bus?
B The next bus ²_____ at ten-thirty.
A ³_____ does it leave from?
B It leaves from gate 6.
A ⁴_____ does it take?
B It ⁵_____ about two hours.

__ / 5

I can ask questions about the future. (p.45) B1

6 Write questions. Then ask your partner.

people / live longer in the future?
Will people live longer in the future?
1 the climate / change?
2 school / exist?
3 people / drive electric cars?
4 vacations in space / be popular?
5 everyone / speak the same language?

__ / 5

Reading, listening, and writing

		Got it?	
	Yes	I'm not sure	No
I can read and answer questions about internships. (pp.36-37) B1	☐	☐	☐
I can understand people talking about their future plans. (p.37) B1	☐	☐	☐
I can write about my future plans. (p.37) B1	☐	☐	☐
I can read and answer questions about future predictions. (pp.44-45) B1	☐	☐	☐
I can understand a radio interview about the future of the world. (p.45) B1	☐	☐	☐
I can write about the future of the world. (p.45) B1	☐	☐	☐

Vocabulary

1 Complete the sentences with the correct noun or adjective.

Karl never works. He's very l_azy____!

1 I went to the h_____ when I broke my leg.
2 I have to load the d_____ after dinner.
3 Clara hates waiting. She isn't a p_____ girl.
4 I borrow books from the city l_____.
5 Peter loves meeting new people. He's very o_____.
6 You can buy stamps at the p_____ o_____.

2 Add three new words or phrases for each category.

Places around town	Housework	Personality adjectives	Life events
bus station	4_____	7_____	10_____
1_____	5_____	8_____	11_____
2_____	6_____	9_____	12_____
3_____			

Grammar

must

3 Look at the information. Then write five more rules with *must / mustn't*.

Stanton Swimming Pool

buy a ticket at the entrance

take a shower before you swim

don't jump into the pool

don't eat food near the pool

leave your clothes in the changing room

don't run near the pool

You must buy a ticket at the entrance.

Compounds: *some- / any- / no- / every-*

4 Complete the compound words with *some-, any-, no-,* or *every-*.

We didn't do _any_ thing interesting last weekend.

1 I think there's _____one upstairs. I can see a light.
2 _____body came to the park with me. I was alone.
3 I can't find my cat _____where.
4 I saw _____thing moving over there. What is it?
5 We looked _____where, but we didn't find him.
6 I have _____thing to do. Let's play tennis.

have to

5 Write five more sentences about Kevin's obligations. Use the correct form of *have to*.

At home	At school
set the table ✓	play sports ✓
clean the bathroom ✗	eat in the cafeteria ✗
feed the dog ✓	go to school on Saturday ✗

He has to set the table.

6 And you? Write about your obligations. Use the activities in activity 5 or your ideas.

mustn't / don't have to

7 Complete the sentences. Use *mustn't, don't have to,* or *doesn't have to*.

You _mustn't____ play soccer in the classroom!

1 She's lucky. She _____ do any housework.
2 I _____ get up early on Saturday because there's no school.
3 Mom says I _____ play loud music at night.
4 We _____ walk. We can get the bus.
5 Tom _____ take out the trash. His dad always does it.
6 You _____ go near the animals. They're dangerous.

be going to

8 Complete the text with the correct form of *be going to* and the verbs in the box. Use short forms of *be* if possible.

be   have   ~~not get~~   stay
travel   visit   you / do

When I finish school, I'**m not going to get**
a job immediately. I ¹_____
a long vacation first. My friend and I
²_____ around the world.
We ³_____ different countries.
Then I ⁴_____ with my
grandparents in the U.S. for a month.
It ⁵_____ a lot of fun. What
⁶_____ when you finish school?

9 Complete the sentences with *be going to* and the verbs in the box. Use short forms of *be* if possible.

play   ~~rain~~   score   take   unload   watch

It'**s going to rain**
tomorrow.

1 He_____

out the trash.

2 She_____

the dishwasher.

3 We_____

a movie.

4 They_____

tennis.

5 She_____

a goal.

Verb + infinitive / -ing form

10 Complete the sentences with the infinitive form or the *-ing* form of the verbs in parentheses.

I hate **taking** out the trash. (take)

1 I'd like _____ biology in college.
(study)

2 Do you enjoy _____ museums? (visit)

3 Maria hopes _____ a summer job.
(get)

4 My friends like _____ to rock music.
(listen)

5 My brother wants _____ a new car.
(buy)

6 _____ irregular verbs is hard.
(remember)

will: future

11 Complete the text with the correct form of *will* and the verbs in the box.

~~change~~   control   do   not go
shine   study   not work

I think a lot of things **will change** in the future.
People ¹_____ the weather. The sun
²_____ all the time on weekends. People
³_____ every day, and robots ⁴_____
all the boring jobs. Children ⁵_____ to
school. They ⁶_____ at home using
computer screens.

will / be going to

12 Choose the correct answers.

~~Are you going to meet~~/ **Will you meet** your
friends tonight?

1 I think everyone **is going to use** / **will use** solar
energy in the future.

2 Do you think people **are going to live** /
will live on the moon one day?

3 It's 8:45! You **are going to miss** / **will miss** the
bus!

4 What **are you going to do** / **will you do** next
weekend?

5 In the future, everyone **is going to live** /
will live to one hundred.

6 I **am not going to study** / **won't study** math in
college.

First conditional

13 Complete the sentences with the correct form of the verbs in parentheses.

If it '**s** (be) wet tomorrow, we
won't go (not go) to the beach.

1 If you _____ (make) a lot of noise, you
_____ (wake up) your brother.

2 If you _____ (not do) your homework,
the teacher _____ (be) angry.

3 If our team _____ (not play) better, it
_____ (not win).

4 The dentist _____ (not be) pleased if
you _____ (eat) a lot of candy.

5 If I _____ (have) time, I _____
(cook) dinner for the family.

5 I've never had so much fun!

Try it Out!
The ultimate ocean sports festival! For fantastic action IN, ON, ABOVE, and OUT OF the water!

Dates: August 19th to August 24th

Many people have tried surfing, or they've been whitewater rafting. But have you tried kitesurfing or wakeboarding? Have you ever heard of coasteering? No? Well, come and try them out! You can be part of the action and try it out!

August 22nd

The **Try it Out!** festival is the biggest ocean sports festival in the U.S. Our reporter, **Linda Spears**, hasn't done ocean sports before, so she went there yesterday and she met **Joe Nichols**, the festival organizer.

Linda So, tell me Joe, what's the most popular sport this year?

Joe Well, a lot of people have tried kitesurfing. It's very exciting. Wakeboarding is very popular, too.

Linda And I see there's something called "coasteering" on the program. What is it? I've never heard of it.

Joe Oh, it's an amazing new sport. We haven't done it at the festival before. You do it on a rocky coast. You climb onto the rocks, and then you jump into the ocean. You also swim into caves. It's great fun.

Linda It sounds crazy! Have you ever had an accident?

Joe No, we haven't. It isn't that dangerous. You have to wear a wetsuit, a life jacket, and a helmet. Even my young daughter has done it.

Linda Did you invent it?

Joe No, I didn't. It comes from the U.K. It started there in the 1970s.

Linda Have you been to the U.K.?

Joe Yes, I have. I went there last year and discovered that coasteering is really popular, so I decided to start it here in the U.S. You have to try it!

Linda OK, I think I will!
…
Wow! Well, I've tried coasteering! And you know what? I've never had so much fun in my life! It's awesome! I'm going to try some other exciting things tomorrow. I haven't been kitesurfing before, and I've never tried wakeboarding. I've chosen both of them. It's going to be a crazy day!

1 🔊 2.02 **Read and listen** Choose the correct answers.
1 Joe Nichols is **a journalist** / **the festival organizer**.
2 The festival is in the **U.S.** / **U.K.**
3 Linda Spears is **a friend of Joe Nichols** / **a journalist**.

Check it out!

Find these words and check their meaning.

rocky (a) / rocks (n)
wetsuit
caves

2 Comprehension Answer the questions.

What can people do at the festival?

People can do surfing, whitewater rafting, kitesurfing, wakeboarding, and coasteering.

1 What sports are popular this year?
2 Which new sport is there at the festival this year?
3 What do you wear to do coasteering?
4 Where does this new sport come from?
5 What does Linda think of coasteering after she has tried it?
6 What sports is Linda planning to try tomorrow?

Language focus

3 Read the article again. Match the beginnings (1–5) and endings (a–e) of the sentences.

1 Many people
2 I've
3 Have you ever
4 Linda Spears
5 Have you been

a had an accident?
b hasn't done ocean sports before.
c to the U.K.?
d have tried surfing.
e never had so much fun in my life!

4 🔊 2.03 Listen to Alice and her friend Hugo. Complete their conversation with the words in the box.

> haven't done   Have you ever done   Have you ever tried
> I have   I haven't   've done

Alice What did you do on the weekend, Hugo?
Hugo I went to an ocean sports festival and I tried coasteering. It was amazing! Have you ever tried it?
Alice No, ¹_____. I think it sounds crazy!
Hugo No, it isn't. It's so much fun, and it's really exciting. ²_____ anything exciting?
Alice Yes, ³_____. I ⁴_____ a parachute jump.
Hugo Wow! A parachute jump?! I ⁵_____ that!

5 Focus on you Check (✓) the things you have done in your life.

I've been scuba diving. ☐
I've ridden a horse. ☐
I've done karaoke. ☐
I've eaten Japanese food. ☐
I've visited a different country. ☐
I've won a competition. ☐

6 Pairwork Tell your partner about the things you have done in your life.

A *I've been scuba diving, I've done karaoke, and I've eaten Japanese food.*
B *I've ridden a horse, and I've visited a different country.*

Experiences

1 🔊 2.04 **Match the experiences with the pictures. Then listen and repeat.**

be in the newspaper   climb a mountain   ~~do a parachute jump~~   fly in an airplane
go whitewater rafting   meet a famous person   ride a horse   sleep in a tent
visit a foreign country   win a competition

do a parachute jump

1 _____

2 _____

3 _____

4 _____

5 _____

6 _____

7 _____

8 _____

9 _____

2 🔊 2.05 **Listen and write what the people are doing.**

He's visiting a foreign country.
1 They_____
2 She_____
3 They_____
4 They_____

3 Pairwork Check (✓) the things in exercise 1 that you have done. Then look at your partner's answers and ask and answer. Use the simple past. 😃

A When did you ride a horse?
B I rode a horse on vacation last year.

4 Pairwork Discuss the questions. 😃

1 Which activities in exercise 1 are …
  • the most / least exciting?
  • the most / least dangerous?
2 Which activities would you like / hate to do? Why?

Workbook p.28   Extra practice online

Present perfect

Affirmative and negative

A lot of people **have tried** kitesurfing.
She **hasn't done** ocean sports before.

Subject	have / has	Past participle
I / You / We / They	have ('ve) / haven't	finished.
He / She / It	has ('s) / hasn't	finished.

Think!

Read the sentences. Then choose the correct alternatives.

She's seen Beyoncé.
They've visited Mexico.

- We ¹**know** / **don't know** when she saw Beyoncé.
- We ²**know** / **don't know** when they visited Mexico.
- We use the present perfect when we ³**know** / **don't know** when a past action happened.

Rules p.W26

Past participles

Regular verbs		
Base form	Simple past	Past participle
finish	finished	finished
visit	visited	visited
Irregular verbs		
Base form	Simple past	Past participle
see	saw	seen
eat	ate	eaten

Rules p. W26   Irregular verbs list

1 Complete the sentences with the affirmative (✓) or negative (✗) present perfect form of the verbs in parentheses.

I **'ve read** this book three times. (read) (✓)
Roberta **hasn't met** Diego. (meet) (✗)

1 Dad _____ his glasses again! (lose) (✓)
2 We _____ this movie before. (see) (✗)
3 Beth _____ some new shoes. (buy) (✓)
4 I _____ all my homework. (do) (✗)
5 My uncle _____ on TV. (be) (✓)
6 You _____ her new song. (hear) (✗)

2 Complete the sentences with the present perfect form of the verbs in the box.

> buy   not clean   ~~not eat~~   not fly
> not meet   read

I **haven't eaten** Indian food before. Let's try it!
1 I_____ this book twice. It's great.
2 Eiji _____ in an airplane before. He's very excited!
3 We _____ Chloe's new boyfriend.
4 Tom's parents _____ him a tablet for his birthday.
5 Ana _____ her room. It's a mess!

been / gone

Think!

Read the sentences and answer the questions.

1 Adam **'s been** to Mexico. He really enjoyed it. Is Adam in Mexico now? _____
2 Adam **'s gone** to Mexico. He's coming home on Friday. Is Adam in Mexico now? _____

Rules p.W26

3 Complete the sentences with *been* or *gone*.

"Are Jack and Sarah at home?" "No, they've **gone** to the movie theater."
1 Jo loves Italy. She's _____ there six times.
2 "Where's Greta?" "She's _____ to bed."
3 My dad's _____ to Chicago. He's staying there until Monday.
4 Ben's _____ to Spain. He showed me his pictures.
5 "Is Mrs. Wilson in her office?" "No, she's _____ to lunch."

4 Game! In groups, talk about the experiences on page 54. Who has done the most things?

I've ridden a horse, and I've flown in an airplane.

Finished?

Write about your experiences using the ideas in the box. Then compare your answers with a partner.

> climb a mountain   eat sushi   ride a camel
> stay in a hotel   swim with a dolphin
> travel abroad   win a competition

I haven't eaten sushi.

Puzzle p.106

At the hotel

1 🔊 2.06 **Heather is checking in to a hotel with her family. Listen to the dialogue and complete the hotel registration form. Then listen and repeat.**

The Grand Hotel

Check in date / time: _08/05_ / _3:15 p.m._

First name: [1]_____ Last name: [2]_____

Number of people: [3]_____ Type of room: [4]_____ (single / double / family)

Number of nights: [5]_____ Room number: [6]_____

Check out date / time: [7]_____ / [8]_____

Receptionist	Good afternoon. Can I help you?
Heather	Yes, please. We'd like to check in.
Receptionist	Certainly. What's your name, please?
Heather	It's Heather Blackwell. I've booked a room for four people for tonight.
Receptionist	OK, I'll just check that. Yes, … a family room for one night. Is that correct?
Heather	Yes, that's right.
Receptionist	Great. Could I have your passports or ID cards?
Heather	Yes, here they are.
Receptionist	Thank you. And, can you sign this form, please?
Heather	Yes, of course.
Receptionist	OK. Here's your key card. It's room 205. That's on the second floor.
Heather	OK, thank you. And what time do we have to check out tomorrow?
Receptionist	You have to leave the room by 11 a.m.
Heather	OK, thank you very much.
Receptionist	You're welcome. Have a nice stay.

Learn it, use it!

You hear	You say
Can I help you?	I / We'd like to check in. I / We've booked a room for …
Could I have your passports or ID cards?	Yes, here they are.
Can you sign this form, please?	Yes, of course.
Here's your key card. It's room …	Thank you. What time do we have to check out?

2 🔊 2.07 **Listen to two people checking in. Complete the charts.**

1

First name:	Janet
Last name:	[1]_____
Number of people:	[2]_____
Type of room:	[3]_____
Number of nights:	[4]_____
Room number:	[5]_____

2

First name:	Rafael
Last name:	[6]_____
Number of people:	[7]_____
Type of room:	[8]_____
Number of nights:	[9]_____
Room number:	[10]_____

3 Pairwork **Imagine that you are checking into a hotel. Invent information for your stay (number of people, type of room, number of nights) and then take it in turns to role-play your conversation with the receptionist.** 😊

Workbook p.30   **Extra practice** online

Present perfect

yes / no questions and short answers

"**Have** you **been** to the U.K.?" "Yes, I **have**."
"**Has** she **done** ocean sports?" "No, she **hasn't**."

Have / Has	Subject	Past participle
Have	I / you / we / they	finished?
Has	he / she / it	finished?
Short answers		
Affirmative		Negative
Yes, I / you / we / they **have**.		No, I / you / we / they **haven't**.
Yes, he / she / it **has**.		No, he / she / it **hasn't**.

Rules p. W27

1 Write questions. Then write affirmative (✓) or negative (✗) short answers.

you / be / to Spain? (✗)
"*Have you been to Spain?*" "*No, I haven't.*"

1 Flora and Ivan / travel / a lot? (✗)
2 I / win / a prize? (✓)
3 Lucy / ride / a horse? (✗)
4 the children / sleep / in a tent? (✓)
5 you / find / your passport? (✗)
6 Tim / be / to Canada? (✓)

ever / never

Think!

Read the sentences. Then complete the rules with *ever* and *never*.

Have you **ever** written a song?
I've **never** written a song.
- We use ¹_____ in yes / no questions.
- We use ²_____ in affirmative sentences with a negative meaning.

Rules p. W27

2 Reorder the words to make questions. Then give true short answers.

the theater / you / ever / have / to / been ?
"*Have you ever been to the theater?*"
"*Yes, I have.*" / "*No, I haven't.*"

1 to / the / U.S. / has / ever / your dad / been ?
2 a / tiger / seen / have / ever / you ?
3 ever / moved / your family / house / has ?
4 ever / have / table tennis / played / you ?
5 pizza / made / ever / have / your parents ?
6 have / in / a lake / you / swum / ever ?

3 Write two negative present perfect sentences.

Lee / visit / Peru.
Lee hasn't visited Peru. Lee has never visited Peru.
1 My parents / meet / my teacher.
2 I / run / ten kilometers.
3 Alice / eat / Thai food.
4 You / be / to Paris.
5 We / try / whitewater rafting.

Present perfect / Simple past

I've **been** to Sydney.   (= sometime before now)
I **went** to Sydney in 2012.

Think!

Read the sentences. Then choose the correct alternatives.

I've **slept** in a tent. I **slept** in a tent last June.
- We use the ¹present perfect / simple past for past actions with a specific time reference.
- We use the ²present perfect / simple past for past actions with no time reference.

Rules p. W27

4 Complete the sentences with the present perfect or simple past form of the verbs in parentheses.

Nate ___went___ (go) to Miami last month.
I _haven't heard_ (not hear) this song before.
1 We _____ (see) Pat yesterday.
2 _____ (they / get) married in 2012?
3 _____ (Li / ever / fly) in a helicopter?
4 Ana _____ (start) school last March.
5 I _____ (not try) snowboarding.

5 Complete the dialogue with the correct form of the verbs or a short answer.

A _Have you ever met_ (you / ever / meet) a famous actor?
B No, I ¹_____, but I ²_____ (see) Lionel Messi.
A When ³_____ (you / see) him?
B I ⁴_____ (see) him at the World Cup last year, but he ⁵_____ (not win).

Finished?

Write five questions for your partner. Then exchange questions and write true answers. Ask about ...

buy   clean   ~~eat~~   fly   lose   meet   read

Have you ever eaten Chinese food?

Puzzle p.106

I've Done That!

Every week, one of our readers tells us about an exciting experience that they've had. This week, Jessica Reed (15) describes how she got her Duke of Edinburgh Award (DofE), and what she has learned from the experience.

What is The Duke of Edinburgh Award?

"The DofE Award is a personal development program for young people aged 14 to 25. To receive it, they have to complete a variety of challenging activities. To date, over 500,000 young Canadians have received the award. The award program has three levels of difficulty: Bronze, Silver, and Gold; with four sections at each level: community service, skills, physical fitness, and an expedition. You choose activities for the first three sections, and do them regularly for at least three months. Then you must organize and complete an expedition.

I've never had so much fun!

The Duke of Edinburgh Award is one of the best things that I've ever done. Thanks to DofE, I've learned new skills, I've started a new sport, I've become a volunteer, and I've made a lot of friends. It's given me confidence and helped me take responsibility.

- I did the Bronze Award last year. For the community service, I volunteered at a computer club for retired people called The Silver Surfers' Club. I showed members how to use a computer and how to go online. I still go there once a week. It's cool to help people!

- For the skills section, I did a Circus Skills course. I learned how to ride a unicycle and how to juggle. I still practice juggling every day and I've learned to juggle with five balls!

- I've never been good at sports, so the physical section wasn't easy. I joined the girls' soccer team at school, and I didn't like it at first because we had to practice outside in the cold, but now I love soccer!

- Finally, for my expedition, I went on a four-day canoeing trip with two friends in the Algonquin Park in Ontario. We carried our canoes between lakes and camped. It was hard sometimes, but we had an awesome experience!

Now I've started the Silver Award and I'd like to do the Gold Award next year, too."

Jessica Reed

Culture

The Duke of Edinburgh Award (DofE) program started in the U.K. in 1956. Its founder was Queen Elizabeth II's husband, the Duke of Edinburgh. Today, the award exists in 130 countries, and it is very popular in Canada and Australia. A DofE award is an excellent thing to have on your résumé for a college application or a job.

Check it out!

Find these words and check their meaning.

award
to date
at least
unicycle
juggle

Reading

1 🔊 2.08 **Read and listen to the magazine article. Check (✓) the activities Jessica mentions in the article.**

bungee jumping	☐	climbing a mountain	☐	volunteering	☐
camping	✓	playing basketball	☐	whitewater rafting	☐
canoeing	☐	playing soccer	☐		

2 Answer the questions.

How old do you have to be to take part in the Duke of Edinburgh Award?

You have to be aged 14 to 25.

1 How many young people in Canada have received an award?
2 What are the three levels of the DofE?
3 What are the four different sections to the award?
4 What level of the award has Jessica done?
5 What two skills did she learn in the Skills section of the award?
6 What did she do for her expedition?
7 Would you like to do the Duke of Edinburgh Award? Why? / Why not?

My listening skills

Choosing the correct answer
When you have a choice between two possible answers, you might hear both words in the dialogue. Only one word is correct, so you need to pay close attention to what the speakers say. A speaker may use one of the options in a question, but this may not be the correct answer.

Listening

3 🔊 2.09 **Listen to Oliver talking about his experience of the Duke of Edinburgh Award. Then listen again and check.**

Oliver has done the **Bronze** / **Silver** Award of the Duke of Edinburgh's Award.

1 The four sections in the Bronze and Silver Awards are **the same** / **different**.
2 Oliver helped at a homework club at **his high school** / **an elementary school**.
3 He had music lessons and learned to play the **guitar** / **drums**.
4 He joined the school **soccer** / **basketball** team.
5 For his expedition, he went **camping** / **hiking** in the Canadian Rocky Mountains.

Speaking

4 Pairwork Ask and answer questions about your partner's experiences. If he / she answers yes, then ask questions to find out more about the experience. 😃

Yes (✓) / No (✗)   If yes: When? Where? Who with?

- do any volunteer work
- try an exciting sport
- go on a school trip
- win an award or a prize
- speak in public
- sleep in a tent
- visit another country
- visit a famous tourist attraction
- have an exciting experience

A *Have you ever done any volunteer work?*
B *Yes, I have. I've helped clean a river.*

A *When did you do that?*
B *Last summer.*

Writing

5 Read the beginning of Dave's postcard. Then imagine you are on vacation and write a postcard (80–100 words) to a friend. Replace the phrases in bold with your experiences. Then write the second paragraph with your ideas.

Hi, Carlos,
Guess what! I'm on vacation in **New Zealand** with **my family**. It's a very beautiful country. I've only been here for **a week**, and I've already done some really exciting things. I've **done a bungee jump**, I've **seen whales**, and I've **climbed a volcano**! …

Have You Seen It Yet?

In May 2007, an Englishman posted a video of his two young sons on the Internet. He called it "Charlie Bit My Finger" because the baby, Charlie, bites his brother's finger, and then laughs. The video is less than a minute long, but it immediately went "viral," and billions of people have watched it since 2007! There are billions of videos online, but very few go viral, and nobody knows why. Have you seen the latest viral video yet?

0:00 / 4:33

I've just watched the new *Singing Dog* video. It's hilarious! It's one of a series of videos by college students in Chicago about a cute dog who loves singing. They only posted the first one a month ago, but they've already made five more videos, and they've become incredibly popular. The new video has been online for a week and it's already gone viral. It's had over 250,000 hits since last Monday. Another great video is *Gangnam Style* by Psy. Psy is a Korean pop singer, and billions of people have watched *Gangnam Style* since 2012.

I posted something last week, but it's only a video of me playing my guitar. There's no chance it'll go viral!

Mike, 15

I love funny animal videos. I haven't seen the new *Singing Dog* video yet, but I've just seen *Greatest Freak Out Ever*. It's a video of a teenager who's angry because his mom stopped him playing video games. It's been on the Internet for a few years now. I don't know if it's fake or not, but it's hilarious! The *Annoying Orange* videos are great, too. If you haven't seen them yet, you should. They're so funny.

Personally, I've only posted two videos on YouTube, but they haven't had many hits. I'm working on a funny one of my cat right now, but I haven't finished it yet. I'd love to post a video that goes viral, and then become famous!

Olivia, 16

Check it out!

Find these words and check their meaning.

hilarious
cute
(to have) hits
no chance
fake

1 🔊 2.10 **Read and listen** What is a viral video?

a It's a very short video.
b It's a very successful video.
c It's a very funny video.

2 Comprehension Answer the questions.

What happens in "Charlie Bit My Finger"?
The baby, Charlie, bites his brother's finger, and then laughs.

1 How long is the video?
2 Does anyone know why some videos go viral?
3 What does Mike think of the new *Singing Dog* video?
4 What video did Mike post online last week?
5 Why is the teenager in *Greatest Freak Out Ever* angry?
6 What's Olivia working on at the moment?
7 What are your favorite online videos? Why?

Language focus

3 Write the words in the correct order.

latest viral video / seen / you / yet / the / have ?
Have you seen the latest viral video yet?

1 *Singing Dog* video / I've / watched / just / new / the
_____

2 already / they've / five more videos / made
_____

3 Monday / it's / last / had / since / 250,000 hits / over
_____

4 since / watched / *Gangnam Style* / billions / 2012 / have / of / people
_____

5 haven't / new / yet / *Singing Dog* video / I / the / seen
_____

6 been / a few years / the Internet / for / on / it's
_____

4 🔊 2.11 **Listen to the dialogues and say what Victor, Lola, and Alice have (✓) or haven't (✗) done.**

Victor		Lola		Alice	
make his bed	✔	do her math homework	☐	take Scooby for a walk	☐
clean his bedroom	☐	do her English homework	☐	feed Scooby	☐

Victor has made his bed.

5 Focus on you Look at the titles of these movies and write if you have already seen them or if you haven't seen them yet.

Captain America   Godzilla   Jurassic World   Noah   Rio 2
The Amazing Spider-Man   The Avengers   Transformers   X-Men

A *I've already seen Captain America and Godzilla.*
B *I haven't seen Godzilla yet.*

6 Pairwork Tell your partner the titles of three movies or online videos you have already seen and three movies or online videos you haven't seen yet. 😊

I've already seen ...
I haven't seen ... yet.

6 Vocabulary

Internet activities

1 🔊 2.12 **Complete the Internet activities with the words in the box. Then listen and repeat.**

commenting on a picture   downloading music   IMing   ~~playing an online game~~
posting a picture   sending an e-mail   updating her antivirus software
using a search engine   watching a video

1 He's _playing an online game_____.
2 She's _____.
3 He's _____.
4 She's _____ to a friend.
5 He's _____.

6 She's _____.
7 She's _____.
8 He's _____ his cousin.
9 He's _____.

2 🔊 2.13 **Complete the sentences. Then listen and check.**

I always _download_ music from the Internet Music Store. The songs are only $1!
1 Is George going to _____ pictures from his vacation on Facebook?
2 A lot of teenagers _____ online games.
3 I often _____ on my friends' posts on Facebook. I usually write something funny.
4 If I want to find some information, I _____ a search engine.
5 I _____ my antivirus software every week.
6 Can you _____ me when you get home?
7 I _____ funny videos on YouTube when I'm bored.
8 I don't often _____ e-mails to my friends. I usually text them.

3 Pairwork **Ask and answer about often you do the Internet activities in exercise 1. Use the adverbs of frequency _always_, _sometimes_, _often_, _rarely_, and _never_.** 😊

A How often do you download music?
B I rarely download music.

Look!

IM = _Instant message_
She IMd me last night.

Workbook p.34   **Extra practice** online

Present perfect + *yet* and *already*

> Have you seen the latest viral video **yet**?
> They've **already** made five more videos.

Think!

Read the sentences. Then complete the rules with *yet* and *already*.

Have you seen the new video **yet**?
No, I haven't. I haven't seen it **yet**.
Yes, I have. I've **already** seen it.

- We usually put ¹_____ in yes / no questions and negative sentences.
- We usually put ²_____ in affirmative sentences.

Rules p.W32

1 Choose the correct answers.

Darren hasn't read his e-mails **already** / **yet**.
1 Clara has **already** / **yet** posted the pictures on her social network page.
2 Have you done your homework **already** / **yet**?
3 We haven't had dinner **already** / **yet**.
4 I've **already** / **yet** spoken to Mia.
5 You're late! The test has **already** / **yet** started.

2 Write the sentences in the correct order.

finished / hasn't / yet / her dance lesson / Maria .
Maria hasn't finished her dance lesson yet.
1 blog / read / yet / have / you / Michael's ?
2 already / my / I've / done / homework .
3 movie / hurry up! / the / already / started / has .
4 you / have / new / yet / student / met / the ?
5 already / some / Jo / songs / downloaded / has .
6 shopping / we / yet / done / the / haven't .

3 Write affirmative sentences (✓) with *already*, and negative sentences (✗) and yes / no questions (?) with *yet*.

Dad / wash the dishes (✗)
Dad hasn't washed the dishes yet.
they / finish their project (?)
Have they finished their project yet?
Katie / see / the video (✓)
Katie has already seen the video.
1 I / make my bed (✓)
2 you / see Sally's new video (?)
3 Mike / post the pictures of his birthday party (✗)
4 the train / arrive (✗)
5 we / downloaded the new *Superman* movie (✓)
6 you / save the document (?)

4 Look at Julia's list. Write about what she has already done (✓) and what she hasn't done yet (✗).

She's already made her bed.
She hasn't cleaned her room yet.

My chores!
make my bed (✓) | IM Ana about tonight (✗)
clean my room (✗) | post pictures on my blog (✓)
do the shopping (✗) | buy Mom's birthday present (✗)
finish my homework (✓) | study for the English test (✓)

5 Complete the message with the words in the box.

already (x3) has haven't have already yet (x2)

Hi, Sylvia,

We're having a great time in New York. We only arrived two days ago, but we've **already** done some exciting things. I've ¹_____ taken a lot of pictures, but I ²_____ posted them on my website yet. We've ³_____ visited the Statue of Liberty, but we haven't been to any museums ⁴_____. We're planning to go tomorrow. On Friday, we're going to see *War Horse* on Broadway. We ⁵_____ bought the tickets. I'm very excited! Have you gotten your test scores ⁶_____? My brother ⁷_____ already received his and they aren't very good. I hope yours are better!

Amy

6 Game! Guess three things your partner has already done and three things he / she hasn't done yet this week. Write them down.

She's already cleaned her room.
She hasn't watched her favorite TV show yet.

Then find out if your guesses are correct. You get one point for a correct guess. The winner is the person with more points.

A Have you cleaned your room yet?
B Yes, I've already cleaned it. / No, I haven't cleaned it yet.

Finished?

Write five sentences about things you have already done or haven't done yet today.

I've cleaned my room today, but I haven't watched my favorite TV show yet.

Puzzle p.106

At the visitor center

1 🔊 2.14 **Jenny is at a visitor center. Listen and choose the correct answer. Then listen and repeat.**

Assistant Good (morning) / afternoon. Can I help you?
Jenny Yes, please. I'd like to do a tour of the ¹city / old town.
Assistant There are a lot of different tours. There's a walking tour, a bike tour, and a bus tour. What type of tour are you looking for?
Jenny What do you recommend?
Assistant The ²walking / bike tour is very good. And I think the best way to see the city is ³on foot / by bike.
Jenny How much does it cost?
Assistant The tickets are ⁴$8 / $18.
Jenny How long does it take?
Assistant It takes ⁵two / a few hours.
Jenny Where does it start?
Assistant It starts here at the visitor center. You visit the most important sights in the city.
Jenny What time does it start?
Assistant There are three tours every day – at 10 a.m., 2 p.m., and 4 p.m. Here's a leaflet with all the ⁶information / telephone numbers.
Jenny Thank you. That's great.

Learn it, use it!

You say	You hear
I'd like to do a tour of the city.	What type of tour are you looking for?
What do you recommend?	I think the best way to see the city is on foot / by bike.
How much does the tour cost?	The tickets are …
How long does the tour take?	It takes …
Where / What time does it start?	It starts at … / There are three tours. They start at …

2 🔊 2.15 **Listen to two more people at the visitor center. Complete the chart.**

	Person 1	Person 2
Type of tour	A bus tour	6 _____
Price of ticket	1 _____	7 _____
Duration of tour	2 _____	8 _____
Departure from	3 _____	9 _____
Times	4 _____, 5 _____	10 _____, 11 _____

3 Pairwork Look at advertisements for tours of San Francisco. Choose a tour and take turns to ask for information at the visitor center. 😊

San Francisco Duck Tour
See San Francisco from land and water!
Duck tours last 90 minutes and depart every hour from the beach.
Tickets: Adults $27, children $20

BAY QUACKERS

Helicopter Tour
See San Francisco from the sky!
Take a Helicopter Tour!
This unique tour lasts 30 minutes.
Tickets: Adults $225, children $170
Departs from the airport at 10 a.m. and 3 p.m.

N197AE

Workbook p.36 **Extra practice** online

Present perfect + *just*

> I've **just** watched the new "Singing Dog" video.

Think!

Read the sentences. Then choose the correct alternatives.

I've **just** watched the new "Singing Dog" video.
He's **just** bought an awesome new video game.
- We use *just* in [1]**affirmative / negative** sentences.
- *Just* comes after [2]***have* or *has* / the verb**.

Rules p.W32

1 Complete the sentences with the present perfect form of the verbs in parentheses and *just*. Use short forms.

My brother is very excited. He 's *just passed* (pass) his driving test.

1 Our team is winning! Diego _____ (score) a goal.
2 They're not hungry. They _____ (have) lunch.
3 I _____ (finish) my homework. It was easy.
4 Sally isn't here. She _____ (take) the dog for a walk.
5 It's Liam's birthday today. I _____ (send) him a text message.

2 Look at the pictures and write sentences with the words in the box. Use the present perfect with *just*.

> break / a bottle   buy / the groceries
> eat / a fish   ~~find / some money~~
> have / a swim   miss / the bus

She's just found some money.

1 _____
2 _____
3 _____
4 _____
5 _____

Present perfect + *for / since*

> It's been on the Internet **for** a few years now. Billions of people have watched *Gangnam Style* **since** 2012.

Think!

Read the sentences. Then complete the rules with *for* and *since*.

The new video has been online **for** a week. It's had over 250,000 hits **since** last Monday.
- We use [1]_____ with the present perfect to talk about the duration of a state or action.
- We use [2]_____ with the present perfect to talk about when a state or action began.

Rules pp.W32–33

3 Complete the time expressions with *for* or *since*.

since April   3 _____ last Saturday
1 _____ twenty minutes   4 _____ 2 o'clock
2 _____ six months   5 _____ a long time

4 Match the sentence halves and complete them with *for* or *since*.

1 I've been a student at this   a the phone _____ hours!
2 Our team hasn't won   b house _____ 2012.
3 We've lived in this   c school *for* two years.
4 Jennifer has been on   d a game _____ November.
5 Olivia hasn't eaten   e teacher _____ two years.
6 Mrs. Watson has been our   f chocolate _____ February.

1 c   I've been a student at this school for two years.

5 Complete the sentences with the present perfect form of the verbs in parentheses and *for* or *since*.

We 've been (be) friends for five years.

1 George _____ (study) Japanese _____ three years.
2 My grandparents _____ (live) in Spain _____ 2013.
3 She's hungry because she _____ (eat) anything _____ breakfast.
4 We _____ (have) our pet iguana _____ six months.
5 I _____ (see) my cousins _____ my birthday party.

Finished?

Write about the things in the box. Use the present perfect with *for* and *since*.

> be at this school   have my cell phone
> know my best friend

I've known my best friend for / since ...

Puzzle p.106

What Type of Internet User are You?

What have you used the Internet for in the past week? The answer to this question can tell you what type of Internet user you are. There are four categories of Internet users: butterflies, dolphins, seals, and squirrels. Read the article and discover what type you are.

1 *It's 8:30 in the morning. Jessie has already checked her Facebook page three times. She has "liked" two photos, and she has sent messages to three friends. And she hasn't had breakfast yet!*

Jessie is an Internet butterfly.

Butterflies use the Internet to keep in touch with friends on social network websites. They send messages, chat, post photos or videos, and comment on their friends' posts.

2 *Simon's playing an online game. To play the game, he enters a virtual world and creates a character who has to complete missions. Simon's character has just killed two dragons!*

Simon is an Internet dolphin.

Dolphins like playing online games. In online games, players often create characters and enter virtual worlds. Multiplayer games are very popular. In them, people from all over the world play the game at the same time.

3 *Carly's spending the evening with two friends. They haven't arrived yet, and Carly is getting ready. She's already downloaded some songs so she can make a playlist. They are going to listen to music and watch a movie online.*

Carly is an Internet seal.

Seals use the Internet for entertainment. They listen to music and watch TV, movies, and videos online. They usually access the Internet via their smartphones, laptops, or tablets so they can listen to music or watch TV shows anytime and anywhere.

4 *Chris and Holly are using the Internet to do some research for their science project. They've just found a great website with interesting information.*

Chris and Holly are Internet squirrels.

Squirrels use the Internet to get information and do research. They read and watch the news online. They use it to help them with their schoolwork. Squirrels have to be careful about choosing the correct website. Not all the information on the Internet is accurate!

Check it out!

Find these words and check their meaning.

keep in touch with
dragons
playlist
entertainment
mixture

So, are you an Internet butterfly, dolphin, seal, or squirrel? Or perhaps you're a mixture of two or more categories – a squirrefly or a dolseal!

Reading

1 🔊 2.16 **Read and listen** to the article. Find the names of the four types of Internet users.

butterfly, ...

2 Answer the questions.

What type of websites do butterflies use? *They use social network websites.*

1 What type of game is Simon playing?
2 What are multiplayer games?
3 Why has Carly downloaded some songs from the Internet?
4 How do seals usually access the Internet?
5 What are Chris and Holly doing research for?
6 Why do squirrels have to be careful?
7 What Internet user category or categories do you belong to? Why?

Listening

3 🔊 2.17 **Listen to Darren talking about how he uses the Internet. The underlined information is false. Listen and write the correct information. Then listen and check.**

I use the Internet every <u>week</u>. *day*

1 I use it at school and at <u>the library</u>.
2 At home, I use the Internet for <u>homework</u>.
3 I have a laptop, but I usually use my <u>tablet</u> to go online.

4 I <u>often</u> play online games.
5 I like <u>adventure</u> and action games.
6 I <u>love</u> social network websites.
7 I prefer chatting to my friends <u>online</u>.

Speaking

4 Pairwork Ask and answer with a partner. Take notes of your partner's answers. 😊

• How often do you use the Internet?
• Where do you usually go online – at home, at school, at the library?
• How do you access the Internet – PC, laptop, smartphone, tablet?
• What do you use the Internet for – social network sites, games, music, videos, schoolwork, other?
• Give an example of how the Internet has helped you with your schoolwork.
• How often do you post things online? What and where?
• How many times have you used the Internet today / this week?
• What sites have you visited? Why?

My speaking skills

Taking notes
When you ask another student questions, and you take notes of their answers, don't write full sentences. Only write one or two key words. You can also use abbreviations and then complete the words when you have finished talking.

5 Tell your classmates about how your partner uses the Internet.

Andrea uses the Internet every day ...

Writing

6 Use your answers in exercise 4 to write a paragraph (70–100 words) about how you use the Internet.

I use the Internet twice or three times a week ...

Review

Vocabulary

1 Match the words in A and B to make six
exciting experiences and six Internet activities.

A		B	
download _h_		a	a horse
1	do ___	b	a mountain
2	post ___	c	a competition
3	ride ___	d	in an airplane
4	use ___	e	whitewater rafting
5	climb ___	f	a search engine
6	comment ___	g	on your friends' pictures
7	win ___	h	music
8	send ___	i	a video
9	fly ___	j	pictures on a website
10	watch ___	k	a parachute jump
11	go ___	l	e-mails

Grammar

2 Write affirmative (✓) and negative (✗)
sentences or questions (?) with the present
perfect.

we / be / to Spain (✗)
We haven't been to Spain.

1 Kevin / answer / my e-mail (✗)
_____

2 you / download / The Script's new album (?)
_____

3 I / see / all of Kirsten Dunst's movies (✓)
_____

4 Mary / post / the pictures of her party on
Facebook (✓)
_____
_____

5 the children / finish / their homework (?)
_____

6 it / stop / raining (✗)
_____

3 Complete the sentences with *been* or *gone*.

"Where's Alice?" "She's _gone_ home."

1 I've _____ to Mexico twice.
2 Tim isn't here. He's _____ to the library.
3 Pete's never _____ to a pop concert.
4 Steve has _____ whitewater rafting in the
mountains. I hope it doesn't rain.
5 She's _____ to eight countries in Asia.

4 Complete the dialogues. Use the present
perfect or simple past.

A _Have you ever eaten_ (you / ever eat)
Chinese food?
B Yes, I _have_ . I _went_ (go) to a
Chinese restaurant last weekend.

1
A ¹_____ (you / ever fly)
in an airplane?
B Yes, I ²_____. I ³_____ (go) to
Australia last year. I ⁴_____ (fly) from Rio
to Perth.

2
A ⁵_____ (your
grandma / ever use) a computer?
B Yes, she ⁶_____. She ⁷_____
(download) the new Adele song last week.

3
A ⁸_____ (you / ever
climb) a mountain?
B Yes, I ⁹_____. I ¹⁰_____ (climb)
Mount Kilimanjaro last summer.

5 Rewrite the sentences in the correct order.

started / just / has / the / movie
The movie has just started.

1 has / Peter / yet / sold / his / laptop ?
_____

2 we've / cousin / your / met / already
_____

3 taken / trash / Jason / yet / hasn't / the / out
_____

4 left / train / just / has / the
_____

5 I've / seen / movie / this / already
_____

6 the / just / students / finished / have / Unit 4
_____

6 Complete the sentences with *for*, *since*,
already, or *yet*.

Jack hasn't woken up _yet_ .

1 I've known my best friends _____ we were
at elementary school.
2 Jill hasn't finished her homework _____.
3 Dad has _____ fed the dog.
4 We've been here _____ Friday.
5 Al has _____ invited 50 people to his party!
6 I've had this phone _____ two years.
7 Have you lived in L.A. _____ a long time?

Communication

7 🔊 2.18 **Complete the dialogues. Then listen and check.**

1

A Good afternoon. *Can I help you?*

B Yes, please. I'd like to check in.

A OK. ¹_____?

B It's Ray, Janet Ray. ²_____ for three nights.

A Ray. OK, that's fine. Could I have ³_____?

B Yes, here's my passport.

A Thank you. Your room number is 26. It's on the second floor.

B Thank you.

A ⁴_____.

2

A Hello. ⁵_____ does a walking tour of the town cost?

B The tickets are $6.

A ⁶_____?

B It takes about two hours.

A ⁷_____?

B It starts at 10 a.m.

A Thank you. That's great.

Pronunciation

/æ/ and /ʌ/

8 🔊 2.19 **Listen to the difference between the two sounds. Then listen and repeat.**

/æ/ began   /ʌ/ begun

9 🔊 2.20 **Complete the chart with the simple past and past participles of the verbs. Listen and check. Then listen and repeat.**

Base form	Simple past /æ/	Past participle /ʌ/
begin	*began*	*begun*
drink	¹_____	²_____
ring	³_____	⁴_____
sing	⁵_____	⁶_____
swim	⁷_____	⁸_____

Listening

10 🔊 2.21 **Listen to Yuki describing her trip to the U.S. Check (✓) the things she has done.**

1 ridden a horse ✓
2 been whitewater rafting ☐
3 visited a museum ☐
4 met Native American people ☐
5 done a parachute jump ☐
6 taken a lot of pictures ☐
7 been to Las Vegas ☐
8 been to a theme park ☐

1 Which is Chloe's bedroom?   a ☐ b ☐ c ☐

2 What has Grandpa never done?   a ☐ b ☐ c ☐

3 Where are the girl's keys?   a ☐ b ☐ c ☐

11 🔊 2.22 **Listen to four conversations and check (✓) the correct answers.**

Where does Paul live now?   a ☐ b ☐ c ✓

C Culture club

The Online Community

1 Teens online

The Internet has become an essential part of a teenager's life in the U.S. Today, about 97 percent of American teenagers use the Internet, and over three quarters of them use social networking websites.

2 _____

Social networking sites first appeared in the late 1990s, and their growth has been incredible. Today, the number one social network in the U.S. is Facebook, but Pinterest and Twitter are also popular. The most popular activities on social networking sites are chatting and instant messaging. People also post comments on their friends' newsfeeds as well as posting pictures and personal updates.

3 _____

The majority of teenagers say that they have had positive online experiences, and people their own age are generally kind to one another on social networks. However, 20 percent say that some people write unkind or rude things on their social networking sites. Also, many young people have experienced online bullying. This is a very serious problem, and you must tell an adult if someone tries to bully you or is unkind to you on the Internet.

4 _____

Many people seem to have different personalities online than in real life. For example, some people may be too shy to say what they think in real life, but they are more confident online and they aren't afraid of giving their opinions. But someone who is usually kind may say unkind things about a friend online, and this can create problems.

5 _____

We are all citizens of a physical community and we have to obey laws. Similarly, Internet users are citizens of the digital community and there are rules of behavior there, too. It is important that all people learn to be responsible digital citizens. They must learn to use the Internet safely and responsibly to help make the Internet a great place to be.

Digital Citizenship Tips

Think before you post something – nothing disappears on the Internet, so never post secrets or personal information.

Respect other people – don't post your friends' personal texts or pictures online.

Be kind and polite – don't say unkind things about other people.

Be responsible – only spread useful and positive information.

Be critical – don't believe everything you read on the Internet.

Check it out!

Find these words and check their meaning.

newsfeeds
one another
bullying
similarly
spread

1 🔊 2.23 **Read and listen to the article. Match the headings with the paragraphs. Then listen and check.**

A Online experiences   C Digital citizenship   E Online identity
B Teens online   D Social networks

2 Comprehension Answer the questions.

What proportion of American teenagers use social networking sites?
Over three quarters of them use social networking websites.

1 When did the first social networking sites appear?
2 What are the most popular social networking activities?
3 What is a serious problem on the Internet?
4 What happens to many people's personalities online?
5 What is a digital citizen?
6 How can people make the Internet a great place to be?

3 Presentation Discuss the questions with your partner. Make notes and then prepare a short presentation about your online experiences.

• What social network websites do you and your friends use?
• What activities do you and your friends use these sites for?
• Have you had mainly positive or negative experiences on the Internet?
• Have you or someone you know ever experienced online bullying? If so, what happened?
• How do you check information you find on the Internet?

Vocabulary and speaking

I can talk about experiences. (p.54) B1

1 Match 1–5 with a–f. Then say true sentences to your partner.

My dad wants to go — a a parachute jump.
1 We flew to Rome — b whitewater rafting.
2 I hate sleeping   c a famous actor.
3 I'd like to do   d in an airplane.
4 My mom likes riding e in a tent.
5 I met   f horses.

___ / 5

I can check into a hotel. (p.56) B1

2 Complete the dialogue. Then practice the dialogue.

A Good evening. Can I h_elp_____ you?
B I'd like to ¹c_____ in. My name's Kim Jones.
A ²C_____ I have your passport, please?
B Yes, ³h_____ you are.
A Can you ⁴s_____ this form, please?
B Yes, of course.
A It's room 302. ⁵H_____ your key card.

___ / 5

I can ask about experiences. (p.59) B1

3 Write questions with *ever*. Then write true answers. Practice the questions.

you / win / an award?
Have you ever won an award?
1 your friends / do / voluntary work?
2 you / speak / in public?
3 your best friend / visit / a foreign country?
4 your mom / be / on TV?
5 you / try / an exciting sport?

___ / 5

I can ask and say how often people do Internet activities. (p.62) B1

4 Reorder the letters and complete the Internet activities.

I often _download_ music. (l a d o d w n o)
1 My friends _____ games online. (l y a p)
2 How often do you _____ e-mails? (n e d s)
3 I rarely _____ on my friends' Facebook posts. (e m n o t m c)
4 I often _____ online videos. (c w h a t)
5 Tim often _____ pictures (s t o p s)

___ / 5

I can ask for information at the visitor center. (p.64) B1

5 Complete the questions.

_What_____ type of tours are there?
1 _____ tour do you recommend?
2 _____ does it cost?
3 _____ does it take?
4 _____ does it start?
5 _____ does it start?

___ / 5

I can ask my partner questions about how he / she uses the Internet. (p.67) B1

6 Reorder the words and write questions. Then write true answers.

often / do / how / Internet / use / you / the ?
How often do you use the Internet?
1 access / how / you / Internet / do / the ?
2 ever / online / anything / have / posted / you ?
3 do / for / you / use / Internet / what / the ?
4 visited / today / what / websites / you / have ?
5 games / play / often / you / online / do ?

___ / 5

Reading, listening, and writing

		Got it?	
	Yes	I'm not sure	No
I can read and understand an article about a person who did the Duke of Edinburgh award. (p.58) B1	☐	☐	☐
I can understand a person talking about his experience of the Duke of Edinburgh Award. (p.59) B1	☐	☐	☐
I can write an e-mail about things I have done on vacation. (p.59) B1	☐	☐	☐
I can understand an article about different types of Internet user. (p.66) B1	☐	☐	☐
I can understand a person talking about how he uses the Internet. (p.67) B1	☐	☐	☐
I can write an article about how I use the Internet. (p.67) B1	☐	☐	☐

7 What were they doing?

💬 comments

BIKE THEFT ON THE RISE

It's a bike rider's worst nightmare – you lock your bike and leave it, but when you come back, it's gone!

Urban biking in the U.S. is increasing everywhere, but bike crime is, too. In New York City last year, thieves stole about 60,000 bikes! Most people don't report bike thefts because the police rarely do anything. Serious crimes like murder and vandalism take up most of their time. Stealing bikes is easy, as filmmakers Casey and Van Neistat discovered. They made a movie that showed it was too easy to steal a bike in New York City. In the movie, Casey stole his own bike in various situations, and the police only stopped him once!

We interviewed two victims of bike theft to find out what happened to them. Were they being careful when their bikes were stolen?

Make it hard for criminals!

- Don't ride alone at night.
- Lock your bike.
- Keep your bike indoors.
- Report thefts to the police.

Check it out!

Find these words and check their meaning.

nightmare
lock
threatening
sidewalk
suspicious

First, we spoke to Steve; was he doing anything wrong?

Steve was riding his bike alone at night: "I was riding on a backstreet when I saw two boys. They were laughing and talking while they were walking towards me. They weren't doing anything threatening. Then, while I was riding past, one of the boys pushed me and I fell off my bike. While I was getting up, the other boy hit me. Then they took my bike and ran away. I reported it to the police, but they never found it."

Eva didn't lock her bike: "I was riding my bike with a friend. We stopped at a store to get some groceries. We left our bikes on the sidewalk while we were shopping. I didn't lock my bike because I was only in the store for a couple of minutes. I was looking out the door while I was waiting in line at the register. A guy was standing near my bike, but he wasn't doing anything suspicious. When I got outside, the guy was riding away fast on my bike! I ran after him, but he disappeared. I reported it to the police, but nothing happened."

1 🔊 2.24 **Read and listen** What did Steve and Eva do wrong?

2 Comprehension Answer the questions.

How many bikes did thieves steal in New York City last year?
They stole about 60,000 bikes.
1 Why don't most people report bike thefts?
2 Where was Steve when the boys stole his bike?
3 What happened when the first boy pushed Steve?
4 Why didn't Eva lock her bike?
5 What happened after Eva reported the theft?

Language focus

3 Complete the sentences from the web page article. Then put them in the correct order to tell Steve and Eva's stories.

Steve's story

They _____ and _____ while they _____ towards me. ___

I _was riding_ on a backstreet when I _saw_ two boys. 1

They _____ anything threatening. ___

Then they _____ my bike and _____ away. ___

While I _____ up, the other boy _____ me. ___

While I _____ past, one of the boys _____ me and I _____ off my bike. ___

Eva's story

We _____ our bikes on the sidewalk while we _____. ___

I _____ out of the door while I _____ in line at the register. ___

I _____ my bike with a friend. 1

A guy _____ near my bike, but he _____ anything suspicious. ___

When I _____ outside, the guy _____ away fast on my bike! ___

We _____ at a store to get some groceries. ___

4 🔊 2.25 Listen to the story. Put the sentences in the correct order.
___ I locked my bike to a post outside.
1 A few weeks ago, I rode my bike to the sports center for basketball practice.
___ He was doing something to my bike.
___ He was running away with the front wheel of my bike.
___ I shouted and ran outside.
___ A guy was standing near my bike, but he wasn't looking at it.
___ When I looked again, the guy was still there.
___ While I was playing, I looked out the window.

5 Focus on you Were you doing these activities at these times yesterday?

7 a.m.	having breakfast	3 p.m.	going home
7:30 a.m.	traveling to school	5 p.m.	doing my homework
10 a.m.	having a science lesson	7 p.m.	watching TV
1 p.m.	having lunch	11 p.m.	sleeping

I was / wasn't having breakfast at 7 a.m. yesterday.

6 Pairwork Tell your partner what activities you were or weren't doing at specific times yesterday. 😊
I was riding my bike to school at 7:45 a.m. yesterday.

Vocabulary

Crime

1 🔊 2.26 **Match the crimes with the pictures. Then listen and repeat.**

> burglary   kidnapping   mugging   murder   pickpocketing
> ~~robbery~~   shoplifting   vandalism

robbery _____

1 _____

2 _____

3 _____

4 _____

5 _____

6 _____

7 _____

2 🔊 2.27 **Complete the chart with the words in the box. Then listen and check.**

> burglar   kidnapper   mugger   murderer
> pickpocket   ~~robber~~   shoplifter   vandal

Look!

Steal (v) (simple past *stole*, past participle *stolen*) – to take something from someone without their permission.
Theft (n) – the act of stealing.
Thief (n) – a general term for a person who steals. Robbers, burglars, pickpockets, and muggers are all *thieves*.

Crime	Criminal	Action
robbery	robber	**robs** a bank or a store
shoplifting	1 _____	**shoplifts / steals things** in a store
burglary	2 _____	enters a house and **burglarizes** it
pickpocketing	3 _____	**picks** people's pockets or steals from bags
murder	4 _____	**murders** someone
mugging	5 _____	**mugs** people in the street
vandalism	6 _____	**vandalizes** property
kidnapping	7 _____	**kidnaps** someone

3 Pairwork **Ask and answer questions about what criminals do.**

A What *does a burglar do?*
B He enters a house and burglarizes it. What does a pickpocket do?
A He takes ...

Workbook p.40   **Extra practice** online

Past progressive

Affirmative and negative

> I was riding my bike with a friend.
> They were walking towards me.

Affirmative	Negative
I was walking.	I wasn't walking.
You were talking.	You weren't talking.
He / She / It was running.	He / She / It wasn't running.
We/ You / They were riding.	We / You / They weren't riding.

Think!

Read the sentences. Then choose the correct alternative.

I was having breakfast at eight o'clock this morning. They weren't listening to the teacher.
- We use the past progressive to describe an action **in progress in the past / that is still happening now.**

Rules p.W38

1 Complete the sentences with the past progressive form of the verbs in parentheses.

The boys <u>were playing</u> (play) soccer on Saturday morning.

1 She _____ (listen) to music in her bedroom all evening.
2 I _____ (not wear) my best clothes yesterday.
3 They _____ (not study) all afternoon.
4 The officer _____ (run) after the robbers.
5 He _____ (watch) a movie at 8 p.m.

yes / no questions and short answers

> Were they walking towards you?
> Yes, they were. / No, they weren't.

yes / no questions	Short answers	
	Affirmative	Negative
Was I talking?	Yes, I was.	No, I wasn't.
Were you walking?	Yes, you were.	No, you weren't.
Was he / she / it sleeping?	Yes, he / she / it was.	No, he / she / it wasn't.
Were we / you / they playing?	Yes, we / you / they were.	No, we / you / they weren't.

2 Write questions in the past progressive. Then write short answers.

Amy / use the tablet / this morning? (✓)
"Was Amy using the tablet this morning?"
"Yes, she was."
it / rain / yesterday? (✗)
"Was it raining yesterday?" "No, it wasn't."

1 the burglar / run away / from the police? (✓)
2 you / talk to Mr. Peters / after the lesson? (✗)
3 James / wait at the bus stop / this morning? (✓)
4 they / copy / during the test / last week? (✗)
5 you / wear / sneakers / yesterday? (✗)

while

Think!

Read the sentences. Then complete the rule.

While he **was studying**, he **was listening** to music.
The boys **were talking while** they **were walking** towards me.
- We use _____ to link two simultaneous actions in the past.

Rules p.W39

3 Write sentences. Use the past progressive.

Juan / play / video games / while / I / wash / the dishes.
Juan was playing video games while I was washing the dishes.

1 You / bike / while / I / run.
2 While / we / play / basketball, / Maria / study.
3 The students / talk / while / they / take / a test.
4 Jason / come / out of the movie theater / while / we / go / in.
5 While / they / have / lunch, / they / watch / TV.

Finished?

Say what you and your friends were and weren't doing at these times.

> 10 a.m. last Saturday   5 p.m. yesterday
> 8 p.m. last night   7:30 a.m. today

I was playing tennis at 10 a.m. last Saturday.
I wasn't sleeping.

Puzzle p.107

At the police station

1 🔊 2.28 **Listen and complete the crime report. Then listen and repeat.**

Date: May 14th	**Full Name:** _Diane_ Clarke
Description of suspect(s):	About 16 or 17, wearing jeans and a ¹_____. Quite tall and had ²_____ brown hair. Had a tattoo on his ³_____.
Item(s) stolen:	⁴_____ ⁵_____
Place: ⁶_____	**Time:** ⁷_____

Officer Can I help you?

Diane Yes. I want to report a crime.

Officer OK. Let's fill out this crime report. What happened?

Diane A boy stole my wallet and my cell phone.

Officer OK. I need a few details. Where were you?

Diane I was walking through Lincoln Park. I was going home from school.

Officer Lincoln Park ... and then what happened?

Diane A boy stopped me. He had a knife and he asked me for money and my cell phone.

Officer What time did this happen?

Diane It happened at around 4:30 this afternoon.

Officer How much money was in your wallet?

Diane There was about $15 and my metro card.

Officer What did the boy look like?

Diane He was about 16 or 17. He was wearing jeans and a black jacket. He was tall, and he had short brown hair. He had a tattoo on his neck.

Learn it, use it!

You hear	You say
Can I help you?	I want to report a crime.
What happened?	A boy / girl stole my cell phone.
Where / When did it happen?	It happened in Lincoln Park / this afternoon ...
What was he / were they wearing?	He was wearing ... / They were wearing ...

2 🔊 2.29 **Listen to the conversation in a police station and complete Rachael's crime report. Listen again and complete the description of the crime and suspect.**

Incident and Crime Report

Date:	December 17th	Item(s) stolen:	¹_____
Name:	Rachael Hall	Place:	²_____
Type of crime:	_theft_	Time:	³_____

Description of the crime:

I was sitting on the bus when ⁴_____. I took it out of my backpack and while I ⁵_____, a girl sat down next to me. My ⁶_____ was open on my knee. At the next bus stop, the girl ⁷_____ suddenly and ⁸_____ the bus. I knew something was wrong so I checked my backpack and my ⁹_____.

Description of the suspect(s):

She was ¹⁰_____ and slim, and she had blond, ¹¹_____ hair. She was wearing jeans and ¹²_____. She was about ¹³_____ years old.

3 Pairwork **Role-play a scene at a police station. Take turns to play the parts of the officer and the victim. Use the dialogue in exercise 1 as a model.** 🙂

Workbook p.42 **Extra practice** online

Past progressive and simple past + *when / while*

Think!

Read the sentences. Then complete the sentences with *past progressive* or *simple past*.

While I **was riding** past them, one of the boys **pushed** me.
I **was sitting** on the bus **when** my phone **rang**.

- We use the ¹_____ for a short action which interrupts a longer action.
- We use the ²_____ for the longer action.

Rules p.W39

1 Match the sentence halves.

1 I was sleeping <u>d</u>
2 While Katia was cleaning her room, ___
3 Tom was skateboarding in the park ___
4 When I saw the burglar, ___
5 While we were walking home, ___
6 Mom burned her hand ___

a her pet mouse escaped.
b while she was cooking.
c we saw an accident.
d when my alarm went off.
e he was climbing out of a window
f when he fell and broke his arm.

2 Read the text and choose the correct answers.

It was 8 p.m. and I was in my bedroom. I was listening / listened to music and I ¹was sending / sent text messages to my friends. It was very hot, so I decided to open the window. While I ²was opening / opened the window, I ³was looking / looked at the sky and I ⁴was seeing / saw two big red circular lights. They ⁵were moving / moved slowly towards the house. I was very excited! I ⁶was running / ran downstairs into the yard. While I ⁷was running / ran through the kitchen, I ⁸was calling / called my dad. He ⁹was watching / watched TV in the living room. When Dad ¹⁰was coming / came into the yard, the lights ¹¹were moving / moved over the house. It was incredible. Dad said, "Quick! Film them with your phone." I ¹²ran / was running to my room and got my phone, but when I ¹³was getting / got back, the lights ¹⁴were disappearing / disappeared in the distance. I tried to film them, but it was too dark!

3 Complete the sentences with the past progressive or simple past form of the verbs in parentheses.

I <u>was reading</u> in bed when I <u>heard</u> someone outside. (read / hear)

1 Two boys _____ Oscar's backpack while he _____ home from school. (steal / walk)
2 While we _____ in Brazil, we _____ a lot of friendly people. (travel / meet)
3 When I _____ up, it _____. (wake / snow)
4 While Alicia _____ in her room, a bird _____ in through the open window. (study / fly)
5 Lucas _____ his leg while he _____ in Canada. (break / ski)
6 Aunt Katie _____ at the train station when I _____. (wait / arrive)
7 We _____ to the bus stop when it _____ to rain. (walk / start)
8 Our cat _____ on the sofa when we _____ home. (sleep / get)

4 Complete the sentences with your ideas. Use the past progressive or the simple past.

I was getting on the bus when <u>my cell phone rang.</u>

1 _____ when the teacher called his name.
2 While my friend was walking home, _____
3 _____ when it started to rain.
4 While my parents were watching TV, _____
5 I fell asleep while I _____

Finished?

Write a crime story. Use the words in the box. Then exchange stories with a partner.

call look see vandalize wait watch

Last night, I was waiting for the bus when I saw ...

Puzzle p.107

The Founding of Modern Australia

The Story of Mary Wade

Mary Wade was born in London in 1777. Her family was very poor, and Mary was a street beggar and a thief. One day while Mary was begging, she saw her friend Jane Whiting. Jane was a beggar, too. The two girls decided to spend the day together. It was a day that changed Mary's life.

While Mary and Jane were begging, they saw an 8-year-old girl. She was filling a bottle at a water fountain, and she was wearing expensive clothes. Mary and Jane offered to fill the bottle for the girl. Mary took the bottle and she broke it. The little girl was very upset, but Mary and Jane had a plan. They told the girl that they had another bottle and they asked her to follow them. Mary and Jane stole the little girl's clothes, and their plan was to sell the clothes and make some money.

The police found the little girl's scarf in Mary's house and arrested her for theft. She went on trial. Mary was only 11 years old, but the judge sentenced her to death. At that time, the death penalty was the punishment for 160 crimes in Britain, including sheep stealing and pickpocketing.

Facts
Britain sent over 165,000 convicts to Australia.
The oldest convict was 60 and the youngest 9 years old.
About 22 percent of Australians have at least one convict ancestor.

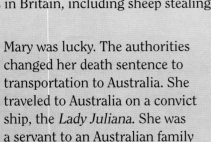
Prime Minister Kevin Rudd

Mary was lucky. The authorities changed her death sentence to transportation to Australia. She traveled to Australia on a convict ship, the *Lady Juliana*. She was a servant to an Australian family when she was only 13. When she became free again, she met Jonathan Brooker. Mary had 21 children. One of her descendents, Kevin Rudd, became Prime Minister of Australia in 2007.

Between 1788 and 1868, Australia was a British penal colony. British prisons were full, so the authorities sent convicts to the colonies. The journey to Australia took eleven months, and conditions on the convict ships were terrible, and many prisoners died. Life in the penal colonies was very hard. The men built roads or worked in factories or on farms. The women and girls became servants. At the end of their sentences, many stayed in Australia. Every year, Australians remember the first convicts on January 26th, Australia Day. It's the country's national holiday and it celebrates the arrival of the first convict ships in January 1788.

Check it out!

Find these words and check their meaning.
beggar / to beg
arrested
sentence / to sentence
punishment
descendents

My reading skills

Overviewing a text
It is useful to get an overview of a text before you read it in detail. Look at the title, any pictures, and the organization to find out what type of text it is. Read the introduction, headings, and topic sentences to get a general idea of its content. Then read in detail to answer specific questions.

Reading

1 Before you read, look quickly at the text and check (✓) what type of text it is.
a a magazine article ___   b an educational text ___   c a tourist brochure ___

2 🔊 2.30 Read and listen **to The Story of Mary Wade. Answer the questions.**

Why did Mary beg on the streets when she was a child? *Because her family was poor.*
1 What was the young girl doing when Mary and Jane saw her?
2 What did Mary and Jane steal?
3 What sentence did the judge give Mary?
4 Why was Mary lucky?
5 How many children did Mary have?
6 What is your personal reaction to Mary's story? Is it shocking, surprising, interesting, inspirational, …? Why?

3 🔊 2.31 Read and listen **to the second part of the text. When is Australia Day? What does it celebrate?**

Listening

4 🔊 2.32 **Emily saw two girls committing a crime. Listen and complete the sentences with one or two words. Then listen and check.**

Emily was in a <u>shoe store</u> .
1 She was buying a pair of _____.
2 She saw _____ girls walking quickly towards the door of the store.
3 One of the girls was carrying a _____.

4 The _____ stopped them.
5 He found _____ pairs of shoes.
6 He took the girls to _____ at the back of the store.
7 The sales clerk called the _____.

Speaking

5 **Pairwork** **How observant are you? Would you make a good witness? Follow the instructions and find out.** 😀

Look at the picture for one minute. Then cover the picture. Use the prompts to ask each other questions.
• Number of robbers
• Description of robbers (clothes, etc.)
• Time and place of robbery
• People at the crime scene
    (What were they doing? / What were they wearing?)
• Other important information for the police

A *How many robbers were there?*
B *I think there were three robbers.*
A *What were they wearing?*

Now uncover the picture and check your answers.

Writing

6 **Imagine you were in a store when a robbery took place. Write an e-mail to a friend about the robbery (100–120 words). Include information about:**
• the time and place and type of store
• what you / other people were doing
• the description of the robber(s)

• what happened
• what they stole
• how you felt

I saw a robbery yesterday! I was in …

Women Who Have Made History

In the last 100 years, more women have become scientists, writers, and politicians than ever before. For example, Rachel Carson was a scientist and writer who started the environmental movement in the 1960s. Indira Gandhi was a politician who became the first female Indian Prime Minister in 1966. The achievements of these extraordinary women and many others have changed the world.

This week, we present Marie Curie, the Polish-French physicist and chemist who was one of the greatest scientists of the 20th century. She was also the first woman to win a Nobel Prize, and the only person ever to win two Nobel Prizes in different subjects, physics and chemistry.

Maria Sklodowska was born in Warsaw, Poland in 1867. Maria went to Paris to study mathematics and physics. She met Pierre Curie, who was a well-known scientist. They got married in 1895.

Marie Curie is famous for her work on radiation, which she named "radioactivity." She used the word "radioactive" to describe substances that produce rays. Scientists already knew about the existence of "X-rays," but they didn't know what they were. Marie Curie's research showed that these radioactive rays come from atoms. She discovered polonium and radium, which are both radioactive elements. Her research was essential for the use of X-rays in medicine. She knew that doctors could use X-rays to reveal broken bones. During World War One, she organized twenty mobile X-ray units to help doctors. Marie also discovered that doctors could use another radioactive element, called radon, to treat cancer.

Marie Curie faced great opposition from male scientists in France, but she never gave up her research. She died in 1934 from leukemia that she developed because of her exposure to radiation. In those days, the health dangers of radioactivity were unknown. Her daughter Irene Curie was also a great scientist who won the Nobel Prize for chemistry in 1935.

Check it out!

Find these words and check their meaning.

elements
reveal
treat
gave up
exposure

1 🔊 2.33 **Read and listen** Complete the chart about Marie Curie.

Marie Curie	
Occupation:	*physicist and chemist*
Nationality:	1 _____
Famous for:	2 _____

2 Comprehension Answer the questions.

What have more women done in the last 100 years?

More women have become scientists, writers, and politicians (than ever before).

1 How many subjects did Marie Curie win Nobel prizes for?
2 Why did she go to Paris?
3 What did she discover about radioactive rays?
4 What radioactive elements did she discover?
5 What did she do during World War One?
6 How did she die?

Language focus

3 Rewrite the two sentences with one sentence. Start with the words given and find the endings in the article.

Rachel Carson was a scientist and writer. She started the environmental movement in the 1960s.

Rachel Carson was a scientist and writer *who started the environmental movement in the 1960s.*

1 Indira Gandhi was a politician. She became the first female Indian Prime Minister in 1966.
Indira Gandhi was a politician _____.
2 She met Pierre Curie. He was a well-known scientist.
She met Pierre Curie, _____.
3 Marie Curie is famous for her work on radiation. She named it "radioactivity."
Marie Curie is famous for her work on radiation, _____.
4 She used the word "radioactive" to describe substances. They produce rays.
She used the word "radioactive" to describe substances _____.
5 She discovered polonium and radium. They are both radioactive elements.
She discovered polonium and radium, _____.
6 She died from leukemia. It developed because of her exposure to radiation.
She died from leukemia _____.
7 Her daughter Irene Curie was also a great scientist. She won the Nobel Prize for chemistry in 1935.
Her daughter Irene Curie was also a great scientist _____
_____.

4 Read the article again. Complete the sentences.

She went to Paris *to study mathematics and physics*.

1 She knew that doctors could use X-rays _____.
2 She organized twenty mobile X-ray units _____.
3 Marie also discovered that doctors could use radon _____.

5 Focus on you Why do you do these things? Choose the most important reasons.

I go to school	a to study	b to meet friends	c to see the teachers
I use the Internet	a to do homework	b to chat	c to play games
I watch TV	a to relax	b to get the news	c to learn new things
I meet friends	a to play sports	b to hang out	c to listen to music
I save money	a to buy candy	b to buy clothes	c to buy presents

6 Pairwork Discuss your answers to exercise 5.

A I go to school to study.
B So do I. / Really? I go to school to meet my friends.

Human achievement

1 🔊 2.34 **Label the people with the professions in the box. Then listen and repeat.**

> architect   artist   composer   explorer   ~~inventor~~
> musician   politician   scientist   writer

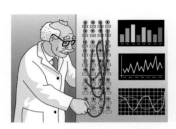

inventor

1 _____
2 _____
3 _____
4 _____
5 _____
6 _____
7 _____
8 _____

2 🔊 2.35 **Match the people with the verbs. Then listen and check.**

1 inventor	a travel / explore
2 scientist	b negotiate / debate
3 artist	c write
4 composer	d invent
5 explorer	e play music
6 writer	f discover
7 architect	g compose music
8 politician	h paint / draw
9 musician	i build / design

3 **Match the famous people with their professions and achievements. Then write two sentences about each person.**

1 Cervantes	explorer	Niteroi museum
2 Marie Curie	architect	*Guernica* (1937)
3 Roald Amundsen	artist	radioactivity
4 Oscar Niemeyer	writer	*Don Quixote* (1605)
5 Picasso	scientist	the South Pole (1912)

1 *Cervantes was a famous writer. He wrote Don Quixote.*

4 **Pairwork** **Think of a famous person for each category in exercise 1. Find out if your partner knows why they are famous.** 😊

A Who was Oscar Niemeyer?
B He was a Brazilian architect.

Workbook p.46   Extra practice online

Relative pronouns: *who / which / that*

People

> Marie Curie was a scientist. She discovered radium.
> Marie Curie was the scientist **who / that** discovered radium.

Things

> Radium is an element. It is very radioactive.
> Radium is an element **which / that** is very radioactive.

Think!

Read the sentences. Then complete the rules with *who* and *which*.

Alexander Fleming was the scientist **who** discovered penicillin.
Penicillin is a drug **which** kills bacteria.
- The relative pronoun [1]_____ refers to people.
- The relative pronoun [2]_____ refers to animals or things.

Rules p.W44

1 Choose the correct answers.

Oscar Niemeyer was the architect (who) / that designed the National Museum in Brasilia.
1 Charles Darwin was the man **who / which** described the theory of evolution.
2 DNA is a molecule **which / who** contains genetic code.
3 An explorer is a person **who / which** discovers new places.
4 The TV was an invention **who / which** changed the world.
5 Tim Berners-Lee was the person **which / who** invented the World Wide Web.
6 The Internet is a network **who / which** connects computers.

2 Complete the definitions with *who* or *which* and a phrase from the box.

> ~~debate and make laws~~   designed the Eiffel Tower
> discovered DNA   made the *Star Wars* movies
> is radioactive   stores and plays music files

Politicians are people
who debate and make laws.

1 George Lucas is the director
_____.
2 Uranium is an atom
_____.
3 Crick and Watson were the scientists
_____.
4 An MP3 player is an electronic device
_____.
5 Gustave Eiffel is the man
_____.

3 Join the sentences together. Rewrite them with *who*, *which*, or *that*.

Laurel and Hardy were actors. They appeared in silent movies.
Laurel and Hardy were actors who appeared in silent movies.

1 Frida Kahlo was a Mexican artist. She painted a lot of self-portraits.
_____

2 A hard drive is a part of a computer. It stores computer files.
_____

3 Vasco da Gama was an explorer. He came from Portugal.
_____

4 A vacuum cleaner is a machine. It cleans the floor.
_____

5 That is the dog. It bit my brother.
_____

4 Game! Take turns to define one of the people or things in the box. See if your partner can guess who or what you are describing.

> an airplane   a cat   a dog   a DVD player
> an iron   a pickpocket   a salesclerk
> a student   a teacher   ~~an umbrella~~   a vandal

A It is an object that is very useful when it rains.
B An umbrella!

Finished?

Write five more definitions for people and things.

A nurse is a person who works in a hospital.
A tablet is a computer that's small and easy to carry.

Puzzle p.107

Discussing what things are for

1 🔊 2.36 **Read and listen** to the dialogues. Match the dialogues with the pictures. **Listen again and repeat.**

 ___

 ___

 1

1
A What's this gadget?
B It's a solar cell phone charger.
A What's it for?
B It's for charging your cell phone. You attach it to your backpack and you use it to charge your cell phone outside in sunny weather.

2
A What's this?
B It's an automatic dog bowl.
A What's it for?
B It's for feeding your dog. You put dog food in it and you use it to feed your dog when you're not there.

3
A What are these?
B They're ice grippers.
A What are they for?
B They're for walking on ice. You put them over your shoes and you use them to walk on icy roads.

Learn it, use it!

You ask	You answer
What's this / are these?	It's a/an … . / They're … .
What's it for?	It's for (feeding your dog). / You use it to (feed your dog).
What are they for?	They're for (charging your cell phone). / You use them to (walk on icy roads).

2 🔊 2.37 **Pronunciation** /ð/ **Listen and repeat.**

   1 this   **2** these   **3** they   **4** then   **5** them

3 🔊 2.38 **Listen to three more conversations. Complete the notes about the gadgets.**

   1 A USB memory stick_____   Use: for _____ information.
   2 A money _____   Use: for _____ your passport and money safe.
   3 Touch screen _____   Use: for _____ your smartphone in cold weather.

4 Pairwork **Ask and answer questions about these gadgets.**

1 Universal phone charger
   Use: charges all types of cell phone!

2 DVD for cats
   Use: for indoor cats – keeps your cat happy when you're out!

3 Runaway alarm clock
   Use: wakes you up and runs away! Can you catch it?

4 Headphone hat
   Use: listen to music in cold weather – keeps your head and ears warm!

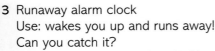

Workbook p.48   **Extra practice** online

The infinitive of purpose

Think!

Read the sentences. Then check (✓) the correct answers.

She went to Paris **to study physics**.
I use the Internet **to find information**.

1 What is the function of the **bold** phrases?
  a to describe an event ☐
  b to describe a reason or purpose ☐
2 What form does the verb in the phrases take?
  a the infinitive ☐
  b the base form ☐

Rules p.W45

1 Match the sentence halves.

1 She went to the museum
2 Pedro called the police
3 I went to the store
4 Lucas called Sofia
5 We organized a party
6 Olivia went online

a to report a crime.
b to celebrate Mom's birthday.
c to see an exhibition.
d to check her e-mails.
e to buy some groceries.
f to invite her to a concert.

2 Look at the pictures and complete the sentences.

She went to the store _to buy sneakers_.

1 He went to the park _____.

2 Ana went to the beach _____.

3 They went to the movie theater _____.

4 Aya went to the library _____.

5 Bruno got a knife _____.

Which one ...? / Which ones ...?

Singular
A These T-shirts are cool!
B **Which one** do you like best?
A I like the blue **one**.
Plural
A Help me choose some boots. **Which ones** do you prefer?
B I prefer the black **ones**.

Think!

Read the sentences. Then choose the correct alternative.

I like the black shirt. I don't like the green **one**. These video games are great. Those **ones** are boring.

• You can use *one* or *ones* to avoid repeating **an adjective / a countable noun**.

Rules p.W45

3 Rewrite the sentences. Substitute the underlined words with *one* or *ones*.

Which coat is more expensive? The red <u>coat</u> or the blue <u>coat</u>?

Which coat is more expensive? The red one or the blue one?

1 There are some books on the desk. Which <u>books</u> are yours?
2 Which sandwich do you want? The <u>sandwich</u> with cheese, or the <u>sandwich</u> with chicken?
3 A Look at these watches. Which <u>watch</u> do you prefer?
  B I prefer the black <u>watch</u>. It's smaller.
4 A Which sandals do you like best? The blue <u>sandals,</u> or the brown <u>sandals</u>?
  B I like the brown <u>sandals</u>. They're more fashionable.
5 A Which of those girls is your cousin?
  B The <u>girl</u> on the right.
6 This DVD isn't as good as that <u>DVD</u>.

Finished?

Look for three examples of these things in your book. Say which one you prefer.

animals   boys   gadgets   girls   sports

There are pictures of animals on pages 30, 36, and 60. I prefer the one on page 60.

Puzzle p.107

The Genius Who Changed the Way We See the World

Charles Darwin was a British scientist. He was born on February 12th, 1809. Darwin is famous because he described the theory of evolution, which transformed the way people think about life on Earth.

As a child, Darwin was very interested in nature, and he collected insects and plants. Later, he went to college to study medicine, but he hated it. His life changed in 1831 when he joined a scientific voyage around the world as a naturalist on a ship called the HMS *Beagle*. During the trip, he collected an enormous number of birds, plants, and fossils, and he found South America and the Galapagos Islands particularly interesting. He studied the animals and plants there, and noticed small but important differences between species on different islands. It was then that he started to develop his ideas about evolution.

Darwin returned to England in 1836, and continued to collect evidence to support his theory. He worked hard for over twenty years until, in 1859, he published his famous book *On the Origin of Species* on his theory of evolution by the process of natural selection. According to his theory, animals (or plants) that are

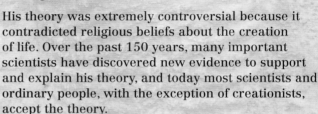

best adapted to the environment are more likely to survive and pass on to their offspring the characteristics that helped them to survive. Gradually, over very long periods of time, species change and new species develop.

His theory was extremely controversial because it contradicted religious beliefs about the creation of life. Over the past 150 years, many important scientists have discovered new evidence to support and explain his theory, and today most scientists and ordinary people, with the exception of creationists, accept the theory.

Darwin did not know how inheritance worked because the science of genetics was unknown in his lifetime. The later discoveries of genes and DNA have helped explain exactly how inheritance works.

Charles Darwin died on April 19th, 1882, but his ideas live on. His theories have revolutionized science, and he is one of the greatest scientists in history.

Check it out!

Find these words and check their meaning.

offspring
species
evidence
controversial
inheritance

Reading

1 🔊 2.39 **Read and listen** **Answer the question.**

What was the title of Charles Darwin's famous book?

2 Answer the questions.

What nationality was Charles Darwin? He was British.

1 When was he born?
2 What was he interested in as a child?
3 Why did his life change in 1831?
4 What did he collect during his trip on the *Beagle*?
5 What theory did he present in his book?
6 Why was his book controversial?
7 What discoveries helped explain Darwin's theory of evolution?

Listening

3 🔊 2.40 **Listen to two conversations. Choose the correct answers.**

In conversation 1 …
1 there are **two / three** people.
2 they are **friends / two of the people are friends.**
3 they are **at home / in a store.**

In conversation 2 …
4 there are **two / three** people.
5 they are **strangers / friends.**
6 they are **at home / in a store.**

My listening skills

Identifying context
Listening can be difficult when you can't see the speakers. If the question doesn't give you information about the context, listen carefully and find out …
• who the people are
• what their relationship is
• where they are

4 🔊 2.40 **Listen again and check (✓) the objects the people buy.**

1 ✓ 2 ☐ 3 ☐ 4 ☐ 5 ☐ 6 ☐

Speaking

5 Pairwork **Look at the objects in exercise 4 again. Discuss which ones you prefer.** 😊

A *What do you think of the cell phone cases? Which one do you prefer?*
B *I like the red one best, of course! It has …*
A *I like that one, too. The other one is … / Really? I prefer the green one. It's …*

Writing

6 **Read the factfile about Louis Daguerre. Then complete the biography.**

Factfile

Louis Daguerre
Nationality: French
Born: November 18th, 1787
Education: did an apprenticeship in theater design
Worked: 1804, theater designer at the Paris Opera
Occupation: Artist and inventor
Achievement: 1839 – invented the daguerreotype
Died: July 10th, 1851
Influence today: modern cameras are digital electronic devices; cameras on cell phones

Louis Daguerre was a French __artist__ *and*
1_____. *He was born on November 18th,* 2_____.
He did an apprenticeship in theater design. He became a theater designer at the Paris Opera. Daguerre is famous today because he was an artist and 3_____. *In* 4_____, *he invented a camera which he called the daguerreotype. He died on*
5_____, *1851.*

Today, 6_____ *are one of the most common electronic devices in the world and most people have digital cameras on their cell phones.*

7 **Write a biography of Sir Alexander Fleming. Use the information in the factfile.**

Factfile

Alexander Fleming
Nationality: Scottish
Born: August 6th, 1881
Education: studied medicine at University of London
Occupation: scientist
Worked: University of London
Awards: 1945, won the Nobel Prize in Medicine
Achievement: discovered penicillin, the first antibiotic
Died: March 11th, 1955
Influence today: many antibiotics; save millions of lives

Workbook p.49   **Writing builder** p.95

Vocabulary

1 Complete the chart with the missing crimes or criminals.

Crime	Criminal
robbery	robber
1 _____	vandal
burglary	2 _____
3 _____	mugger
shoplifting	4 _____
5 _____	murderer

2 Answer the questions.

What do you call someone who …

creates new machines?   an i_nventor_

1 writes novels and plays?   a w_____
2 writes music?   a c_____
3 plays music?   a m_____
4 travels to unknown places?   an e_____
5 designs buildings?   an a_____
6 debates and makes new laws?   a p_____
7 paints and draws pictures?   an a_____

Grammar

3 Complete the dialogues with the past progressive form of the verbs and short answers.

1
Police   What _were you doing_ (do) at 7 p.m.?
Suspect 1   I ¹_____ (watch) TV at home. My wife ²_____ (cook) dinner and the children ³_____ (play) video games.

2
Police   ⁴_____ (you / sit) in your car in Lyme Street at 8 p.m.?
Suspect 2   No, I ⁵_____. I ⁶_____ (walk) my dog. We ⁷_____ (go) to the park.

3
Police   ⁸_____ (the men / look) through the window?
Witness   No, they ⁹_____. They ¹⁰_____ (stand) on the sidewalk.
Police   What ¹¹_____ (they / wear)?
Witness   They ¹²_____ (wear) dark hoodies and jeans.

4 Complete the sentences with the simple past or the past progressive form of the verbs in parentheses.

I _was watching_ TV (watch) when the doorbell _rang_ (ring).

1 While I _____ (wait) for the bus, a pickpocket _____ (steal) my wallet.
2 Jake _____ (eat) candy when he _____ (break) his tooth.
3 When the phone _____ (ring), I _____ (take) a shower.
4 While they _____ (shop), they _____ (see) a bank robbery.
5 Daniel _____ (play) tennis when he _____ (hurt) his arm.
6 Mom's friend _____ (arrive) while we _____ (cook) dinner.

5 Write complete sentences using **who** or **which**.

I met a woman. (the woman was a famous writer)
I met a woman _who was a famous writer_ .

1 Ichiro wrote to his uncle. (his uncle lives in Tokyo)
2 A chef is a person. (a chef cooks in a restaurant)
3 Jack bought a car. (the car was ten years old)
4 Katie has a brother. (her brother is a pilot)
5 This is the photograph. (the photograph was in the newspaper)
6 Salvador Dali was a Spanish painter. (he was an important surrealist artist)

6 Choose the correct answers.

You use a search engine for /(to) find information.

1 He went to the hospital **for** / **to** see his grandpa.
2 Which **one** / **ones** do you prefer? The red or the blue wallet?
3 I called Maria **for** / **to** invite her to my party.
4 "Which of these sweaters is yours?" "The **one** / **ones** with the hood."
5 A USB stick is **for** / **to** storing information from your computer.
6 I prefer these drawings to those **one** / **ones** .
7 A book light is **for** / **to** reading in the dark.

Communication

7 🔊 2.41 **Choose the correct answers. Then listen and check.**

1 A Hello. Can I help you?
B Yes, please. I want to ¹tell / **report** a crime.
A Let's ² **fill out** / do this crime report. What happened?
B I was skateboarding in the park when a boy ³ **stole** / was stealing my camera.
A When did this happen?
B It ⁴ **happened** / was happening about an hour ago.
A How old was he, and what ⁵ **did he wear** / was he wearing?
B He was about 16, and he was wearing jeans and a blue jacket.
A OK, ⁶ **write** / sign here, please.

2 C What's ⁷ **this** / these?
D It's a GPS dog locator.
C What's it ⁸ about / **for**?
D It's ⁹ to / **for** locating your dog. You use it to ¹⁰ **find** / finding your dog when it runs away. You put it on the dog's collar and it tells you where your dog is. It sends a text message to your cell phone.
C Cool!

Pronunciation

Strong and weak forms of *was / were*

8 🔊 2.42 *Was / Were* can have a weak form or a strong form.

In affirmative sentences and questions, we usually use the weak form. Listen.

I **was** walking along the road.
They **were** talking and laughing.

But in short answers, we use the strong form of *was / were*.

Was he running?   **Were** they going into the store?
Yes, he **was**.   Yes, they **were**.

Now listen again and repeat.

9 🔊 2.43 **Listen to a police officer talking to a person who witnessed a crime. Underline the examples of *was / were* and decide if the pronunciation is strong (*S*) or weak (*W*). Then listen and repeat.**

		W
A Where <u>were</u> the girls?		
B They were in the café.	1	___
A Was the boy with them?	2	___
B Yes, he was.	3	___
A Were they sitting at the same table?	4	___
B Yes, they were.	5	___

Listening

10 🔊 2.44 **Listen to five short dialogues and choose the best picture for each conversation.**

Which girl are the people talking about?

a ☐   b ☐   c ✓

1 What did the thief steal?

a ☐   b ☐   c ☐

2 What type of crime did the girl see?

a ☐   b ☐   c ☐

3 What does Rebecca use her head lamp for?

a ☐   b ☐   c ☐

4 Which is Amelia Earhart's flight map?

a ☐   b ☐   c ☐

From Slavery to Presidency:
Great People Who Changed America

For millions of African Americans, the election of Barack Obama in 2008 was an achievement beyond their wildest dreams. For the first time in history, a black American was President of the United States.

For black Americans, the long road to freedom started in 1863 with the Proclamation of Emancipation by President Abraham Lincoln. The Proclamation of Emancipation gave black slaves their freedom, but it didn't give them the same rights as white people. It took over 100 years for black Americans to achieve equality. Read about the Little Rock Nine and Martin Luther King, heroes of the civil rights movement in the 1950s and 60s.

In 1957, segregation in schools was still common in many southern states of the U.S. In Little Rock, Arkansas, nine black students were determined to change this and attend the Central High School, which was for whites only. On the first day of school, the governor of Arkansas sent the state's soldiers to stop the black students from entering the school. President Eisenhower had to send federal soldiers to protect the students. It took a lot of courage to continue attending school because every morning, angry crowds of whites insulted the students and they even made death threats. But the Little Rock Nine didn't give up, and several graduated from Central High. Their example gave other students the courage to fight for equality. Nine courageous African-American teenagers challenged segregation in the south and won.

Americans celebrate Martin Luther King Day each year in January. Dr. Martin Luther King was a church minister who was the leader of the civil rights movement in the 1950s and 60s. He was born on January 15th, 1929 in Atlanta. After graduating, King became a church minister in Alabama. Dr. King helped organize the Montgomery bus boycott, which another famous black American named Rosa Parks started. He was sent to jail for his participation. On August 28th, 1963, King made a speech which became very famous. It is called the "I have a dream" speech. His actions resulted in the Civil Rights Act of 1964, which made all forms of discrimination and segregation illegal. Dr. King won the Nobel Peace Prize in 1964. He was assassinated on April 4th, 1968. In the U.S., August 28th, which is the anniversary of Dr. King's speech, is called "Dream Day."

Check it out!

Find these words and check their meaning.

wildest
freedom
equality
boycott
assassinated

Culture Focus

Extract from Dr. Martin Luther King's famous speech.

"I have a dream that my four little children will one day live in a nation where they will not be judged by their color of their skin, but by the content of their character."

1 🔊 2.45 Read and listen to the magazine article. Why are The Little Rock Nine and Martin Luther King famous?

a They were the first black American politicians.
b Their actions helped black Americans get equality.
c They both went to prison for their ideas.

2 Answer the questions.

When did Barack Obama first become President? *He first became President in 2008.*
1 What did the Proclamation of Emancipation do?
2 Why did President Eisenhower send federal soldiers?
3 How did the crowds of white people react?
4 How did the actions of the Little Rock Nine influence other people?
5 Who was Dr. Martin Luther King?
6 What did the Civil Rights Act of 1964 do?
7 What is Dream Day?

3 Presentation Prepare a presentation about an important person in the history of your country. Include the following information.

• Who is / was the person?
• Why is / was the person famous?
• What has changed as a result of his / her actions?

Vocabulary and speaking

I can identify crimes and criminals. (p.74)   B1

1 Complete the words.

A p<u>ickpocke</u>t stole my cell phone.
1 M_____g people is a violent crime.
2 There was a b_____y in our street yesterday.
3 V_____s painted on the school wall.
4 The guard caught a s_____r in the mall.
5 There was a bank r_____y this morning.

___ / 5

I can ask and answer questions about a crime. (p.76)   B1

2 Complete the questions.

A <u>What</u> happened?
B A man stole my wallet.
A ¹_____ were you? ²_____ did it happen?
B I was walking through the park at around 3 p.m.
A ³_____ money did he steal?
B About $20.
A ⁴_____ did he look like? ⁵_____ was he wearing?
B He was tall and he was wearing a red sweater.

___ / 5

I can describe a crime and criminals. (p.79)   B1

3 Reorder the words.

4 p.m. / took / robbery / at / the / place / around .
The robbery took place at around 4 p.m.
1 were / six / bank / there / people / in / the .
2 wearing / robbers / were / masks / the .
3 door / a / was / woman / near / standing / the .
4 robber / carrying / one / gun / a / was .
5 money / the / gave / clerk / all / them / the .

___ / 5

I can identify different professions. (p.82)   B1

4 Complete the sentences with professions.

Bill Clinton was an American <u>politician</u> .
1 Picasso was a Spanish _____.
2 Mozart was an Austrian _____.
3 Mark Twain was an American _____.
4 Marie Curie was a Polish _____.
5 Magellan was a Portuguese _____.

___ / 5

I can identify gadgets and say what they are for. (p.84)   B1

5 Choose the correct answers.

A What's (this) / those gadget?
B ¹It's / They're a memory stick.
A What's it ²for / used?
B It's for ³store / storing computer information.
A And what are ⁴these / that?
B They're Google glasses. You use ⁵it / them to go online.

___ / 5

I can discuss preferences. (p.87)   B1

6 Complete the dialogue with the words in the box.

| has   I'd prefer   ones   other one |
| ~~think~~   this one |

A I like this cell phone. What do you <u>think</u>
B It's OK. But I prefer ¹_____.
A Mmm. It's cheaper than the ²_____.
B It ³_____ a big screen and it's quite light.
A But ⁴_____ a colored one.
B There are some colored ⁵_____ here.

___ / 5

Reading, listening, and writing

	Got it?		
	Yes	I'm not sure	No
I can read two texts about the founding of Australia. (p.78) B1	☐	☐	☐
I can understand a person describing a crime she saw. (p.79) B1	☐	☐	☐
I can write an article for a website about a crime I saw. (p.79) B1	☐	☐	☐
I can read and understand an article about a great scientist. (p.86) B1	☐	☐	☐
I can understand people comparing objects and discussing preferences. (p.87) B1	☐	☐	☐
I can write the biography of a famous scientist. (p.87) B1	☐	☐	☐

1 An informal e-mail

1 Read the rules.

> **Informal expressions in e-mails**
>
> We can use informal language in e-mails and letters to friends and family.
>
> **Starting your message**
> *Hi, (name), / Hello! / Hi there! / Hey,*
> **Asking for news and expressing excitement**
> *How are you? / How are things? / Great to hear from you. / Thanks for your e-mail. Guess what (I'm doing)! / I can't wait (to see you)!*
> **Ending your message**
> *See you next weekend / later / soon.*
> *Talk to you later / tomorrow / next week. Call me ... / Text me ...*
> *Bye (for now)! / All the best / Love (name)*

2 Read Oliver's e-mail. Find five more informal expressions.

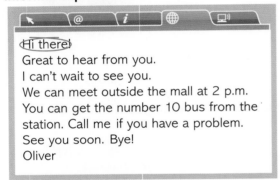

Hi there!
Great to hear from you.
I can't wait to see you.
We can meet outside the mall at 2 p.m.
You can get the number 10 bus from the station. Call me if you have a problem.
See you soon. Bye!
Oliver

3 Read Pedro's e-mail. Replace the underlined words with informal expressions. There is more than one possible answer.

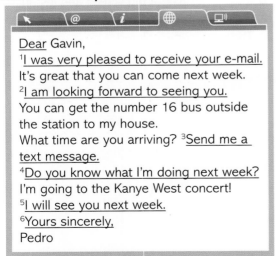

Dear Gavin,
¹I was very pleased to receive your e-mail.
It's great that you can come next week.
²I am looking forward to seeing you.
You can get the number 16 bus outside the station to my house.
What time are you arriving? ³Send me a text message.
⁴Do you know what I'm doing next week?
I'm going to the Kanye West concert!
⁵I will see you next week.
⁶Yours sincerely,
Pedro

Hi,

4 Now do exercise 6 on page 17.

2 A school trip

1 Read the rules.

> ***because* and *so***
>
> We use *because* to introduce a reason.
> *I usually go to bed early **because** I have to get up early.*
> We use *so* to introduce a result.
> *The cabins are small, **so** we have to keep them clean.*
> There is a comma before *so*, but not before *because*.

2 Write *reason* or *result* and label the underlined clauses. Then complete the sentences with *because* or *so*.

We're camping <u>because</u> <u>there aren't any hotels near here</u>.   <u>reason</u>

1 I wanted to learn scuba diving, _____ <u>I joined a diving club</u>. _____

2 I hate cleaning, _____ <u>my room is a total mess</u>! _____

3 I'm going on an adventure vacation _____ <u>I love sports</u>. _____

4 I have to study _____ <u>I have a test tomorrow</u>. _____

3 Match sentences 1–5 with a–e. Combine the sentences using *because* or *so*.

1 I can't learn to dive ...   *e*
2 You have to walk or ride a bike ...   ___
3 We're very busy all day ...   ___
4 I'm going camping ...   ___
5 Bring some bottles with you ...   ___

a we don't mind going to bed early.
b there isn't much water.
c I must buy a tent and a sleeping bag.
d there aren't any buses.
e I can't swim!
1 e I can't learn to dive because I can't swim!

4 Complete the text with *because* and *so*.

> Hi! I'm camping for a week. It's great fun, but there are a lot of rules. I don't mind <u>because</u> they're safety rules. I have to wear a shirt and long trousers ¹_____ there are mosquitoes. They're horrible! The water here isn't clean, ²_____ we mustn't drink it. We cook all our food on a fire, ³_____ it is very basic, but delicious. I have to wear boots ⁴_____ there are snakes. It sounds dangerous, but it isn't really! See you soon. *Tracy*

5 Now do exercise 7 on page 25.

3 Future plans

1 Read the rules.

Articles

We use the definite article *the*:

a when there is only one of a thing,
   e.g., *the future*, *the world*, *the law*, etc.
   *I have plans for **the** future.*

We use the indefinite article *a / an*:

b with jobs.
   *My uncle is **an** engineer.*

c with some expressions of quantity,
   e.g., *a lot of, a few, a little.*
   *I have **a lot of** plans for my next vacation.*

d instead of the number *one*.
   *I'm going to stay for **a** week.*

We use no article:

e with towns, most countries, languages,
   sports, and expressions with *school /
   college / home / work.*
   *I love playing **tennis**.*

2 Look at these sentences. Match the use of articles with rules a–e.

I'm going to L.A. for a week.   d

1 The weather is very cold today.   __
2 I want to be a dentist.   __
3 There are already a few people here.   __
4 We went to Australia last summer.   __

3 Complete these sentences with your own ideas.

Last week, I bought _a skateboard_ .

1 I can't speak _____, but I can understand it.
2 My sister wants to be _____ when she leaves school.
3 I have a lot of _____ in my room.
4 I got _____ for my birthday.

4 Complete the text with *a / an*, *the*, or no article (Ø).

I'm Javier, and I'm _Ø_ Spanish. I live in
¹_____ small town in ²_____ Spain. I am
going to study ³_____ journalism when I
go to ⁴_____ college. I'd like to be ⁵_____
political journalist. Last summer, I did ⁶_____
internship with ⁷_____ national newspaper.
It has ⁸_____ largest number of readers in
Spain. My work was varied and I even wrote
⁹_____ few articles!

5 Now do exercise 7 on page 37.

4 Future predictions

1 Read the rules.

Giving opinions

We use *In my opinion / view, ...* and *I
(don't) think ...* to give an opinion. These
expressions go at the beginning of the
sentence.
*I (don't) think a lot of things will be different
in 20 years.*
*In my opinion, / In my view, students won't
go to school every day.*
We use the adverbs *definitely* and *probably*,
and the expressions *It is possible that ... / It's
unlikely that ...* , to express different degrees
of certainty.
*I think that people will **definitely** live longer.*
*Most people will **probably** live to over
100 years old.*
It's possible that humans will visit Mars.
It's unlikely that people will live on Mars.

2 Match the sentence halves.

1 In my opinion, new technology   c
2 I don't think students   __
3 In my view, people will live   __
4 I think there will be   __

a longer and be healthier.
b a lot more old people.
c will improve our lives.
d will have to go to school every day.

3 Complete the sentences with your opinions.

I think space travel _will become easier_ .

1 I don't think people will _____.
2 I think robots will _____.
3 In my opinion, food will _____.
4 In my view, there won't be _____.

4 Rewrite these sentences so they express your opinions. Use *It's possible that / unlikely that ...*, *probably*, or *definitely (not)*.

Scientists will control the weather.
*Scientists will probably control the
weather.*

1 Robots will do all the boring jobs.
2 Families will be smaller than today.
3 Humans will live on different planets.
4 There will be treatments for most illnesses.
5 Scientists will clone humans.

5 Now do exercise 6 on page 45.

5 A postcard

1 Read the rules.

Adverbs of degree

We can use adverbs of degree before adjectives.
a bit, quite, really, very, extremely, incredibly
They change the meaning of the adjective by **making it weaker:**
*We were **a bit** tired.*
*It was **quite** interesting.*
making it stronger:
*It's a **very** old place.*
*It was **really** interesting.*
*I was **extremely** bored.*
*They were **incredibly** friendly.*

2 Choose the correct answers.

I ate two huge sandwiches. I was **a bit /** **really** hungry.

1 We wore coats, gloves, and boots. It was **really / quite** cold.

2 He was **quite / extremely** lucky. He won a million dollars on the lottery.

3 It was **a bit / incredibly** dark, so we couldn't see anything.

4 I got a B in the test and I was **quite /** **extremely** happy.

5 The view was **quite / really** beautiful and I took a lot of pictures.

3 Look at the text and find seven more adverbs of degree.

Hi, Carlos,
Guess what! I'm on vacation in Australia with my cousin. It's a **really** interesting country. I've done some very exciting things. I've been diving on the Great Barrier Reef, I've swum with sharks, and I've done a parachute jump! I went diving last weekend. The fish and the coral were incredibly beautiful. It's quite easy to take pictures because the sea is really clear. On Sunday, I was diving when two sharks swam past me. I was really scared! Yesterday, I did a parachute jump from an airplane. I was extremely frightened before the jump, but I'm very proud I did it!
Bye for now!
Dave

4 Now do exercise 5 on page 59.

6 How I use the Internet

1 Read the rules.

Expressions of frequency

We use adverbs of frequency and phrases to say how often things happen.
never, rarely, hardly ever, sometimes, usually, generally, often, always
every day / month / year
once / twice / three times a week
Frequency adverbs go between the subject and the verb.
*She **never** posts comments.*
Adverb phrases go at the end of the sentence.
*Tom plays video games **three times a week**.*

2 Where does the adverb or adverb phrase go in these sentences? Check (✓) the correct position.

___ I ✓ access ___ the Internet ___ with my smartphone ___. (rarely)

1 Maria ___ chats ___ to her friends ___. (every day)

2 I ___ read ___ the newspaper ___ on Sundays ___. (sometimes)

3 ___ Those students ___ go ___ to the movies ___. (once a month)

4 We ___ buy ___ things ___ online ___. (often)

3 Reorder the words to make sentences.

phone / online / go / Mom / her / never / to / uses
Mom never uses her phone to go online.

1 week / a / I / room / clean / my / once

2 month / visits / Lucia / her / twice / grandparents / a

3 TV / my / night / is / on / every / show / favorite

4 three / week / I / soccer / play / a / times

5 computers / in / ever / class / use / hardly / math / we

4 Rewrite the sentences so they are true for you. Use expressions of frequency.

I go online.
I go online twice a week.

1 I download music.

2 I post comments on other people's social network sites.

3 I use the Internet at school.

4 I have used the Internet for schoolwork.

5 I watch online videos.

5 Now do exercise 6 on page 67.

7 A crime

1 Read the rules.

Time expressions in stories

We use time expressions like *Last week* and *Yesterday* to say when something happened.
Last month, I saw a crime in the street.
We use *when* and *while* to talk about actions and situations that take place at the same time.
I was walking home **when** *a man stole my purse.*
The man was watching me **while** *I was waiting for the bus.*
We use time expressions like *First, Suddenly, Then, Next, Just then, After that, Next, Later, In the end*, and *Finally* to order events in a story.
The man bought a ticket. **Then** *he sat down.*
Suddenly, *a woman started shouting.*
In the end, *the thief ran away.*

2 Choose the correct answers.

I was so mad (when) / while someone stole my phone at school. **After that,** / (At first,) I thought it was at home, but it wasn't.

1 **While / When** I was looking at my watch, a man took my bag. **Suddenly / Then** he ran down the street and disappeared.

2 **Last night,** / **Next,** I was walking down the street **when / then** I heard a noise behind me. **Suddenly / Later,** a man ran past me.

3 Complete the texts with the time expressions in the box. There is more than one possible answer.

> After that   Finally   Suddenly
> Then   ~~Yesterday~~

1 _Yesterday_, I was standing in the bank. [1]_____, two robbers came in and told everyone to lie on the floor. [2]_____, they told the clerk to give them the money. [3]_____, they ran out of the bank. [4]_____, the police arrived, but it was too late.

> After that   In the end   Just then
> Last night   Then   when

2 [5]_____, Sophie and I were waiting for the bus. [6]_____, a man grabbed my sister's purse. [7]_____, he ran away. [8]_____, the man stole a car. [9]_____, the police arrested him [10]_____ he crashed the car.

4 Now do exercise 6 on page 79.

8 A biography

1 Read the rules.

Time expressions in biographies

We can use these time expressions in biographies:
He was born **on April 6th**.
She died **in 1867**.
She studied architecture **for three years**.
After college, *he worked for a software company.*
Today / Now, *most people use the Internet.*

2 Match the sentence halves

1 Galileo was born   _c_
2 He studied medicine   ___
3 After that, he   ___
4 He died   ___

a on January 8th, 1642.
b became a professor of mathematics.
c in 1564.
d for a year at Pisa University.

3 Look at the factfile for Hubert Booth. Answer the questions.

When was Hubert Booth born?
He was born on July 4th, 1871.

1 What did he do after college?
2 When did he die?
3 When did he invent the vacuum cleaner?

> Name: Hubert Booth
> Nationality: British
> Born: July 4th, 1871
> Education: engineering in London
> Worked: engineering company – designed bridges and ship engines
> Occupation: engineer and inventor
> Died: January 14th, 1955
> Achievement: 1901, invented the vacuum cleaner

4 Complete the time expressions in the text.

Hubert Booth was a British engineer and inventor. He was born _on_ July 4th, 1871. He studied engineering in London. [1]_____ college, he worked for an engineering company, and he designed bridges and ship engines. He died [2]_____ January 14th, 1955. Booth is famous because he invented the vacuum cleaner [3]_____ 1901. All modern machines are based on Booth's idea. [4]_____, the vacuum cleaner is one of the most common household machines.

5 Now do exercise 7 on page 87.

1 Food poisoning

Every year, about 48 million people in the U.S. get food poisoning, and about 3,000 Americans die from it. Dangerous microbes are responsible for food poisoning. Microbes are microscopic organisms, including fungi, viruses, and bacteria. Bacteria are the most common microbes (often called "germs") that cause food poisoning.

2 _____

Bacteria are one-cell living organisms. They need food, water, and the right temperature to grow and multiply. In the right conditions, one cell can multiply to nearly 17 million cells in eight hours. A bacterium is like a normal animal cell, but it is smaller and it doesn't have a nucleus. Some bacteria have a tail (a flagellum). This helps them move about.

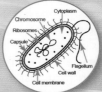

3 _____

There are thousands of different types of bacteria. Scientists classify them according to their shape.

Bacteria are everywhere, and most of them are harmless. There are ten times more bacteria cells in your body than there are body cells. Some bacteria are helpful, for example, enteric bacteria in our intestines help our bodies digest food. Only a few bacteria are pathogenic (cause disease).

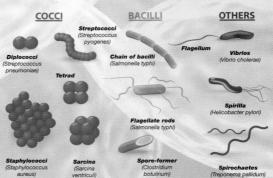

COCCI
- Diplococci (Streptococcus pneumoniae)
- Tetrad
- Staphylococci (Staphylococcus aureus)
- Sarcina (Sarcina ventriculi)

BACILLI
- Streptococci (Streptococcus pyogenes)
- Chain of bacilli (Salmonella typhi)
- Flagellate rods (Salmonella typhi)
- Spore-former (Clostridium botulinum)

OTHERS
- Flagellum
- Vibrios (Vibrio cholerae)
- Spirilla (Helicobacter pylori)
- Spirochaetes (Treponema pallidum)

4 _____

Pathogenic bacteria multiply inside our body, and they release toxins or poisons that make us ill. Five bacteria are responsible for most cases of food poisoning.

- **Campylobacter jejuni** is spiral shaped. It develops in chicken, milk, and other dairy foods. It is the most common cause of food poisoning, but it isn't usually serious.
- **Clostridium perfringens** is rod shaped. It lives in human intestines, and develops in cooked food at room temperature. It makes you feel ill for about 24 hours.
- **Escherichia coli** or **E.coli** is rod shaped. It lives in human and animal intestines, and it gets into food that is in contact with animal or human feces. It can be very serious, and causes about 400 deaths in the U.S. every year.
- **Salmonella** is rod shaped. You can get it from eggs or chicken. There are about 1.2 million cases every year, and it kills over 1,000 people.
- **Staphylococcus aureus** is round. It lives in our noses and skin. It gets into food that we make with our hands, or if we cough on food. It multiplies very quickly at room temperature, but it is rarely serious.

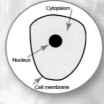

Campylobacter jejuni

Clostridium perfringens

E.coli

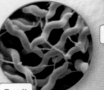

Salmonella

Staphylococcus aureus

5 _____

Germs get into food when we don't follow basic safety rules. Cold or hot temperatures kill most bacteria, so it's important to keep food in the refrigerator, and to cook it well. And, of course, we must always wash our hands before we touch food, and after visiting the toilet.

1 **Read the article quickly. Match the titles with the paragraphs.**

  A Different types of bacteria
  B Bacteria
  C Prevention
  D Pathogens
  E ~~Food poisoning~~

2 **Read the article again. Find and correct the mistakes.**

Bacteria are the only microbes that cause food poisoning.
  Bacteria are the most common microbes that cause food poisoning.

1 Bacteria are larger than normal cells, and they have a nucleus.
  _____

2 Most bacteria are dangerous.
  _____

3 Campylobacter jejuni is a very rare cause of food poisoning.
  _____

4 Salmonella food poisoning is rarely serious.
  _____

5 Staphylococcus aureus is a rod-shaped bacteria.
  _____

3 **Complete the sentences.**

In the U.S., about _3,000_ people die from food poisoning every year.
1 Microbes include bacteria, _____, and _____.
2 Bacteria can only grow and multiply if they have _____, _____, and the _____.
3 Enteric bacteria live in our intestines and they help us _____.
4 Staphylococcus aureus lives in our _____.
5 It's important to keep food in the refrigerator because _____ kill most bacteria.

4 **Match the words with the definitions.**

1 microbe   a to break down food in your intestines so your body can use it
2 germ   b poison that bacteria release into our bodies
3 toxin   c a dangerous microbe
4 digest   d a microscopic organism
5 pathogenic   e can cause disease

Project

Design and write a poster with food safety rules for a school canteen. Find out about the following:

cleaning the kitchen and appliances
hand-washing
clothes
preparing and cooking food
storing food

The Melting Pot

Who are the American people?

1 Indigenous People

The first people to come to North America probably arrived about 30,000 years ago. They walked across the Bering Strait between Asia and North America, and then moved south. The arrival of the first Europeans in 1500 was a disaster for these indigenous people. The newcomers brought diseases which killed native people, and they killed many more for their land. Historians estimate that by 1900 there were only 200,000 Native Americans left in the U.S. Today, there are about five million people of native origin. Famous Native Americans from history include Sitting Bull and Pocahontas.

2 _____

The British were the first Europeans to arrive in North America. They settled on the East Coast from around 1600. Some Spanish immigrants settled in modern-day California and Texas, and French immigrants went to the area that is now Louisiana and Florida. Many settlers became farmers because there was a lot of land. Towards the end of the 19th century, immigrants from all over Europe came to the U.S. looking for a better life. These new Americans included many Jews. They were escaping discrimination in Europe. Famous Jewish Americans include the singer Bob Dylan and Mark Zuckerberg, a co-founder of Facebook.

3 _____

From around 1650, Europeans started transporting the first African slaves to work on the sugar and cotton plantations of the South. When the U.S. became independent, in 1776, about 20 percent of the population was African-American. In 1860, there were about 3.5 million slaves in the south and half a million free African-Americans in the north. Today there are about 40 million African-Americans. Famous African-Americans include civil rights campaigner Martin Luther King and President Barack Obama.

4 _____

Latin American immigration to the U.S. started to increase in the early 20th century when large numbers of Mexicans arrived in Texas, California, and Arizona. After the Cuban Revolution in 1959, many Cubans came to America, too. Later, people from other Central American countries such as Honduras, the Dominican Republic, and El Salvador emigrated to the U.S. Today, there are more than 50 million Hispanic-Americans living in the United States. Famous Hispanic-Americans include the actress Cameron Diaz and the singer Jennifer Lopez.

Check it out!

Find these words and check their meaning.

melting pot
newcomers
diseases
settlers
emigrated

5 _____

At the end of the 20th century, large numbers of immigrants came from Asia. They came from countries like the Philippines, Vietnam, India, China, and Pakistan. Many were economic immigrants, attracted by the promise of a better life.

Its unique mix of people from different origins is what makes the United States a melting pot of cultural diversity.

1 **Read the article quickly. Then answer the question.**

Why do people call the United States of America a melting pot?

2 **Read the article again. Match the headings with the paragraphs.**

A New Immigration

B Indigenous People

C Hispanic Immigration

D The First Africans

E European Settlers

3 **Read the article again. Answer the questions.**

Where did the first inhabitants of North America come from?

The first inhabitants of North America came from Asia.

1 Why was the arrival of Europeans a disaster for Native Americans?

_____

_____

2 When did the first European settlers arrive?

_____

_____

3 Why did Europeans bring African slaves to America?

_____

_____

4 How many African-Americans are there in the U.S. today?

_____

_____

5 When did Hispanic immigration to the U.S. start to increase?

_____

_____

6 Where do the most recent immigrants come from?

_____

_____

_____

4 **Read the article again and complete the sentences with the correct dates.**

1500   1650   1860   1900   1959

After _1959_, a lot of Cubans came to the U.S.

1 In _____, African slaves started to arrive.

2 In _____, the first Europeans arrived.

3 In _____, there were about four million African-Americans.

4 In _____, there were 200,000 Native Americans.

Project

Find out about the origins of the population of your country, or another country. Include the following:

Who were the first people?

Where did they come from?

What other people have immigrated to your country? Why?

What are the proportions of people of different origins today?

How to Build a Website

Home   About Us   Contact Us   Blog   FAQ   Search

Before you start

Ask yourself: *Who is your site for? Why will they visit the site?* This will influence the way you design the site and what you put on it. It's a good idea to look at similar websites for ideas.

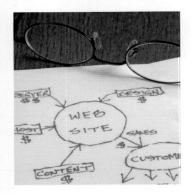

1 Choose a name and a web host

You must choose the domain name for your site as this is your Internet address. First, check that the domain is available, and then register it. Next, you must choose a web host company. These companies keep websites on their computers and make them available on the Internet. You usually have to pay to register your domain, as well as pay the web host company.

2 _____

Choose the content for your site. Most sites have text, images, and videos, so it's a good idea to have all three. Plan the content of your homepage carefully because this is the first thing that visitors to your site will see. It should be attractive and clear.

3 _____

Decide what pages you want on your site. It should have a clear structure, so visitors can navigate and find what they want easily. Almost all websites have the following pages, so you should include them:

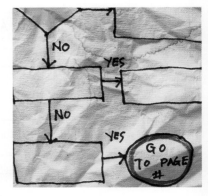

Home This first page often has a short description of the person and their interests.

About Us This page explains the purpose of the website.

Contact Us Include your e-mail address, but not a phone number.

You need to decide what other pages you want on your site, for example, photos, a blog, news, or FAQ (Frequently Asked Questions). Next, create your site map and decide which pages you want to include on the main menu bar. This can be at the top or on the side.

4 _____

The easiest way to create a website is to use a web editor. This is a special software program for creating websites. There are a lot of web editors, for example, Dreamweaver, Komodo Edit, and HTML-Kit. These web editors offer a variety of model web pages, or templates. You can choose the one you like best and use it for your website.

5 _____

Then upload your content onto the template you have chosen. You can personalize, or customize, your content by choosing the colors and fonts for your pages. All web editors have editing tools. You can use these editing tools to name the different pages of your site and to add the text, images, and videos.

Now let people know

Use social networking sites like Facebook and Twitter to tell your friends about it.

Check it out!

Find these words and check their meaning.

influence   upload
available   fonts

1 Read the website quickly. Then answer the question.

What pages are there on almost all websites? _____

2 Read the website again. Match the headings with the paragraphs.

A Choose a web editor

B Choose the content

C Edit your website

D ~~Choose a name and a web host~~

E Create a site map

3 Answer the questions.

What is a domain name?
It is the Internet address.

1 What does a web host company do?

_____

_____

2 What three types of content can you find on a website?

_____

3 Where is the main menu bar of a website?

_____

4 What do web editors offer?

_____

5 How can you tell other people about your website?

_____

4 Match the web pages in the box with pages 1–5 from a school website.

Home page   ~~Photos~~   Contact Us   About Us   News

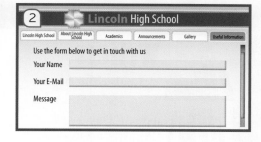

Photos _____

_____

_____

_____

_____

Project

Design a website for your class or school. Think about the following:

Who is the site for, and why will they visit it?

What pages are there on the website?

What photos and videos are there?

What other pages are there?

American Writers and Their Novels

Novels

Many great novels come from the U.S. Some of the famous novels below are over 100 years old, but they are still popular today.

1 *Adventures of Huckleberry Finn*
by <u>Mark Twain</u> **(1885)**
A young boy runs away from home. He makes friends with an African-American slave, Jim. Together, they travel down the Mississippi River. They have lots of adventures, some good and some bad. At the end of the story, Jim becomes a free man.

2 *Little Women*
by _____ **(1868)**
Four sisters – Meg, Jo, Beth, and Amy – live with their mother in Boston during the 1860s. Their father is away fighting in the American Civil War. The four girls are all very different, but they all help each other during a very difficult time.

3 *A Farewell to Arms*
by _____ **(1929)**
This is the story of an American ambulance driver in the Italian army during World War One. Lieutenant Frederic Henry falls in love with an English nurse named Catherine. The story is tragic. Catherine dies after giving birth to their stillborn child.

4 *The Grapes of Wrath*
by _____ **(1939)**
Life is very difficult in Oklahoma in the 1930s. Tom Joad and his family leave their farm. They drive across America to California. Tom and his family try to find work on farms in California, but this is not easy.

Writers

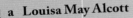

a Louisa May Alcott
Louisa May Alcott was born in Philadelphia, Pennsylvania in 1832. She moved to Boston when she was young. She had three sisters. In her novel, she describes a family very similar to hers. She never got married, and she died in 1888.

b John Steinbeck
John Steinbeck was born in 1902 in Salinas, California. Many of his novels are about poor people who live in California in the 1930s, for example *Of Mice and Men*. He won the Nobel Prize in 1962. He got married three times and had two children. He died in New York in 1968.

c Ernest Hemingway
Ernest Hemingway was born near Chicago in 1899. As a young man, he worked for a newspaper. During World War One, he drove an ambulance in Italy. He lived in Paris, Florida, Spain, and Cuba. Many of his novels describe the places that he visited. He died in Idaho in 1961.

d Mark Twain
Samuel Clemens, which is the real name of Mark Twain, was born in Missouri in 1835. When he was four, his family moved to the town of Hannibal, by the Mississippi River. He worked in a newspaper office, and then on a boat on the Mississippi. He loved the river, and many of his books tell stories about it. He died in 1910.

Check it out!

Find these words and check their meaning.

runs away from home
each other
stillborn

1 Read the descriptions and biographies quickly. Then write the names of the writers (a–d) with their novels (1–4).

2 Write the titles of the novels. Then write the names of the characters.

Novel:
Little Women

Characters:
Meg, Jo, Beth, and Amy

1 Novel:

Characters:

2 Novel:

Characters:

3 Novel:

Characters:

3 Answer the questions.

What happens to Jim at the end of *Huckleberry Finn?*
He becomes a free man.

1 Who is the novel *Little Women* about?

2 Why is the story in *A Farewell to Arms* tragic?

3 When does the story *The Grapes of Wrath* take place?

Project

Find out about a famous writer and one of his / her novels in your language. Think about the following:

Who is the writer?
Where was he / she born and where did he / she live?
When did he / she write the novel?
Who are the main characters?
Where does it take place?
What happens?

Got it! Puzzles 1-2

1A Match the letters to make different places in a town.

chu	po	al	ca	of	ba
sp	rch	nk	st	ho	ra
ce	ry	fé	it	lib	fi

church

1 _____
2 _____
3 _____
4 _____
5 _____

1B Copy the words with the same color. Reorder the words to make a sentence.

pen	know	mistakes	use	talk
mustn't	you	anyone	library	makes
you	everyone	in	do	must
a	the	here?	black	you

Green _you must use a black pen_____

Red _____

Purple _____

Blue _____

2A Draw lines to connect the words and make sentences. Use each box only once. ✔ | ✔ ╲ ✗ ╱ ✗

I	is	does	has	1. He	listen	are	here
don't	make	to	to	think	working	5. They	good
have	to	do	unload	the	dishwasher	love	trash?
hates	2. She	the	4. You	mustn't	to	going	the
cleaning	at	laundry	learning	run	the	taking	out
her	room	3. Doing	we	near	movies	mind	you
boring	is	housework	at	the	swimming	pool	6. Do

_____

2B Read the clues and complete the crossword.

Down

1 My room's a mess. I never _clean_____ it.

3 My brother has to _____ out the trash.

6 I _____ the dishwasher after meals.

Across

2 Do you have to _____ the dog?

4 I _____ the dishwasher when the dishes are clean.

5 I always _____ the table after dinner.

7 We don't _____ the dishes by hand. We have a dishwasher.

Crossword grid:
1 C
L
E
2
A
N
3
4
5 6
7

Got it! Puzzles 3-4

3A Find and circle eight more adjectives. Then complete the sentences.

C	O	N	F	I	D	E	N	T	P
H	H	S	I	F	L	E	S	E	A
E	O	R	Y	S	O	L	T	V	T
G	M	N	F	Z	N	H	T	I	I
Q	C	Y	E	B	A	R	O	T	E
Y	H	X	A	S	J	L	M	A	N
S	G	E	N	D	T	E	L	E	T
F	L	E	X	I	B	L	E	R	G
T	N	A	G	O	R	R	A	C	E

Tom never worries about tests. He is always _confident_ he can do well.

1 Joe is very _____. He never does housework.

2 My sister is very _____. She thinks cheating is terrible.

3 Mom spends hours helping my sister. She is really _____.

4 That boy says he's clever. He's very _____.

5 She designs all her own clothes. She's very _____.

6 Tom never helps anyone. He's a _____ boy.

7 I'm _____. I don't mind what time we go.

8 Sara is very _____. She is so nervous with people she doesn't know.

3B Look at the pictures. What are they going to do?

Clara and Steve
Mateus
Lucia
Leo and Amy
Kenji
Minsoo

Clara and Steve are going to _visit New York_ .

1 _____ is going to _____.

2 _____ is going to _____.

3 _____ are going to _____.

4 _____ is going to _____.

5 _____ is going to _____.

4A Copy the words with the same color. Reorder the words to make sentences.

it	last	are	was
get	in	year	retired
he	soon	to	won't
going	rain	born	they
married	2004	She	tomorrow

Green _It won't rain tomorrow._

Purple _____

Red _____

Blue _____

4B Copy alternate letters to make questions about the future. Then answer the questions.

EALRSETYIOGUBGNOFIRNYGPTNOIGVELTUMQADRORKIFEED
MOWNCEGDIABYD?

Are you going to get married one day?

1 TWUHSERNAWPEARKEGYJOBUCBEOHRUNA?

_____

2 HWUIPLFLIYDOTURGEOXTNOBCIOVLOLKESGRES?

_____

3 HWOHRASTAWYIVLOLJYFOPUCDNOTIOFSIZTDRBALIQN
BSITFOPMUOKRIRAODWL?

_____

4 WIYSTINTEGLOPIRNIGUTBOURKAFIDNOLRAVTSEPRY?

_____

5A Write the four things Carla has done, and one thing she has never done.

LRACA SAH TME A SOAFMU TCARO

Carla has met a famous actor.

1 HES ASH NIDERD A SOHRE

_____

2 SEH HSA PELST NI A NTET

_____

3 HSE AHS NOW A INCMTOPEOTI

_____

4 ESH ASH VRENE NEOD A RAHUACETP PMJU

_____

5B Look at the letter code. Write five questions. Then answer the questions.

A	B	C	D	E	F	G	H	I	J	K	L	M
H	I	J	K	L	M	N	O	P	Q	R	S	T

N	O	P	Q	R	S	T	U	V	W	X	Y	Z
U	V	W	X	Y	Z	A	B	C	D	E	F	G

1 ATOX RHN XOXK YEHPG BG TG TBKIETGX?

Have you ____ _____ __ __

_____?

2 ATOX RHN OBLBMXW XNKHIX?

____ ____ ____ _____?

3 ATL RHNK WTW WHGX T ITKTVANMX CNFI?

___ ___ ___ ____ _____

____ ?

4 ATOX RHN UXXG MH MAX N.L.?

____ ___ ____ __ ___ __ __ ?

6A The verbs are in the wrong sentences. Write the correct verbs.

I often ~~post~~ music from the Internet Music Store. download_____

1 How often do you use e-mails? _____

2 Do you chat travel blogs before you visit another country? _____

3 Are you going to download your travel pictures on your blog? _____

4 I often send on my friends' posts on Facebook. _____

5 What search engine do you play? _____

6 We always video read with Dad on his birthday. _____

7 I rarely comment games online. _____

6B Circle the extra letters in each sentence. Use the extra letters to make a secret question. Then answer the question.

Ih'vejoustdownwloaldedsomoemunsigc.

I've just downloaded some music .

1 Whehaven'tadoneovurhomeworekyet.

_____

2 Sheyhasalreadoyseentuhemovie.

_____

3 TshevidetohasbuedenoinlineseinceModnday.

_____

4 Heheasnlivedhegrelforitwsoyehars.

_____

SECRET QUESTION:

How long _____?

7A Complete the puzzle with crime words. What is the mystery word?

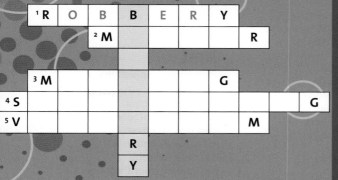

¹R	O	B	B	E	R	Y	

²M _ _ _ _ R

³M _ _ _ _ _ G

⁴S _ _ _ _ _ _ _ G

⁵V _ _ _ _ _ M

R
Y

MYSTERY WORD: _____

7B Break the code and write the questions. Then answer the questions.

1 <u>WHAT</u> _E__ _OU __I__
XIBU XFSF ZPV EPJOH

_I S__ ’_____ ___ ____?
BU TJY P'DMPDL MBU OJHIU

_____

2 ____ ____ _____ _____ __
XFSF ZPVS QBSFOUT XPSLJOH BU

___ ’_____ _____
UFO P'DMPDL ZFTUFSEBZ?

_____

8A Change the underlined words and rewrite the sentences.

<u>An inventor</u> is a person who designs buildings.

An architect is a person who designs buildings.

1 <u>A scientist</u> is a person who travels to new places.

_____

2 <u>A politician</u> is a person who discovers theories and natural laws.

_____
_____

3 <u>A composer</u> is a person who makes the laws of a country.

_____
_____

4 <u>An artist</u> is a person who writes music.

_____

5 <u>An explorer</u> is a person who plays a musical instrument.

_____

6 <u>An architect</u> is a person who invents machines.

_____

7 <u>A writer</u> is a person who draws and paints pictures.

_____

8 <u>A musician</u> is a person who writes novels.

_____

8B Break the code and write the question and answer.

A	B	C	D	E	F	G	H	I	J	K	L	M
	20	✕			✕		6	14	✕	✕	16	10

N	O	P	Q	R	S	T	U	V	W	X	Y	Z
	5		✕					✕		✕		✕

_ H _ ___ ___ __ _____?
3 6 15 8 14 8 15 5 1 2 5 5 4 16 14 4 9

_____

_ ____ _____ __ _____
14 3 9 4 11 5 4 16 14 4 9 11 5 1 12 8 7 11 9

__ ____.
10 15 20 16 5 2

_____

Word list

Unit 1

Places around town
bank /bæŋk/
bus stop /'bʌs stɑp/
café /kə'feɪ/
church /tʃɜrtʃ/
hospital /'hɑspɪtl/
library /'laɪbreri/
park /pɑrk/
parking lot /'pɑrkɪŋ lɑt/
pharmacy /'fɑrməsi/
police station /pə'lis steɪʃn/
post office /'poʊst ɑfəs/
shopping mall /'ʃɑpɪŋ mɔl/
sports center /'spɔrts sentər/
supermarket /'supərmɑrkət/
train station /'treɪn steɪʃn/

Other nouns
anybody /'ɛnibʌdi/
anyone /ɛniwʌn/
anything /'ɛniθɪŋ/
anywhere /'ɛniwer/
atmosphere /'ætməsfɪr/
attraction /ə'trækʃn/
challenge /'tʃæləndʒ/
charity /'tʃærəti/
congratulations /kəngrætʃə'leɪʃnz/
congress /'kɑŋgrəs/
corridor /'kɔrədor/
entry fee /'ɛntri fi/
everybody /'ɛvribɑdi/
everyone /'ɛvriwʌn/
everything /'ɛvriθɪŋ/
everywhere /'ɛvriwer/
front door /frʌnt 'dɔr/
fun run /'fʌn rʌn/
graffiti /grə'fiti/
guide /gaɪd/
hometown /hoʊm'taʊn/
illness /'ɪlnəs /
nobody /'noʊbʌdi/
no one /'noʊ wʌn/
nothing /'nʌθɪŋ/
nowhere /'noʊwer/
puzzle /'nʌθɪŋ/
sightseeing tour /'saɪtsiɪŋ tʊr/
somebody /'sʌmbʌdi/
someone /'sʌmwʌn/
something /'sʌmθɪŋ/
somewhere /'sʌmwer/
starting point /'stɑrtɪŋ pɔint/
tour /tʊr/
traffic light /'træfɪk laɪt/
wheelchair /'wiltʃer/
wish /wɪʃ/

Verbs
activate /'æktəveɪt/
care /ker/
come true /kʌm 'tru/
cover /'kʌvər/
cross /krɔs/
excuse /ɪk'skyuz/
participate /pɑr'tɪsəpeɪt/
register /'rɛdʒəstər/
support /sə'pɔrt/

Adjectives
crazy /'kreɪzi/

interactive /ɪntər'æktɪv/
urban /'ɜrbən/

Adverbs
straight /streɪt/
unfortunately /ʌn'fɔrtʃənətli/

Unit 2

Housework
clean my bedroom /klin maɪ 'bɛdrum/
clean the bathroom /klin ðə 'bæθrum/
clear the table /klɪr ðə 'teɪbl/
do the cooking /du ðə 'kʊkɪŋ/
do the ironing /du ðə 'aɪərnɪŋ/
do the laundry /du ðə 'lɔndri/
do the vacuuming /du ðə 'vækyumɪŋ/
feed the dog /fid ðə 'dɑg/
load the dishwasher /loʊd ðə 'dɪʃwɑʃər/
make my bed /meɪk maɪ 'bɛd/
set the table /set ðə 'teɪbl/
take out the trash /teɪk aʊt ðə 'træʃ/
unload the dishwasher /ʌnloʊd ðə 'dɪʃwɑʃər/
wash the dishes /wɑʃ ðə 'dɪʃɪz/

Nouns
basket /'bæskət/
bowling /'boʊlɪŋ/
cabin /'kæbən/
chef /ʃɛf/
choir /'kwaɪər/
chore /tʃɔr/
credit /'krɛdət/
dentist /'dɛntɪst/
dryer /'draɪər/
garbage /'gɑrbɪdʒ/
gopher /'goʊfər/
housework /'haʊswɜrk/
laundry /'lɔndri/
life jacket /'laɪf dʒækət/
navigator /'nævəgeɪtər/
scuba-diving /'skubə daɪvɪŋ/
skipper /'skɪpər/
sky /skaɪ/
sous-chef /'su ʃɛf/
vacuum cleaner /'vækyum klinər/
waste /weɪst/

Verbs
focus on /'foʊkəs/
hang out /'hæŋ 'aʊt/
last /læst/
push /pʊʃ/
put away /pʊt ə'weɪ/
respect /rɪ'spɛkt/
ride /raɪd/
sail /seɪl/
train /treɪn/

Adjectives
disgusting /dɪs'gʌstɪŋ/
fair /fer/
household /'haʊshoʊld/
messy /'mɛsi/
rough /rʌf/
self-cleaning /self 'klinɪŋ/

Review A

Nouns
flour /'flaʊər/
umbrella /ʌm'brɛlə/

Culture club A

Nouns
civil service /sɪvl 'sɜrvəs/
community service /kəmyunəti 'sɜrvəs/
military service /mɪlətɛri 'sɜrvəs/
reference /'rɛfrəns/
volunteer /vɑlən'tɪr/

Adjectives
elderly /'ɛldərli/
grateful /'greɪtfl/
lonely /'loʊnli/
voluntary /'vɑləntɛri/
younger /'yʌŋgər/

Unit 3

Personality adjectives
ambitious /æm'bɪʃəs/
arrogant /'ærəgənt/
confident /'kɑnfədənt/
creative /kri'eɪtɪv/
enthusiastic /ɪnθuzi'æstɪk/
flexible /'flɛksəbl/
hardworking /hɑrd'wɜrkɪŋ/
honest /'ɑnəst/
lazy /'leɪzi/
organized /'ɔrgənaɪzd/
outgoing /'aʊtgoʊɪŋ/
patient /'peɪʃnt/
selfish /'sɛlfɪʃ/
shy /ʃaɪ/
stubborn /'stʌbərn/

Nouns
aisle /aɪl/
attorney /ə'tɜrni/
audio engineer /'ɔdioʊ ɛndʒənɪr/
biological sciences /baɪə'lɑdʒɪkl 'saɪənsɪz/
boarding pass /'bɔrdɪŋ pæs/
career /kə'rɪr/
chance /tʃæns/
check-in /'tʃɛk ɪn/
conservation /kɑnsər'veɪʃn/
environmental studies /ɪnvaɪərn'mɛntl stʌdiz/
fitness coach /'fɪtnəs koʊtʃ/
gap year /'gæp yɪr/
garden center /'gɑrdn sɛntər/
hand baggage /'hænd bægɪdʒ/
hand-to-hand combat /hænd tə hænd 'kɑmbæt/
intention /ɪn'tɛnʃn/
internship /'ɪntərnʃɪp/
landscape design /'lændskeɪp dɪzaɪn/
law /lɔ/
martial arts /mɑrʃl 'ɑrts/
mechanic /mə'kænɪk/
operation /ɑpə'reɪʃn/
passion /'pæʃn/
pocket /'pɑkət/
poem /'poʊəm/
profession /prə'fɛʃn/
salon /sə'lɑn/
security checkpoint /sɪ'kyurəti tʃɛkpɔint/
software developer /'sɔftwer dɪvɛləpər/
sound engineering /'saʊnd ɛndʒənɪrɪŋ/
stunt artist /'stʌnt ɑrtɪst/
stuntman /'stʌntmæn/
technique /tɛk'nik/
vet /vɛt/
wildlife biologist /'waɪldlaɪf baɪ'ɑlədʒɪst/

work experience /ˈwɜrk ɪkspɪriəns/
working hours /ˈwɜrkɪŋ ˈaʊərz/

Verbs

board /bɔrd/

Other adjectives

devastated /ˈdɛvəsteɪt̮əd/
extreme /ɪkˈstrim/
metal /ˈmɛt̮l/
passionate /ˈpæʃənət/
real-life /ˈriəl laɪf/
technical /ˈtɛknɪkl/
varied /ˈvɛrid/
veterinary /ˈvɛt̮ərənɛri/

Adverbs

behind the scenes /bɪhaɪnd ðə ˈsinz/
outdoors /aʊtˈdɔrz/

Unit 4

Life events

apply for a job /əplaɪ fɔr ə ˈdʒɑb/
apply to college /əplaɪ tə ˈkɑlɪdʒ/
be born /bi ˈbɔrn/
die /daɪ/
get a job /gɛt ə ˈdʒɑb/
get married /gɛt ˈmærid/
graduate /ˈgrædʒueɪt/
have a baby /hæv ə ˈbeɪbi/
have children / hæv ˈtʃɪldrən/
pass your driving test /pæs yɔr ˈdraɪvɪŋ tɛst/
retire /rɪˈtaɪər/
start school /stɑrt ˈskul/

Nouns

architect /ˈɑrkətɛkt/
billion /ˈbɪlyən/
destination /dɛstəˈneɪʃn/
engineering /ɛndʒəˈnɪrɪŋ/
fly /flaɪ/
gate /geɪt/
generation /dʒɛnəˈreɪʃn/
life expectancy /laɪf ɪkˈspɛktənsi/
malaria /məˈlɛriə/
medical school /ˈmɛdɪkl skul/
miniskirt /ˈmɪniskərt/
one-way /wʌn weɪ/
open return /oʊpən rɪˈtərn/
overpopulation /oʊvərpɑpyəˈleɪʃn/
prediction /prɪˈdɪkʃn/
procedure /prəˈsidʒər/
prophecy /ˈprɑfəsi/
ray /reɪ/
round-trip /ˈraʊnd trɪp/
space travel /ˈspeɪs trævl/
timeline /ˈtaɪmlaɪn/
wireless /ˈwaɪərləs/

Other verbs

criticize /ˈkrɪt̮əsaɪz/
manipulate /məˈnɪpyəleɪt/
publish /ˈpʌblɪʃ/

Adjectives

accurate /ˈækyərət/
definite /ˈdɛfənət/
enthusiastic /ɪnθuziˈæstɪk/
internal /ɪnˈtərnl/
sustainable /səˈsteɪnəbl/

Adverbs

however /haʊˈɛvər/

nevertheless /nɛvərðəˈlɛs/

Review B

Nouns

astronaut /ˈæstrənɔt/
fashion designer /ˈfæʃn dɪzaɪnər/
pensioner /ˈpɛnʃənər/

Culture club B

Nouns

coast /koʊst/
contract /ˈkɑntrækt/
global warming /gloʊbl ˈwɔrmɪŋ/
polar ice /poʊlər ˈaɪs/
sea level /ˈsi lɛvl/
wealth /wɛlθ/

Adjectives

underwater /ʌndərˈwɔt̮ər/
wealthy /ˈwɛlθi/

Verbs

melt /mɛlt/
rise /raɪz/

Unit 5

Experiences

be in the newspaper /bi ɪn ðə ˈnuzpeɪpər/
climb a mountain /klaɪm ə ˈmaʊntn/
do a parachute jump /də ə ˈpærəʃut dʒʌmp/
fly in an airplane /flaɪ ɪn æn ˈɛrpleɪn/
go whitewater rafting /goʊ waɪtwɔt̮ər ˈræftɪŋ/
meet a famous person /mit ə feɪməs ˈpərsn/
ride a horse /raɪd ə ˈhɔrs/
sleep in a tent /slip ɪn ə ˈtɛnt/
visit a foreign country /vɪzət ə fɔrən ˈkʌntri/
win a competition /wɪn ə kɑmpəˈtɪʃn/

Nouns

award /əˈwɔrd/
bungee jumping /ˈbʌndʒi dʒʌmpɪŋ/
camel /ˈkæml/
canoe /kəˈnu/
canoeing /kəˈnuɪŋ/
cave /keɪv/
circus /ˈsərkəs/
coasteering /koʊstˈɪrɪŋ/
dolphin /ˈdɑlfən/
expedition /ɛkspəˈdɪʃn/
family room /ˈfæməli rum/
ID card /aɪ ˈdi kɑrd/
key card /ˈki kɑrd/
kitesurfing /ˈkaɪtsərfɪŋ/
New Zealand /nu ˈzilənd/
registration form /rɛdʒəˈstreɪʃn fɔrm/
rock /rɑk/
snowboarding /ˈsnoʊbɔrdɪŋ/
unicycle /ˈyunəsaɪkl/
wakeboarding /ˈweɪkbɔrdɪŋ/
wetsuit /ˈwɛtsut/
whale /weɪl/

Other verbs

book /bʊk/
check in /tʃɛk ˈɪn/
check out /ˈtʃɛk ˈaʊt/
juggle /ˈdʒʌgl/

Adjectives

retired /rɪˈtaɪərd/
rocky /ˈrɑki/
Thai /taɪ/

Unit 6

Internet activities

commenting on a picture /kɑmɛntɪŋ ɑn ə ˈpɪktʃər/
downloading music /daʊnloʊdɪŋ ˈmyuzɪk/
IMing /ˈaɪˈɛmɪŋ/
playing an online game /pleɪɪŋ æn ɑnlaɪn ˈgeɪm/
posting a picture /poʊstɪŋ ə ˈpɪktʃər/
sending an e-mail /sɛndɪŋ æn ˈimeɪl/
updating antivirus software /ʌpdeɪtɪŋ æntaɪˈvaɪrəs sɔftwɛr/
using a search engine /yuzɪŋ ə ˈsərtʃ ɛndʒən/
watching a video /wɑtʃɪŋ ə ˈvɪdioʊ/

Nouns

butterfly /ˈbʌt̮ərflaɪ/
category /ˈkæt̮əgɔri/
dragon /ˈdrægən/
entertainment /ɛntərˈteɪnmənt/
helicopter /ˈhɛləkɑptər/
mission /ˈmɪʃn/
mixture /ˈmɪkstʃər/
playlist /ˈpleɪlɪst/
seal /sil/
squirrel /ˈskwərəl/

Other verbs

go viral /goʊ ˈvaɪrəl/
have hits /həv hɪts/
keep in touch with /kip ɪn ˈtʌtʃ wɪð/

Adjectives

accurate /ˈækyərət/
cute /kyut/
fake /feɪk/
hilarious /hɪˈlɛriəs/
multiplayer /ˈmʌltipleɪər/
unique /yuˈnik/
viral /ˈvaɪrəl/
virtual /ˈvərtʃuəl/

Culture club C

Nouns

bullying /ˈbʊliɪŋ/
citizenship /ˈsɪt̮əzənʃɪp/
growth /groʊθ/
newsfeed /ˈnuzfid/
secret /ˈsikrət/

Verbs

obey /oʊˈbeɪ/

Unit 7

Crime

burglar /ˈbərglər/
burglarize /ˈbərgləraɪz/
burglary /ˈbərgləri/
kidnapper /ˈkɪdnæpər/
kidnapping /ˈkɪdnæpɪŋ/
mugger /ˈmʌgər/
mugging /ˈmʌgɪŋ/
murder /ˈmərdər/
murderer /ˈmərdərər/
pickpocket /ˈpɪkpɑkət/
pickpocketing /ˈpɪkpɑkət̮ɪŋ/
robber /ˈrɑbər/

robbery /ˈrɑbəri/
shoplifter /ˈʃɑplɪftər/
shoplifting /ˈʃɑplɪftɪŋ/
steal /stil/
vandal /ˈvændl/
vandalism /ˈvændlɪzəm/
vandalize /ˈvændlaɪz/

Other nouns

backstreet /ˈbækstrit/
beggar /ˈbɛgər/
colony /ˈkɑləni/
convict /ˈkɑnvɪkt/
criminal /ˈkrɪmənl/
death penalty /ˈdɛθ pɛnlti/
death sentence /ˈdɛθ sɛntns/
descendant /dɪˈsɛndənt/
filmmaker /ˈfɪlmˈmeɪkər/
knife /naɪf/
metro card /ˈmɛtroʊ kɑrd/
nightmare /ˈnaɪtmɛr/
penal colony /ˈpinl kɑləni/
punishment /ˈpʌnɪʃmənt/
servant /ˈsɜrvənt/
sheep stealing /ˈʃip stilɪŋ/
sidewalk /ˈsaɪdwɔk/
tattoo /tæˈtu/
theft /θɛft/
transportation /trænspərˈteɪʃn/
wallet /ˈwɑlət/
water fountain /ˈwɔțər faʊntn/

Other verbs

arrest /əˈrɛst/
beg /bɛg/
lock /lɑk/
report /rɪˈpɔrt/

Adjectives

circular /ˈsɜrkyələr/
suspicious /səˈspɪʃəs/
threatening /ˈθrɛtnɪŋ/
various /ˈvɛriəs/

Adverbs

indoors /ɪnˈdɔrz/
rarely /ˈrɛrli/

Unit 8

Human achievement

architect /ˈɑrkətɛkt/
artist /ˈɑrțɪst/
composer /kəmˈpoʊzər/
explorer /ɪkˈsplɔrər/
inventor /ɪnˈvɛntər/
musician /myuˈzɪʃn/
politician /pɑləˈtɪʃn/
scientist /ˈsaɪəntɪst/
writer /ˈraɪțər/

Other nouns

apprenticeship /əˈprɛntəʃɪp/
atom /ˈæțəm/
bacteria /bækˈtɪriə/
bone /boʊn/
cancer /ˈkænsər/
characteristic /kærəktəˈrɪstɪk/
charger /ˈtʃɑrdʒər/
chemistry /ˈkɛməstri/
creationist /kriˈeɪʃnɪst/
daguerreotype /dəˈgɛrətaɪp/
device /dɪˈvaɪs/

DNA /di ɛn ˈeɪ/
element/ /ˈɛləmənt/
evidence /ˈɛvədəns/
evolution /ɛvəˈluʃn/
exposure /ɪkˈspoʊʒər/
fossil /ˈfɑsl/
genetic code /dʒənɛțɪk ˈkoʊd/
genetics /dʒəˈnɛțɪks/
genius /ˈdʒinyəs/
ice gripper /ˈaɪs grɪpər /
inheritance /ɪnˈhɛrəțəns/
iron /ˈaɪərn/
leukemia /luˈkimiə/
memory stick /ˈmɛməri stɪk/
molecule /ˈmɑləkyul/
movement /ˈmuvmənt/
naturalist /ˈnætʃrəlɪst/
network /ˈnɛtwərk/
Nobel prize /noʊbɛl ˈpraɪz/
offspring /ˈɔfsprɪŋ/
opposition /ɑpəˈzɪʃn/
penicillin /pɛnəˈsɪlən/
physicist /ˈfɪzəsɪst/
physics /ˈfɪzɪks/
polonium /pəˈloʊniəm/
radiation /reɪdiˈeɪʃn/
radioactivity /reɪdioʊækˈtɪvəți/
radium /ˈreɪdiəm/
radon /ˈreɪdɑn/
ray /reɪ/
self-portrait /sɛlf ˈpɔrtrət/
species /ˈspiʃiz/
substance /ˈsʌbstəns/
theory /ˈθɪri/
touch screen /ˈtʌtʃ skrin/
X-ray /ˈɛks reɪ/

Verbs

attach /əˈtætʃ/
compose /kəmˈpoʊz/
debate /dɪˈbeɪt/
give up /gɪv ˈʌp/
invent /ɪnˈvɛnt/
negotiate /nɪˈgoʊʃieɪt/
reveal /rɪˈvil/
revolutionize /rɛvəˈluʃənaɪz/
treat /trit/

Adjectives

controversial /kɑntrəˈvərʃl/
extraordinary /ɪkˈstrɔrdnɛri/
radioactive /reɪdioʊˈæktɪv/
runaway /ˈrʌnəweɪ/
solar /ˈsoʊlər/

Review D

Nouns

collar /ˈkɑlər/
GPS /dʒi pi ˈɛs/
head lamp /ˈhɛd læmp/

Adjectives

surrealist /səˈriəlɪst/
unknown /ʌnˈnoʊn/

Culture club D

Nouns

anniversary /ænəˈvərsəri/
boycott /ˈbɔɪkɑt/
courage /ˈkərɪdʒ/
equality /ɪˈkwɑləți/
freedom /ˈfridəm/

governor /ˈgʌvənər/
jail /dʒeɪl/
slave /sleɪv/

Verbs

assassinate /əˈsæsəneɪt/

Adjectives

courageous /kəˈreɪdʒəs/
federal /ˈfɛdərəl/
wildest /ˈwaɪldəst/

Curriculum extra A

Nouns

bacterium /bækˈtɪriəm/
food poisoning /ˈfud pɔɪzənɪŋ/
fungi /ˈfʌŋgaɪ/
intestine /ɪnˈtɛstən/
microbe /ˈmaɪkroʊb/
nucleus /ˈnukliəs/
organism /ˈɔrgənɪzəm/
virus /ˈvaɪrəs/

Verbs

classify /ˈklæsəfaɪ/
digest /daɪˈdʒɛst/
multiply /ˈmʌltəplaɪ/

Adjectives

microscopic /maɪkrəˈskɑpɪk/
spiral /ˈspaɪrəl/

Curriculum extra B

Nouns

discrimination /dɪskrɪməˈneɪʃn/
Jew /dʒu/
melting pot /ˈmɛltɪŋ pɑt/
newcomer /ˈnukʌmər/
plantation /plænˈteɪʃn/

Verbs

settle /ˈsɛtl/
transport /trænsˈpɔrt/

Adjectives

indigenous /ɪnˈdɪdʒənəs/
Jewish /ˈdʒuɪʃ/
native /ˈneɪțɪv/

Curriculum extra C

Nouns

domain name /dəˈmeɪn neɪm/
template /ˈtɛmplət/
web editor /ˈwɛb ɛdəțər/
web host /ˈwɛb hoʊst/

Verbs

customize /ˈkʌstəmaɪz/
influence /ˈɪnfluəns/
navigate /ˈnævəgeɪt/
upload /ˈʌploʊd/

Adjectives

available /əˈveɪləbl/
font /fɑnt/

Curriculum extra D

Nouns

ambulance /ˈæmbyələns/
civil war /sɪvl ˈwɔr/

Adjectives

stillborn /ˈstɪlbɔrn/
tragic /ˈtrædʒɪk/

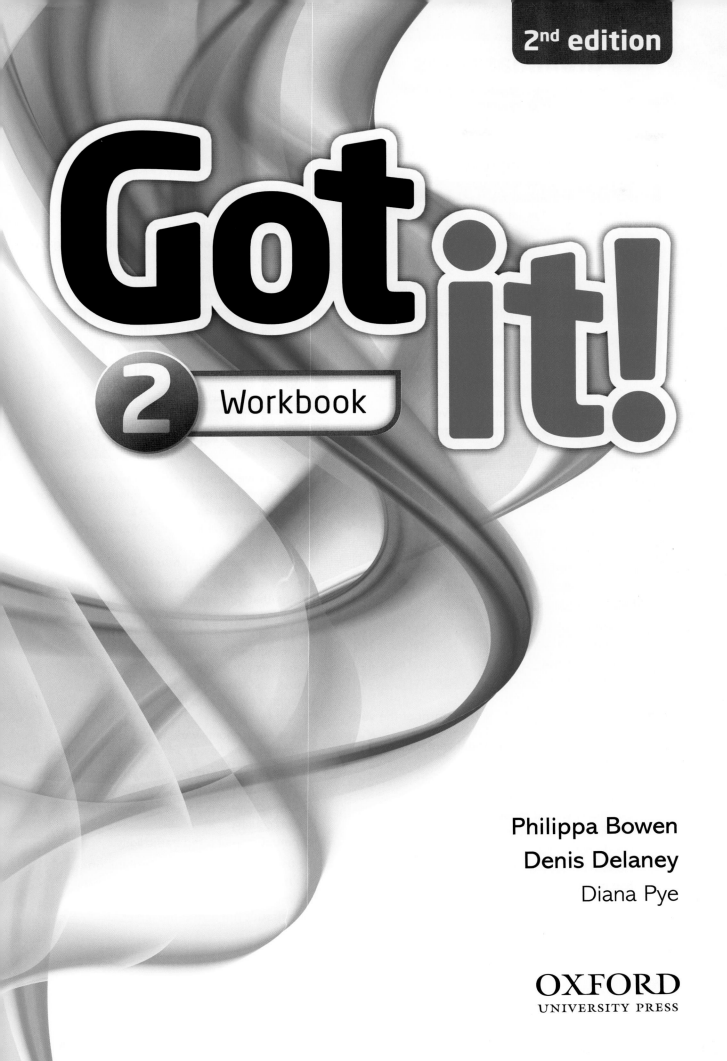

2nd edition

Got it!

2 Workbook

Philippa Bowen
Denis Delaney
Diana Pye

OXFORD
UNIVERSITY PRESS

1 Grammar rules

must
Affirmative and negative

Affirmative
I **must** study.
You **must** listen.
He **must** stop talking.
She **must** clean her room.
It **must** be turned off in class.
We **must** go to class.
You **must** do your homework.
They **must** have tickets.

Subject + *must* + base form of the verb

Negative	
Full forms	**Short forms**
I **must not** be late.	I **mustn't** be late.
You **must not** talk.	You **mustn't** talk.
He **must not** come home late.	He **mustn't** come home late.
She **must not** eat a lot of candy.	She **mustn't** eat a lot of candy.
It **must not** be loud.	It **mustn't** be loud.
We **must not** take photographs.	We **mustn't** take photographs.
You **must not** swim here.	You **mustn't** swim here.

Subject + | *must not* / *mustn't* | + base form of the verb

1 *Must* is a modal verb. All modal verbs follow the same rules:
   – We only use one form for all persons.
     I **must** stop. He **must** stop.
     She **must** stop. It **must** stop.
     We **must** stop. They **must** stop.
   – We do not add an *-s* to *must* with *he*, *she*, or *it*.
     He **must** stop. NOT ~~He musts stop.~~
     She **must** stop. NOT ~~She musts stop.~~

– We always follow *must* with another verb in the base form.
   You **must drive** slowly.
   NOT ~~You must to drive slowly.~~
   You **mustn't run** in school.
   NOT ~~You mustn't to run in school.~~
– We don't use *don't / doesn't* with the negative form of modal verbs.
   You **mustn't** come home late.
   NOT ~~You don't must come home late.~~

2 The negative form of *must* is *must not*. In spoken and informal written English, *must not* is usually abbreviated to *mustn't*.
   You **must not** text in class. = You **mustn't** text in class.
   I **must not** be late. = I **mustn't** be late.

3 We use *must* to talk about necessity. Necessity means that you cannot avoid doing something.
   You **must** come home before 9:30 p.m.
   (*You cannot come home after 9:30 p.m.*)
   You **must** be 18 to drive a car.
   (*You cannot drive a car before you are 18.*)
   I **must** call Adam. It's his birthday today.
   (*I cannot call Adam tomorrow because it's his birthday today.*)
   I **must** do my homework now.
   (*I cannot do my homework later because I'm busy.*)

4 We use *must* to express general obligation.
   You **must** drive on the right in the U.S.
   You **must** have a passport to travel to a foreign country.
   You **must** stop at a red traffic light.

5 We use *mustn't* to express prohibition.
   You **mustn't** use a dictionary in the test!
   You **mustn't** use your cell phone in class.
   You **mustn't** run across the street.

Compounds: *some- / any- / no-*

	Person	Thing	Place
some	someone / somebody	something	somewhere
any	anyone / anybody	anything	anywhere
no	no one / nobody	nothing	nowhere

1 We use *-one / -body* to talk about people.

2 We use *-thing* to talk about things and objects.

3 We use *-where* to talk about places.

4 We use the compound *some-* in affirmative sentences.

   Someone / Somebody is at the door.
   I need **something** cool to wear for the party.
   I want to go **somewhere** fun this weekend.

5 We use the compound *any-* in negative sentences and questions.

   I don't know **anyone / anybody** at my new school.
   Do you know **anyone / anybody** at your new school?

   There isn't **anything** interesting to watch on TV.
   Is there **anything** interesting to watch on TV?

   I didn't go **anywhere** interesting on vacation.
   Do you want to go **anywhere** special on vacation?

6 We use the compound *no-* in affirmative sentences to mean something does not exist.

   There's **no one / nobody** in the movie theater.
   I like to do **nothing** on Sunday mornings.
   There's **nowhere** to go skateboarding in this town.

Watch out!

In English, only one negative is used. In a sentence with *no*, we use the verb in the affirmative form.
There's **nothing** on at the movie theater.
NOT ~~There isn't nothing on at the movie theater.~~

Compounds: *every-*

	Person	Thing	Place
every	everyone / everybody	everything	everywhere

1 We use the compound *every-* to talk about all people, things, or places.
   Everyone / Everybody is here.
   Everything is ready.
   We went **everywhere** in the town.

2 We use the compound *every-* in affirmative, negative, and question forms.
   Everyone / Everybody went to the concert.
   We didn't have **everything** ready.
   Did you go **everywhere** in the town?

Student Book p.15

Word list

Review the Vocabulary. Write your own study notes (or translation) for each word.

Places around town
bank _____
bus stop _____
café _____
church _____
hospital _____
library _____
park _____
parking lot _____
pharmacy _____
police station _____
post office _____
shopping mall _____
sports center _____
supermarket _____
train station _____

Check it out!
anyone _____
challenges _____
come true _____
entry fee _____
guide _____
hometown _____
illness _____
nobody cared _____
puzzles _____
wish _____

Learn it, use it!
Excuse me. How do I get to …?
_____
Excuse me. Can you tell me the way to …? _____

Go up / down (Market Street).
_____
Go past (the bank). _____
Go straight as far as (the traffic circle).
_____
At the end of the road / traffic lights / bank, … _____
Turn right / left. _____
Take the first / second turn on the right / left. _____
Cross the road / street. _____
It's on the right / left. _____
The … is on the right / left.
_____

Student Book pp.12, 10, 16, 14

W3

1 Exercises

Vocabulary
Places around town

1 Complete the places around town with the words from the box.

center lot mall office ~~station~~ station stop

police station____
1 parking _____   4 bus _____
2 train _____   5 post _____
3 sports _____   6 shopping _____

2 Complete the sentences with the missing place names.

I must go to the p_ost office_____. I want to send this parcel to my aunt in France.

1 "I'm hungry. I want to eat something."
"OK, there's a new c_____ downtown. Let's go there."
2 A man took my purse this morning. I must go to the p_____.
3 I want to go to the l_____. I need to return some books.
4 It's a nice day. Let's go for a walk in the p_____.
5 My family is quite religious. We usually go to c_____ on Sundays.
6 I brought some bread, cheese, and milk from the s_____.
7 My grandma isn't well. She's in the h_____ at the moment.
8 Dad went to the b_____ to get some Euros for our vacation.
9 Are you sick? You should go to the p_____ to buy some medicine.
10 You can get the number eight in West Street. There's a b_____ in front of the library.

Grammar
must
Affirmative and negative

3 Write the sentences in the correct order. Use *must* and *mustn't*.

you / library / talk / the / in / mustn't
You mustn't talk in the library._____

1 early / you / home / come / must / today
_____
2 volleyball / practice / mustn't / late / Tom / be / for
_____

3 must / the / students / in / class / be / quiet
_____
4 classroom / cell phone / use / mustn't / your / you / in / the
_____
5 buy / must / new / notebook / I / a
_____
6 uniform / wear / we / a / must / to / school
_____

4 Complete the sentences with *must* or *mustn't*.

You have a test tomorrow. You _must_ study for it.
1 This is a "no parking" area. You _____ leave your car here.
2 The train leaves at 9 a.m. We _____ be at the train station at 8:45 a.m.
3 Parents _____ leave small children alone at home.
4 You _____ be 16 years old to drive a car in Iowa, U.S.
5 You _____ stop at a red traffic light.
6 Be quiet, Ricky! It's a test. You _____ talk!

5 Read the information about Fairview Art Gallery. Then complete the rules with *must* or *mustn't* and a verb.

Fairview Art Museum

RULES FOR VISITORS

Leave your bags at the reception desk.
Do not touch the pictures.
Parents stay with your children.
Don't bring dogs into the museum.
Eat and drink in the café area only.
Don't take photos of pictures.
No smoking in the museum.   *Thank you!*

Open from 10 a.m. to 5 p.m. every day

You _must leave_ your bags at the reception desk.
You ¹_____ the pictures.
Parents ²_____ with their children.
You ³_____ dogs into the museum.
You ⁴_____ in the café area only.
You ⁵_____ photos of pictures.
You ⁶_____ in the museum.

W4

Student Book pp.12-13   **Extra practice** online

Compounds: some- / any- / no-

6 Choose the correct compound.

Do you know **someone** / ~~anyone~~ from the U.S.?

1 There's **somebody** / **anybody** at the front door.
2 I can't find my cell phone **somewhere** / **anywhere**.
3 **Anybody** / **Nobody** knows about the party. It's a secret.
4 Ouch! I've got **something** / **anything** in my eye.
5 Liam said **anything** / **nothing** about the movie.
6 Did you do **anywhere** / **anything** interesting on the weekend?

7 Complete the sentences with compounds of some-, any-, or no- using -thing, -where, or -body.

Does <u>anybody</u> have my calculator?

1 Let's do _____ after school on Friday.
2 I can't see my brother _____.
3 I live a long way from school. _____ in my class lives near me.
4 There's a pen _____ in my bag.
5 I don't have any money. I can't buy _____.
6 Is _____ using the computer?
7 Oh, no! I have _____ to wear to Maria's party!
8 I have _____ important to tell you.

Compounds: every-

8 Write five sentences with the phrases in A and B and everything, everyone, and everywhere.

A	B
I don't know	on your bike.
Mom does	in my bag.
You can go	in our house.
I put	at my school.
Did he go	to her party?
Is she inviting	in Spain?

<u>I don't know everyone at my school.</u>

1 _____
2 _____
3 _____
4 _____
5 _____

9 Read the Pirates' Treasure Game rules. Then choose the correct answers.

Urban Games
The Pirates' Treasure Game

Hi, **somebody** / ~~everybody~~!

Are you doing ¹**anything** / **anywhere** special on Saturday, June 16th? No? Then come and play our Pirates' Treasure Game. There are ten medals for you to find in secret places around town. ²**Everyone** / **Someone** gets instructions for the game with ten puzzles. Complete the puzzles to find the medals, and you can win big prizes! First prize is a day out for two people at Disney World!

The Pirates' Treasure Game starts at the parking lot between the Mega Supermarket and the National Bank. Participants ³**must be** / **must to be** in the parking lot before 10 a.m.

Do you need to bring ⁴**anyone** / **anything**? Yes, energy and enthusiasm!

Is there ⁵**anything** / **something** to eat? Yes, there are free drinks and snacks for ⁶**everyone** / **no one**.

Competition Rules

You ⁷**must playing** / **must play** in teams of four people. There ⁸**mustn't** / **must** be at least one person over 16 in each team.

Each team ⁹**musts register** / **must register** before 4 p.m. on Friday, June 15th. That's the final entry date! ¹⁰**Anybody** / **Nobody** can register on the day of the competition.

You ¹¹**must** / **mustn't** use your car in the game – you must walk (or run!).

Does ¹²**somebody** / **anybody** have any questions? Contact us at urbangames@winger.com

10 Use the words in parentheses to complete the second sentence so that it has the same meaning as the first sentence.

You mustn't run in the corridors at school. (walk)
You <u>must walk in the corridors at school.</u>

I didn't have anything to do on Friday night. (nothing)
I <u>had nothing to do on Friday night.</u>

1 You must be quiet in the library. (talk)
You _____.

2 I know all the people in my class. (everyone)
I _____.

3 You mustn't forget to phone your grandma. (remember)
You _____.

4 I knew nobody at the party. (anyone)
I _____.

5 The students mustn't stay in the classroom at lunchtime. (leave)
The students _____.

6 We went nowhere interesting on the weekend. (anywhere)
We _____.

Asking for and giving directions

1 Match the directions with the pictures.

1 Take the third turn on the left.   _d_
2 Go straight as far as the traffic lights.   ___
3 Take the second turn on the right.   ___
4 Go past the bank and turn right.   ___
5 At the end of the road, turn left.   ___
6 Cross the road at the crosswalk, then   ___
   turn right.

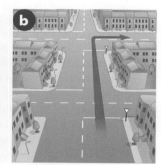
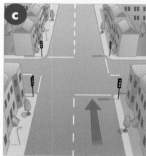
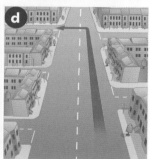

2 Complete the dialogue with the phrases in the box.

as far as   first turn   How do I get to
left   opposite   traffic lights   turn

A Excuse me. _How do I get to_ the hospital, please?

B Go down this street. Go ¹_____
the church and then ²_____ left.
At the ³_____, turn right, and
then take the ⁴_____ on the left.
The hospital is on the ⁵_____. It's
⁶_____ the park.

A Thanks.

3 Three people ask you for directions. Look at the map. Complete the directions.

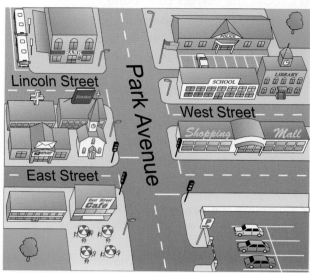

You are at the parking lot.

Man   Excuse me. Can you tell me the way to the post office, please?

You   Go out of the parking lot and turn
_right_____. ¹_____
Park Avenue ²_____ the
traffic lights. Then ³_____
and ⁴_____ East Street. The
post office is on ⁵_____. It's
⁶_____ a church.

Man   Thank you.

You are at the pharmacy.

Woman Excuse me. How do I get to the shopping mall, please?

You   Go out of the pharmacy and turn
right. Go down Lincoln Street. Turn
⁷_____ onto Park Avenue.
Go ⁸_____ on Park Avenue
and take the second ⁹_____
on the left. The shopping mall is
on the ¹⁰_____. It's
¹¹_____ a parking lot.

Woman Thank you.

You are at the post office.

Boy   Excuse me. Can you tell me the way to the bus station, please?

You   Sure. Go to ¹²_____ of
this road. ¹³_____ at
the traffic lights and go down Park
Avenue. ¹⁴_____ the next
turn on the ¹⁵_____. Go
¹⁶_____ the bookstore.
¹⁷_____ the road in front
of the pharmacy.

Boy   Thanks.

Student Book p.14   Extra practice online

| Home | The Race | Registration | Course maps | Results | FAQs |

RACE FOR THE KIDS

Sunday, June 9th, London, U.K.

Do something different on June 9th this year! Run in the Race for the Kids in London. Race for the Kids is a 5 km fun run. It raises money for a special children's hospital in London. Anyone can enter the race, so bring your family and friends, too! Last year, over 3,000 people ran in the race, and everyone has their own story of the day.

This is Lucy's story:

Five students from my class entered the Race for the Kids. Our family and friends sponsored us for the race. Before the race day, we also went downtown with our teacher and we collected money outside the supermarket and post office. In the end, we raised a total of £682 ($1,116) for the hospital!

Unfortunately, it rained on the day of the race, but nobody cared. Everybody had a good time! There were runners everywhere in the park, and we all had blue T-shirts with the name of the race on them. The atmosphere was amazing! I ran 5 km in 39 minutes, and I was very happy about that! Some people walked from start to finish!

ARE YOU INTERESTED?

Everyone is welcome to enter, but there are a few simple rules:

1 You must register online.
2 You must register before June 4th.
3 You must pay an entry fee when you register: adults £15 ($25), children (under 16) £10 ($16).
4 Children under 16 must have their parents' permission.

Reading

1 Read the web page. Then complete the chart.

Event:	Race for the Kids
Location:	1 _____
Date:	2 _____
Raises money for:	3 _____
Entry fee:	4 _____

2 Read the web page again. Answer the questions.

Who can enter the Race for the Kids?

Anyone can enter the race.

1 How many students from Lucy's class entered the Race for the Kids?

2 How much money did they raise for the hospital?

3 What was the weather like on the day of the race?

4 How long did it take Lucy to run 5 km?

5 Where must you register for the race?

Writing

3 Imagine your class is organizing a sports event to raise money for charity. Write a short description of your event for the school website. Think about the following:

- What type of event is it?
- What charity are you raising money for?
- When and where is it taking place?
- Who can take part?
- How and when must you register?
- How much is the entry fee?
- What other rules are there?

2 Grammar rules

have to
Affirmative and negative

Affirmative
I **have to** leave early.
You **have to** clean your room.
He **has to** do chores on weekends.
She **has to** make her bed every day.
It **has to** be 100 words long.
We **have to** go to school.
You **have to** wear sneakers in the gym.
They **have to be** home before 10 p.m.

Subject +	have / has to	+	base form of the verb

1 We use *have to* to express an external necessity or obligation.
  Juan **has to** go the dentist's.
  We **have to** leave now. Our bus is in ten minutes.

2 We use *have to* to express a necessity in the present or in the future.
  I **have to** send this e-mail now.
  Remy **has to** get up early tomorrow morning for school.

Negative
I **don't have to** get up early on Sunday.
You **don't have to** load the dishwasher.
He **doesn't have to** play soccer today.
She **doesn't have to** do the vacuuming.
It **doesn't have to** be perfect.
We **don't have to** clean the classroom.
You **don't have to** wear school uniform.
They **don't have to** go to school on Saturday.

Subject +	don't have to / doesn't have to	+	base form of the verb

1 We use the negative forms *don't have to* / *doesn't have to* when there is no necessity or obligation.
  In the U.S., students **don't have to** wear school uniform.
  She **doesn't have to** do the ironing. Her dad does it.

yes / no questions and short answers

yes / no questions
Do I **have to** feed the dog?
Do you **have to** do chores?
Does he **have to** set the table?
Does she **have to** do the laundry?
Does it **have to** be 100 words long?
Do we **have to** read this for class?
Do you **have to** wear a school uniform?
Do they **have to** clean their rooms?

Do / Does	+ subject +	have to	+	base form of the verb?

Short answers	
Affirmative	**Negative**
Yes, you **do**.	No, you **don't**.
Yes, I **do**.	No, I **don't**.
Yes, he **does**.	No, he **doesn't**.
Yes, she **does**.	No, she **doesn't**.
Yes, it **does**.	No, it **doesn't**.
Yes, you **do**.	No, you **don't**.
Yes, we **do**.	No, we **don't**.
Yes, they **do**.	No, they **don't**.

Yes, No,	+ subject pronoun +	do / does. don't / doesn't.

- We use the auxiliary verb *do* with *have to* in *yes / no* questions and short answer forms.
  Do I have to get up early tomorrow?
  NOT ~~Have I to get up early tomorrow?~~
  Yes, you **do**. / No, you **don't**.
  NOT ~~Yes, you have. / No, you don't have.~~
  Does Rosie have to do the laundry?
  NOT ~~Has Rosie to do the laundry?~~
  Yes, she **does**. / No, she **doesn't**.
  NOT ~~Yes, she has. / No, she hasn't.~~

have to / must

- *Have to* and *must* have a similar meaning. Both forms show a necessity or an obligation, but their uses are different.
  - We use *have to* to show an obligation which the speaker sees as external (for example, a regulation or an order from someone else).

    In my job I **have to** work from nine o'clock to five o'clock.

    (The obligation comes from "outside" the speaker. The speaker sees the obligation to work from nine o'clock to five o'clock as an external obligation.)
  - We use *must* to show something which the speaker sees as necessary.

    I **must** study some more – I have an exam tomorrow.

    (The obligation comes from the speaker. The speaker sees the obligation to study some more as something which is necessary to do.)

mustn't / don't have to

- *Mustn't* and *don't have to* have different meanings.
  - We use *mustn't* when we are not allowed to do something.

    You **mustn't** copy during tests.

    You **mustn't** ride your bike on the sidewalk.
  - We use *don't have to* when there is no necessity to do something.

    He **doesn't have to** play soccer. He can play basketball.

    We **don't have to** pay. It's free.

Gerunds

- A gerund is the *-ing* form of the verb. We use the gerund as the subject of a sentence.

  Eating fruit and vegetables is healthy.

  Skateboarding is fun.

  Doing chores is boring.

Verb + *-ing* form

Subject	Verb	*-ing* form
I / you / he / she / it / we / you / they	love	swimming.
	like	
	enjoy	
	prefer	
	don't mind	
	don't like	
	hate	

- We use the *-ing* form of the verb after a verb of preference such as *love*, *like*, *enjoy*, *prefer*, *don't mind*, *don't like*, and *hate*.

  I love do**ing** the cooking, but I hate clean**ing** my room.

  I don't like walk**ing** to school.

  I hate wash**ing** the dishes, but I don't mind tak**ing** out the trash.

Student Book p.23

Word list

Review the Vocabulary. Write your own study notes (or translation) for each word.

Housework
clean my bedroom _____
clean the bathroom _____
do the cooking _____
do the ironing _____
do the laundry _____
do the vacuuming _____
feed the dog _____
load / unload the dishwasher _____
make my bed _____
set / clear the table _____
take out the trash _____
wash the dishes _____

Check it out
disgusting _____
dishes _____
focus on _____
lasts _____
life jackets _____
messy _____
push _____
respects _____
rough _____
smell _____

Learn it, use it!
Can I (watch this movie), please?
_____
Yes, (of course) you can. / No, (I'm sorry,) you can't. _____
_____
Could I (borrow your cell phone), please? _____
Yes, of course. / (I'm) sorry, but …
_____
May I (go to the bathroom), please?
_____

Student Book pp.20, 18, 24, 22

Vocabulary
Housework

1 Look at the pictures. Complete the housework phrases with the words in the box.

cooking   dishes   dishwasher
ironing   trash   vacuuming

do the
cooking

1 do the
_____

2 wash the
_____

3 do the
_____

4 load the
_____

5 take out the
_____

2 Complete the housework phrases.

set / clear the table

1 _____ the dog
2 _____ / _____ the dishwasher
3 _____ the bathroom
4 _____ out the trash
5 _____ my bed
6 _____ the laundry
7 _____ my bedroom

Grammar
have to

Affirmative and negative

3 Complete the sentences with the correct form of *have to* and the verbs in the box.

clear   do   feed   make   set   take   wash

We <u>don't have to set</u> the table before meals. (✗)

1 He _____ the table. (✓)
2 They _____ the dishes. (✓)
3 I _____ my bed every day. (✗)
4 My brother _____ the dog on school days. (✗)
5 My sister _____ out the trash on weekends. (✓)
6 You _____ the laundry. (✗)

yes / no questions and short answers

4 Look at the chart. Write questions and short answers with *have to*.

	Leah	Rob
set the table	✗	✗
load the dishwasher	✗	✓
clean the bathroom	✓	✓
take out the trash	✓	✗
feed the dog	✗	✗

Leah / set the table?
<u>Does Leah have to set the table?</u>
<u>No, she doesn't.</u>

1 Rob / load the dishwasher?
_____
_____

2 they / clean the bathroom?
_____
_____

3 Rob / take out the trash?
_____
_____

4 they / feed the dog?
_____
_____

Student Book pp.20-21   Extra practice   online

mustn't / don't have to

5 Complete the sentences with *mustn't, don't have to*, or *doesn't have to*.

You <u>mustn't</u> use calculators in this test. It's not allowed.

1 You _____ buy any bread. We have a lot of bread.

2 You _____ cross the road here. It's very dangerous!

3 Marcus _____ study French in his new school. It's optional.

4 You _____ eat at the cafeteria. You can take sandwiches.

5 It's an exam! Students _____ use their cell phones.

6 Sally _____ do the ironing. Her mom did it this morning.

Gerunds

6 Complete the sentences with the gerund form of the verbs in the box.

> get   learn   play   ~~ski~~   travel   wash

<u>Skiing</u> is my favorite sport.

1 _____ new languages is useful.

2 _____ the dishes is the worst household chore.

3 _____ to foreign countries is exciting.

4 _____ video games is more fun than chess.

5 _____ up early is horrible!

Verb + *-ing* form

7 Write sentences.

Yasmin / love / swim.
<u>Yasmin loves swimming.</u>

1 Sofia / not like / walk in the mountains.
_____

2 Kenna / love / play on his game console.
_____

3 Josh / like / run?
_____

4 The boys / not mind / do housework.
_____

5 you / enjoy / listen to classical music?
_____

6 Ella / hate / be late.
_____

8 Read Megan's e-mail. Then choose the correct answers.

| Message | Options | + |

Hi, Silvia,

Are you enjoying the school vacation? I'm not! My parents are working at the moment, so I have to (go)/ **going** to Grandma's every day. I ¹**have to / mustn't** get up early because Mom takes me and my baby brother Lucas to Grandma's at 8:30! I don't like ²**get up / getting up** early on schooldays, but I ³**hate / hating** it when I'm on vacation! I don't mind ⁴**visit / visiting** my grandma, but she's very strict! In the mornings, Mom says I ⁵**mustn't / don't have to** watch TV because I ⁶**have to / has to** study. Then in the afternoon, I ⁷**don't have to / mustn't** make any noise because Grandma and Lucas sleep. It's boring! Next week, Mom and Dad ⁸**mustn't / don't have to** work and we are going camping in Florida. I like ⁹**camp / camping**. It's relaxing! (I ¹⁰**mustn't / don't have to** clean my bedroom, or wash the dishes!) There's an activity club at the campsite. Lucas loves ¹¹**to go / going** to it, so I ¹²**mustn't / don't have to** play with him all day!

What are you doing? Are you relaxing, or ¹³**do you have to / have you to** do your vacation homework?

See you soon!
Megan

9 Read Megan's e-mail again. Correct the mistakes in the sentences below.

Megan's parents are on vacation at the moment.
<u>Megan's parents are working at the moment.</u>

1 Megan doesn't mind getting up early on schooldays.
_____

2 She mustn't sleep in the afternoon.
_____

3 She has to wash the dishes at the camp.
_____

4 Lucas doesn't like going to the activity club.
_____

5 She has to play with Lucas every day.
_____

2 Communication

Asking for permission

1 Complete the dialogues with the phrases in the box.

> ~~can I go to~~   Could I borrow   have to
> have to do   No, you can't
> of course   you can go

1

Lisa Mom, _can I go to_____ Alice's house?

Mom ¹_____, Lisa. You have to practice the piano.

Lisa But Mom, we ²_____ our science project.

Mom Lisa, your piano exam is next week!

Lisa But my science project is more important.

Mom Do piano practice first. Then ³_____ to Alice's house.

Lisa That isn't fair!

2

John ⁴_____ your cell phone, Matt? I forgot my phone today and I ⁵_____ call my dad.

Matt Yes, ⁶_____, John. But don't use all my credit.

John Thanks.

2 Match the questions and answers.

1 May I open the window, Miss Kelly?   _d_
2 Can I use your laptop, Bruno?   ___
3 Dad, I need a new sweater. Can you give me some money?   ___
4 Could I have some cookies? I'm hungry.   ___
5 May I sit next to Silvia, Mr. Jones?   ___
6 Can I send a text with your cell phone?   ___

a Sure. I'm not using it now.
b I'm sorry, you can't. I don't have any credit.
c Yes, of course. Take my bag off the chair.
d No, you can't. It's cold in here.
e OK. How much is it?
f Sorry, but it's nearly lunchtime.

3 Write the dialogue in the correct order.

___ Because we're having dinner with Grandma this evening.

___ But why?

___ Could I stay at Dan's house tonight? He has an awesome new video game.

___ Yes, of course.

_1_ Can I go to Dan's house later to watch the soccer game?

___ No, you can't. You have to come home after the game.

___ Oh, OK.

4 Complete the dialogues with the phrases in the box.

> Could I make a sandwich?
> Can I watch the news?
> Can I sit here, Miss Green?
> Can I borrow your MP3 player?
> ~~Can I use the computer?~~
> May I use your calculator?

A _Can I use the computer?_____
B No, you can't. I'm answering my e-mails.

1
A _____
B Yes, of course. There's bread in the cupboard and cheese in the fridge.

2
A _____
B Sure. I'm not listening to it right now.

3
A _____
B I'm sorry, you can't. I need it for my math homework.

4
A _____
B No, you can't. I'm watching the tennis final.

5
A _____
B No, you can't. Sit next to Jamie.

Student Book p.22   **Extra practice** online

International Backpackers – the best hostel in Melbourne!

International Backpackers is a hostel for international travelers with jobs.

Everyone at the hostel works in Melbourne. The hostel is fifteen minutes by bus from the city center, and the bus station is only a few minutes away. There are cafés, banks, and a shopping mall nearby, and there's a park only two bus stops away. It's a small hostel for only 30 guests, and this means you don't have to share a room with someone different every night. There are bedrooms with two, four, six, and eight beds. All the bedrooms are clean and comfortable, and you mustn't bring any pets. There are shared bathrooms with showers on every floor. There is a communal kitchen, a dining room, and a TV room. You don't have to pay for breakfast – it's free. You have to pay extra for Internet access and a space in the parking lot. The café on the roof garden is open every day.

★★★ **Like:** I arrived here last February. I enjoy meeting people from different countries, so this place is perfect. I don't have to clean my room or the bathroom because the hostel does it. The roof garden is cool, but we mustn't stay outside after 11 p.m.
Don't like: We mustn't listen to music in our bedrooms, and we have to wash the dishes and clean the kitchen after meals. *Sam*

★★ **Like:** I arrived here four months ago and I'm still sharing a room with the same girl. I have a job, so it's great that I don't have to change roommates. I love being near the beach.
Don't like: I don't like paying a lot for the Internet, and some people make a lot of noise at night. *Tina*

Reading

1 Read the web page. Then check (✓) the facilities in the backpackers' hostel.

Single rooms ___   Free breakfast ___
Animals welcome ___   Free Wi-Fi ___
Individual bathrooms ___ Free parking ___
Shared kitchen ✓   Outdoor garden ___

2 Read the web page again. Answer the questions.

What type of people stay at this hostel?
International travelers with jobs stay in the hostel.

1 How far is it from the center of Melbourne?
2 How many people can stay at International Backpackers?
3 What mustn't backpackers do in the hostel?
4 What chores do backpackers have to do?
5 What doesn't Tina like about this hostel?

Writing

3 Imagine you are staying at a backpackers' hostel. Look at the factfile. Write an e-mail to your best friend. Say:

- where the hostel is
- what facilities there are
- what you like about the hostel
- what you don't like about it

Factfile

Green Palace Hostel, Melbourne

5 km from city center

Short-stay hostel for travelers

Bedrooms for 4, 6, or 8 guests

Guests must clean bedrooms and kitchen

Party atmosphere

Free parking

No garden

Breakfast extra

Wi-Fi extra

3 Grammar rules

be going to (1)
Affirmative

Full form	Short form
I **am going to** go to college.	**I'm going to** go to college.
You **are going to** go on vacation.	**You're going to** go on vacation.
He **is going to** have a party.	**He's going to** have a party.
She **is going to** be a doctor.	**She's going to** be a doctor.
It **is going to** bite you.	**It's going to** bite you.
We **are going to** take a test.	**We're going to** take a test.
You **are going to** play soccer.	**You're going to** play soccer.
They **are going to** watch a movie.	**They're going to** watch a movie.

Subject +	am are is	going to	+ base form of the verb

1 We use *be going to* to:
 − talk about people's intentions.
  She**'s going to** become a biologist.
  I**'m going to** be a dentist.
 − talk about things which people have decided to do in the future.
  I**'m going to** play basketball tonight.
  We**'re going to** see a movie tomorrow.

2 We usually use the short form of *be* with *be going to*.
 They**'re going to** go to Kim's party on Saturday.
 He**'s going to** study history in college.

Negative

Full form
I am **not going to** go to college.
You **are not going to** go on vacation.
He **is not going to** have a party.
She **is not going to** be a doctor.
It **is not going to** bite you.
We **are not going to** take a test.
You **are not going to** play soccer.
They **are not going to** watch a movie.

Short form
I'm not going to go to college.
You **aren't going to** go on vacation.
He **isn't going to** have a party.
She **isn't going to** be a doctor.
It **isn't going to** bite you.
We **aren't going to** take a test.
You **aren't going to** play soccer.
They **aren't going to** watch a movie.

Subject +	'm not aren't isn't	going to	+ base form of the verb

• We usually use the short form of *be* with *be going to*.
 They **aren't going to** Sue's party on Saturday.

yes / no questions and short answers

yes / no questions
Am I **going to** go to college?
Are you **going to** go on vacation?
Is he **going to** have a party?
Is she **going to** be a doctor?
Is it **going to** bite you?
Are we **going to** take a test?
Are you **going to** play soccer?
Are they **going to** watch a movie?

Am Are Is	+ subject	going to	+ base form of the verb?

Short answers	
Affirmative	**Negative**
Yes, I **am**.	No, **I'm not**.
Yes, you **are**.	No, you **aren't**.
Yes, he / she / it **is**.	No, he / she / it **isn't**.
Yes, we **are**.	No, we **aren't**.
Yes, you **are**.	No, you **aren't**.
Yes, they **are**.	No, they **aren't**.

Student Book p.33

Yes,	+ subject	+ *am / are / is.*
No,	pronoun	+ *'m not / aren't / isn't.*

- We usually use the short form of *be* in the negative short answer.

  Are they **going to** Sue's party on Saturday?
  Yes, they **are**. / No, they **aren't**.
  Is Sofia **going to** have a party?
  Yes, she **is**. No, she **isn't**.

be going to (2)

- We also use *be going to* to make predictions when there is something in the present which tells us about the future.

  Watch out! The cat**'s going to** steal some fish!
  Look at the big, black clouds. It**'s going to** rain.
  We're late! The teacher**'s going to** be angry!

Verb + infinitive / -ing form

Verb + infinitive	Verb + *-ing* form
I **hope to become** a lawyer.	I **love** playing video games.
	I **like** traveling.
I **want to go** on vacation.	I **enjoy** learning languages.
	I **prefer** being outside.
I'**d like to go** to college.	I **don't mind** studying.
	I **hate** running.

- After some verbs we use the infinitive, and after some verbs we use the *-ing* form.

  I **hope to visit** Australia next summer.
  She **wants to buy** a new bike.
  We'**d like to leave** early because we're tired.
  I **enjoy playing** baseball.
  I **don't mind visiting** my cousins on the weekend.
  I **hate learning** irregular verbs.
  Our dog **loves playing** with balls.

Watch out!

Notice the difference between *like* and *'d like*:
I **like** go**ing** to the mountains.
(*I often go to the mountains and I like it.*)
I'**d like to go** to the mountains.
(*In the future, I want to go to the mountains.*)

(**Student Book** pp.33, 35

Word list

Review the Vocabulary. Write your own study notes (or translation) for each word.

Personality adjectives
ambitious ___
arrogant ___
confident ___
creative ___
enthusiastic ___
flexible ___
hard-working ___
honest ___
lazy ___
organized ___
outgoing ___
patient ___
selfish ___
shy ___
stubborn ___

Check it out!
behind the scenes ___
career ___
chance ___
operations ___
real-life ___
stunt ___
wildlife ___

Learn it, use it!
Can I see your ticket and passport, please?
___
Yes, here you are.
___
Would you like a window or an aisle seat?
___
I'd like a window / an aisle seat, please.
___
Do you have any baggage to check in?
___
Do you have any liquids or a laptop in your hand baggage?
___
Do you have anything in your pockets?
___
No, I don't. / Yes, I do. ___
Are you wearing a watch or a belt?
___
Yes, I am. / No, I'm not. ___

(**Student Book** pp.32, 30, 36, 34

W15

Vocabulary
Personality adjectives

1 Complete the personality adjectives.

Steve is very s _e_ _l_ _f_ _i_ _s_ h. He never shares anything with anyone.

1 I'm f __ __ __ __ __ __ e. I don't mind what time we leave.
2 Maria is very o __ __ __ __ __ __ g. She loves meeting new people.
3 Don't be so l __ __ y! You can't watch TV all day!
4 Carla designs all her friends' clothes. She's very c __ __ __ __ __ __ e.
5 Juan isn't worried about his exams. He seems very c __ __ __ __ __ __ __ __ t.
6 My sister is very a __ __ __ __ __ __ __ s. She wants to be an astronaut for NASA!
7 Tom is very p __ __ __ __ __ t. He always helps his brother with his homework.
8 That girl is very h __ __ __ __ __ t. She found a cell phone on the bus and she gave it to the driver.

Grammar
be going to (1)

Affirmative and negative

2 Complete the sentences with *be going to* and the verbs in the box.

> buy   cook   find   have   play
> ~~see~~   stay   work   write

I _'m going to see_ my grandparents on the weekend.

1 We _____ a party on Tuesday.
2 I _____ home this weekend.
3 My dad _____ dinner tonight.
4 Pablo and Ivan _____ in a basketball game tonight.
5 My mom _____ a new job.
6 Beth _____ harder next semester.
7 He _____ an e-mail to his cousin in Australia.
8 My parents _____ a new car.

3 Write sentences. Use short forms.

Alison / not play tennis / do homework.
Alison isn't going to play tennis. She's going
to do her homework.

1 We / not watch TV / play soccer.
_____
_____

2 Mateus / not ride his bike to school / walk.
_____
_____

3 It / not rain tomorrow / snow.
_____
_____

4 They / not watch a movie / study for a test.
_____
_____

5 I / not wear shorts / jeans.
_____
_____

yes / no questions and short answers

4 Complete the questions and short answers. Use the correct form of *be going to*.

A _Are you going to_ _____ come with us?
B No I _'m not_ _____. I'm busy.

1
A _____
(you / finish) your soda?
B Yes, _____. I'm really thirsty.

2
A _____
(you and Kate / watch) a DVD?
B Yes, _____. There's nothing on TV.

3
A _____
(Juan / study) in college next year?
B No, _____. He wants to get a job.

4
A _____
(Ana and Isabel / stay) the night?
B No, _____. They have to go home.

5
A _____
(Mrs. Harris / give) us homework?
B Yes, _____. She always gives us homework.

6
A What _____ (you / do) on the weekend?
B I don't know.

Student Book pp.32-33   **Extra practice** online

be going to (2)

5 Complete the sentences with the correct affirmative and negative forms of *be going to* and the verbs in the box.

> break   get   have   jump   ~~rain~~   win

It'<u>s going to rain</u>.

1 Number 5 _____ the race!

2 He _____ out of the airplane.

3 She _____ a baby soon.

4 The desk _____.

5 You _____ wet.

Verb + infinitive / -ing form

6 Complete the sentences in the questionnaire. Check (✓) the sentences that are true for you.

What type of person are you?

I don't mind <u>changing</u> my plans at the last minute. (change)   __

1 I don't want _____ in a big city. (live)   __

2 I'd like _____ a lot of foreign countries. (visit)   __

3 I enjoy _____ new people. (meet)   __

4 I love _____ video games. (play)   __

5 I hope _____ famous one day. (be)   __

6 I don't like _____ sports on TV. (watch)   __

Round-up

7 Complete the text with *be going to*, and the infinitive or the *-ing* form of the verbs in parentheses.

oneworld.com

What <u>are you going to do</u> (you / do) in your vacation? Do you want ¹_____ (travel)? What countries would you like ²_____ (see)? With a Oneworld airplane ticket, you can travel anywhere for two months. Read about Ana's experience.

Hi! I didn't want ³_____ (stay) home this summer, so I bought a Oneworld airplane ticket. I love ⁴_____ (see) new cities, and I wanted ⁵_____ (visit) Los Angeles, New York, London, Paris, and Madrid. I'm on my own, but I don't mind ⁶_____ (travel) alone. My first stop was L.A., and now I'm in New York. Tomorrow, I ⁷_____ (fly) to London. My aunt lives there, and she ⁸_____ (meet) me at the airport. She ⁹_____ (show) me London. After that, the two of us ¹⁰_____ (spend) a week in Paris. But we ¹¹_____ (not travel) by airplane because my aunt hates ¹²_____ (fly). We ¹³_____ (take) a train called the Eurostar which goes under the sea!

3 Communication

At the airport

1 Complete the dialogues with the phrases in the box.

> a watch or a belt   boarding pass   ~~Can I see~~
> Do you have   here you are   in your pockets
> put it   remove   to check in   Would you like

At the check-in desk

A Good morning. <u>Can I see</u>_____ your ticket
  and passport or ID card, please?
B Yes, [1]_____.
A Thank you. [2]_____ a window or an
  aisle seat?
B I'd like an aisle seat, please.
A OK. Do you have any baggage
  [3]_____?
B Yes, I have this suitcase.
A OK, here's your [4]_____.
  You're boarding at gate 7.

At the security checkpoint

A [5]_____ any liquids or a laptop in
  your hand baggage?
B Yes, I have a laptop.
A Please [6]_____ in this tray. Do you
  have any metal items [7]_____?
B No, I don't.
A Are you wearing [8]_____?
B I'm wearing a belt.
A Please [9]_____ it.

2 Write the dialogues in the correct order.

1
__ Two suitcases. OK, and would you like a
   window or an aisle seat?
__ Yes, here you are.
__ OK. Here are your boarding passes.
__ Thank you. Do you have any baggage to
   check in?

1 Good morning. Can I see your tickets and
   passports, please?
__ Yes, we have two suitcases.
__ A window seat, please.

2
__ Please put them in this tray. And are you
   wearing a watch or a belt?
__ I'm wearing a belt.
__ Please put it in the tray with the other things.
__ Please remove it.
1 Do you have any metal items in your pockets?
__ OK. Here it is.
__ Yes, I have. I have some coins and my keys.

3 Match the question halves.

1 Do you have a	<u>e</u>
2 Can I see	__
3 Would you like	__
4 Where are you	__
5 Are you wearing	__
6 Do you have any	__
7 Do you have any metal items	__

a your passport or ID card, please?
b in your pockets?
c a watch or a belt?
d liquids in your hand baggage?
e laptop in your hand baggage?
f a window or an aisle seat?
g flying to?

4 Complete the dialogues.

1
A Good morning. <u>Where are you flying to?</u>_____
B To London.
A [1]_____
B Yes, here's my ticket and my passport.
A Thank you. [2]_____
B Yes, I have a backpack.
A [3]_____
B I'd like a window seat, please.
A OK, you have seat 7A, near the front.
B Thank you!

2
A Are you wearing a belt or a watch?
B I'm wearing a belt.
A Please [4]_____ and put it in
  the tray. [5]_____
B Yes, I have a bottle of soda.
A OK, please put it in this tray.
  [6]_____
B Yes, I have some coins and my keys.
A Please [7]_____.

Student Book p.34   Extra practice   online

teen issues

fashion | beauty | love life | health | celebrities | real life | fun | FAQs

Ambitious People

It's good to be ambitious because it helps us work hard. This week, reader Maria Turner writes about her ambition and how she hopes to make it come true.

I love playing soccer and, like thousands of other teenagers, my dream is to become a famous soccer player and mix with the top players. Of course, I know that this isn't going to happen, because professional soccer is very competitive! But I have a plan. I'm going to become a professional referee.

The referee makes all the decisions about a game, but he or she is also responsible for safety in the stadium. He or she can stop a game if there are problems with the weather or the crowd. A good referee must have a strong personality and be able to take difficult decisions – with thousands of fans shouting at you, this isn't easy. A good referee must also be confident and good at talking to people. Most players are easy to talk to, but some behave badly. Referees are well-paid because pressure from sponsors and managers make it a stressful job.

I am sure that I have the right qualities to become a good referee. I like making decisions, and I enjoy telling people what to do. I am outgoing and good with people. Also, I don't mind working in stressful situations. But most of all, I am passionate about soccer.

How am I going to achieve my ambition? First, I'm going to do a course to become a referee for my local club. After that, I'm going to work hard and pass exams so that I can work with more important teams. It isn't going to be easy, but I'm confident and excited about the future.

Write and tell us about your ambitions.

Reading

1 Read the article. Then complete the sentences.

Maria Turner would like to be a _____.
She is going to be a _____.

2 Read the article again. Are the sentences true or false? Correct the false sentences.

Thousands of teenagers dream of becoming famous referees.

False. Thousands of teenagers dream of becoming famous soccer players.

1 Maria has a plan to become a professional player.
2 The referee can't cancel a game if the weather is bad.
3 Refereeing is a difficult job because most players behave badly.
4 Good referees earn a lot of money because they have a lot of stress.
5 Maria wants to be a referee because she wants to be rich.
6 She is going to start her career by playing for a local club.
7 She must do a course to become a referee.

Writing

3 Think about your ambition. Write a paragraph or short text for the magazine feature "Ambitious People." Think about the following:

- What is your ambition, e.g., astronaut, actor, pop star, etc.?
- What qualities does the work require?
- What qualities do you have?
- How are you going to achieve your ambition?

will: future
Affirmative and negative

Affirmative	
Full form	**Short form**
I **will go** to college when I'm older.	I**'ll go** to college when I'm older.
You **will be** happy at your new school.	You**'ll be** happy at your new school.
He / She **will be** famous one day.	He / She**'ll be** famous one day.
It **will rain** later.	It**'ll rain** later.
We **will be** healthier in the future.	We**'ll be** healthier in the future.
You **will be** tired tomorrow.	You**'ll be** tired tomorrow.
They **will win** the big game tomorrow.	They**'ll win** the big game tomorrow.

Subject + *will* / *'ll* + base form of the verb

Negative	
Full form	**Short form**
I **will not go** to college when I'm older.	I **won't go** to college when I'm older.
You **will not be** happy at your new school.	You **won't be** happy at your new school.
He / She **will not be** famous one day.	He / She **won't be** famous one day.
It **will not rain** later.	It **won't rain** later.
We **will not be** healthier in the future.	We **won't be** healthier in the future.
You **will not be** tired tomorrow.	You **won't be** tired tomorrow.
They **will not win** the big game tomorrow.	They **won't win** the big game tomorrow.

Subject + *will not / won't* + base form of the verb

- We use *will*:
  - to predict or suppose.
    It**'ll be** awesome! The weather **will be** hot.
  - to talk about future facts.
    They**'ll arrive** on the 11 a.m. train.
  - to express decisions taken at the moment.
    It's raining hard. I**'ll wait** until it stops.
  - to offer to do something at the moment or later.
    Don't worry, I**'ll help** you with your chores.
  - to make a request with *you*.
    Will you **help** me with my homework?

yes / no questions and short answers

yes / no questions
Will I **go** to college when I'm older?
Will you **be** happy at your new school?
Will he / she **be** famous one day?
Will it **rain** later?
Will we **be** healthier in the future?
Will you **be** tired tomorrow?
Will they **win** the big game tomorrow?

Will + subject + base form of the verb?

Short answers	
Affirmative	**Negative**
Yes, I will.	No, I won't.
Yes, you will.	No, you won't.
Yes, he / she / it will.	No, he / she / it won't.
Yes, we will.	No, we won't.
Yes, you will.	No, you won't.
Yes, they will.	No, they won't.

Yes, / No, + subject + *will. / won't.*

will / be going to

1 We can talk about the future using three different verb forms: *will* + base form of the verb, *be going to* + base form of the verb, and present progressive.

2 We use *will* + base form of the verb to talk about:
  - things we cannot control.
    I think it**'ll be** sunny tomorrow.
  - when we decide to do something at the moment of speaking.
    I**'ll call** you back this afternoon.

Student Book p.41

3 We use *be going to* + base form of the verb to talk about:
- – intentions, things we have already decided to do.

  I'm **going to watch** a movie with my friends.
- – something in the present that tells us something about the future.

  There's a lot of traffic. We'**re going to be** late.

  Look at those black clouds. It'**s going to rain**.

4 We use the present progressive to talk about things that we arrange to do in the future.

"What **are** you **doing** tonight?"

"I'**m going** to the movies with Rachael."

First conditional

Affirmative
If we study, we'll pass our exams.

Hypothesis	Consequence
If we study,	we'll pass our exams.

If + subject + simple present, subject + *will* / *'ll* + base form of the verb.

Negative
If you don't play, the team won't win.

Hypothesis	Consequence
If you don't play,	the team won't win.

If + subject + simple present, subject + *will not* / *won't* + base form of the verb.

1 We use the first conditional to talk about future situations that the speaker thinks are probable.

If she **leaves** before ten o'clock, she'**ll catch** the bus.

(The speaker thinks it is probable that she will leave before ten o'clock and as a consequence catch the bus.)

2 We make first conditional sentences with two parts: an *if* clause (the hypothesis) and a main clause (the consequence).

3 We make the *if* clause with *if* + subject + the simple present form of the verb + comma (,).

<u>If we **see** Alice</u>, we will tell her.

4 We make the main clause with subject + *will* / *won't* + base form of the verb.

If we see Alice, <u>we **will tell** her</u>.

5 We can put the *if* clause at the beginning or end of a sentence. When the *if* clause is at the beginning of a sentence, we put a comma (,) after it.

If the weather **is** nice, we'**ll go** to the beach.

We'**ll go** to the beach if the weather **is** nice.

6 We can also use imperatives in the main clause when we want to give orders.

Stop working if you're tired.

Don't wear sandals if you want to go walking in the mountains.

(**Student Book** pp.41, 43

Word list

Review the Vocabulary. Write your own study notes (or translation) for each word.

Life events

apply to college / for a job _____

be born _____

die _____

get a job _____

get married _____

graduate _____

have a baby / children _____

pass your driving test _____

retire _____

start school _____

Check it out!

accurate _____

came true _____

criticize _____

flies _____

however _____

in charge of _____

may happen _____

nevertheless _____

overpopulation _____

prophecies _____

sustainable _____

Learn it, use it!

I'd like a ticket to …, please.

_____

Would you like a one-way ticket or a round-trip? _____

Are you leaving today? / When are you coming back? _____

_____

What time is the next bus?

_____

It leaves at … _____

What gate / Where does it leave from?

_____

It leaves from … _____

How long does the trip take?

_____

It takes about … _____

(**Student Book** pp.40, 38, 44, 42

Vocabulary
Life events

1 Complete the sentences with the words in the box.

> apply born die get graduate
> have married pass retire start

My baby brother was <u>born</u> in 2012.

1 My brother is going to _____ to medical college.

2 In the U.S., most children _____ school when they are 5.

3 My sister is going to _____ a baby.

4 Pablo and Lola are going to get _____ in church.

5 I want to live a long and happy life before I _____.

6 I hope you _____ your driving test this time.

7 My grandpa doesn't want to _____. He loves his job.

8 Tom is in his third year in college. He hopes to _____ in July.

9 I want to _____ a job after I leave college.

Grammar

will: future

Affirmative and negative

2 Write sentences with will or won't. Use short forms where possible.

He / play soccer for Brazil / one day.
<u>He'll play soccer for Brazil one day.</u>

1 You / enjoy the food in Mexico.
_____

2 I / not stay for long.
_____

3 He / tell you about his trip to South Africa.
_____

4 We / not go to the shopping mall tomorrow.
_____

5 She / graduate in June.
_____

6 Barcelona / not win next week.
_____

7 It / not rain tomorrow.
_____

8 They / meet us at the airport.
_____

yes / no questions and short answers

3 Write the questions and short answers.

you get a D on the test? ✗
<u>Will you get a D on the test?</u>
<u>No, I won't.</u>

1 Maxine get married this year? ✗
_____
_____

2 the weather be cold in Montreal in December? ✓
_____
_____

3 Mr. Fernandez retire next year? ✗
_____
_____

4 Luis study English in college? ✓
_____
_____

5 your sister get a job this summer? ✗
_____
_____

6 you pass your driving test next week? ✓
_____
_____

will / be going to

4 Complete the sentences with will and be going to. Use short forms where possible.

Sara <u>'s going to</u> apply to Harvard University, but I don't think she <u>'ll</u> get in. Her grades aren't very good.

1 We _____ invite Nick and Sam to our party, but I don't think Sam _____ come – he's very shy.

2 I think I _____ pass my driving test. My grandpa _____ buy me a car next month.

3 We hope the weather _____ be warm tonight because we _____ have a barbecue.

4 I _____ visit Hollywood this summer. Maybe I _____ see a movie star!

5 They _____ play basketball this afternoon, so they _____ be tired tonight!

6 Elena _____ study at the Actors' Studio. Maybe she _____ be a movie star one day.

Student Book pp.40-41 **Extra practice** online

First conditional

5 Match the sentence halves.

1 You'll be late   <u>b</u>
2 Will you come to the beach tomorrow   __
3 Pablo's dad will buy him a car   __
4 We'll be hungry   __
5 Will his parents be angry   __
6 Sarah won't come to the party   __

a if you invite her brother!
b if you don't leave now.
c if he fails the test?
d if the weather is nice?
e if we don't eat something before we go.
f if he passes his driving test.

6 Complete the dialogue with the correct form of the verbs in parentheses. Use short forms where possible.

Mom Be quiet! If you <u>make</u>
(make) a lot of noise, you'll wake your
baby sister.

Justin Yes, Amy, turn the music down! If we
¹_____ (wake) Kate, we
²_____ (have to) look after
her.

Amy You're right! We ³_____ (not
have) time to finish our science project if
we ⁴_____ (look after) Kate.

Justin If we ⁵_____ (not finish) our
project, Mr. Grant ⁶_____
(be) annoyed.

Amy And if he ⁷_____ (be)
annoyed, he ⁸_____ (give)
us extra homework.

Justin We ⁹_____ (not have) time
to watch TV if he ¹⁰_____
(give) us extra homework.

Amy OK, let's go outside! If we
¹¹_____ (go) outside, Kate
¹²_____ (not hear) us.

Round-up

7 Read the text. Then choose the correct answers.

Today there are 7 billion people in the world, and experts predict that by 2050, the population **is** / **will be** 9 billion people. If this ¹ **will happen** / **happens**, growing enough food ² **is** / **will be** a serious problem. How ³ **are we going to feed** / **are we feeding** an extra 2 billion people? There ⁴ **won't be** / **is** enough food if we ⁵ **won't** / **don't** find new solutions. Some people think that urban farms in tall buildings ⁶ **become** / **will become** common. These "vertical farms" ⁷ **will produce** / **produce** most of the vegetables for people in towns. In Singapore, a company called Sky Greens already has 120 vertical farms, and it ⁸ **is going to** / **will build** 2,000 farms in the next few years. Of course, vertical farms ⁹ **aren't solving** / **won't solve** the food problem on their own, but they ¹⁰ **are** / **will be** part of the solution.

8 Read the text again. Correct the mistakes in the sentences.

The world's population will be smaller in 2050.
<u>The world's population will be bigger in 2050.</u>

1 There will be farms in city parks.
_____
_____

2 Vertical farms will produce milk and fish.
_____
_____

3 Sky Greens are going to build 120 vertical farms in Singapore in the next few years.
_____
_____

4 Vertical farms will find a solution to the world food problem.
_____
_____

At the bus station

1 Choose the correct answers.

Luis	Hello. I'd like a (ticket) / trip to Newport, please.
Assistant	¹Do you have / Would you like a one-way or a round-trip ticket?
Luis	I'm leaving today and I'm coming back next Friday.
Assistant	OK, so you'll need a ²one-way / round-trip. That's $28, please.
Luis	Here you are, here's $30.
Assistant	Thank you. Here's your ticket and $2 ³cash / change.
Luis	What time is the next bus?
Assistant	There's a bus for Newport every 30 minutes. The next bus ⁴starts / leaves at eleven thirty.
Luis	OK, thanks. What ⁵gate / station does it leave from?
Assistant	It leaves from gate five.
Luis	Thanks. Oh … how ⁶long / often does the trip take?
Assistant	It takes about three hours.
Luis	OK. Thanks. Goodbye.
Assistant	Goodbye.

2 Match the questions and answers.

1 Do you want a one-way or a round-trip?   b
2 When are you coming back?   __
3 When's the next bus for Miami?   __
4 Is there a bus after that?   __
5 Which gate does it leave from?   __
6 How long does the trip take?   __

a It takes about three hours.
b A round-trip, please.
c It leaves from gate 9.
d I'm coming back next Saturday.
e It leaves in 20 minutes.
f No, there isn't. It's the last bus.

3 Write the questions for the answers.

Are you leaving today?
Yes, I am. I'd like to go on the next bus.
1 _____
I'm coming back on Thursday.
2 _____
I'd like a one-way, please.
3 _____
There's a bus to Denver in 30 minutes.
4 _____
It leaves from gate 3.
5 _____
It takes about two hours.

4 Write the dialogue in the correct order.

__ Thank you. What time's the next bus, please?
__ Are you coming back today?
1 Hello. I'd like a round-trip to Chicago, please.
__ It takes four hours.
__ Um … gate 8.
__ Thank you. Here's your ticket and eleven dollars change.
__ It's at two thirty.
__ OK, so you'll need an open return. That's $39, please.
__ OK, thanks. Goodbye.
__ And what gate does it leave from?
__ No, I'm not. I'm coming back next month.
__ Gate 8. Thanks. And how long does the trip take?
__ Here you are, here's $50.

5 You are going to Stamford today and you are coming back next Friday. Use the information to write a dialogue.

Newtown to Stamford
departure 8 a.m.
arrival 9:30 a.m.
Gate 12
One-way: $7   Round-trip: $13

You	I'd like a ticket to Stamford, please.
Assistant	_____
You	A round-trip, please.
Assistant	_____
You	_____
Assistant	_____
You	_____
Assistant	_____
You	_____

Student Book p.42   Extra practice online

One World Study Abroad Program
Become a global citizen

1 _____

The Study Abroad program is a unique opportunity to meet new people, have an amazing time, and do awesome things. It is the perfect way to explore and experience life in another culture. If you spend a semester or a year in a foreign country, you will have time to become part of a community. What's more, you'll learn a foreign language, and make new friends for life.

2 _____

You will live with a host family and attend classes at the local high school. You will take part in community events and out of school activities. When you first arrive, a One World representative will meet you at the airport and take you to your host family. After that, they will help you if you have any problems during your stay.

3 _____

You will come home a different person! You will be more confident and more independent. You will also learn to be more tolerant as you start to understand and accept other people's customs and cultures. Many students also discover new interests. You will probably have a better idea about what you want to do in life. One thing is certain: if you spend a year abroad, you won't regret it.

"My year in Japan changed my life! It opened my eyes to the world, because everything was different. It also helped me choose a career. I'm going to be a diplomat and live in different countries. I'm going to apply to college and study Arabic and French. I won't get a job immediately after I graduate. I'm going to travel around the world.

My advice: Choose a country that is very different from home. Your experience will be more exciting."

Jake, 17, from Illinois

Reading

1 Read the web page. Then match the paragraphs with the headings.

  a How does it work?

  b What are the benefits?

  c What is the Study Abroad program?

2 Read the web page again. Answer the questions.

  How long do students spend abroad on study abroad programs?

  They spend a semester or a year abroad.

  1 Where do students live?

  2 How will your attitude towards other people change?

  3 Why did Japan open Jake's eyes?

  4 What does Jake plan to do after college?

Writing

3 Answer the questions. Then use your answers to write a short text about your plans and hopes for the future.

- What are you going to do after high school?
- When are you going to get a job?
- When will you leave home?
- Where will you live?
- If you get married, what will your husband / wife be like?
- Will you have children? How many?
- How will you spend your free time?

Student Book pp.44-45   **Extra practice** online

5 Grammar rules

Present perfect
Affirmative

Full form	Short form
I have won a competition.	I've won a competition.
You have read this book.	You've read this book.
He / She has been scuba diving.	He / She's been scuba diving.
It has bitten me!	It's bitten me!
We have been to France.	We've been to France.
You have slept in a tent.	You've slept in a tent.
They have tried skiing.	They've tried skiing.

Subject + | have ('ve) / has ('s) | + past participle

1 We make the present perfect with the simple present form of the auxiliary verb *have* + the past participle of the main verb.
They **have bought** a new laptop.

2 We usually use the short forms of the present perfect in spoken and informal written English.
He**'s done** a parachute jump with a friend.

3 We use the present perfect to talk about:
   – a past action with a present result.
     I**'ve eaten** too much candy – I feel sick.
   – experiences in our life without saying when they happened.
     I**'ve been** to Europe.

Negative

Full form	Short form
I have not won a competition.	I haven't won a competition.
You have not read this book.	You haven't read this book.
He / She has not been scuba diving.	He / She hasn't been scuba diving.
It has not bitten me.	It hasn't bitten me.
We have not been to France.	We haven't been to France.
You have not slept in a tent.	You haven't slept in a tent.
They have not tried skiing.	They haven't tried skiing.

Subject + | have not (haven't) / has not (hasn't) | + past participle

1 We make the negative form of the present perfect with the simple present form of the auxiliary verb *have* + *not* + the past participle of the main verb.
We **have not visited** Los Angeles.

2 We usually use the short forms of the present perfect in spoken and informal written English.
You **haven't seen** my pictures of the party.

Past participles

1 We make the past participle of regular verbs by adding -*ed* to the base form of the verb.

Regular verbs		
Base form	Simple past	Past participle
finish	finished	finished
play	played	played
watch	watched	watched

2 Remember the spelling variations:
   – when the verb ends in -*e*, we only add -*d*.
     live – lived
   – when the verb ends in a vowel and then a consonant, we double the last consonant and then add -*ed*.
     stop – stopped   plan – planned
   – when the verb ends in a consonant and then the letter -*y*, we replace -*y* with an -*i* and then add -*ed*.
     study – studied

3 There are no rules to form the past participles of irregular verbs. Look at the irregular verb list on the inside back cover and try to learn them.

been / gone

1 We use the present perfect of *be* (*have been / has been*) to say that someone went to a place and then returned.
Julio **has been** to Japan. He really liked it.
(*Julio went to Japan. Now he is at home.*)

2 We use the present perfect of *go* (*have gone / has gone*) to say that someone went to a place and they are still there.
Jo **has gone** to the store. She'll come back soon.
(*Jo went to the store. She is at the store now.*)

Present perfect
yes / no questions and short answers

yes / no questions
Have I won a competition?
Have you read this book?
Has he / she been scuba diving?
Has it bitten me?
Have we been to France?
Have you slept in a tent?
Have they tried skiing?

Have / Has	+ subject pronoun +	past participle?

Short answers	
Affirmative	**Negative**
Yes, I have.	No, I haven't.
Yes, you have.	No, you haven't.
Yes, he / she / it has.	No, he / she / it hasn't.
Yes, we have.	No, we haven't.
Yes, you have.	No, you haven't.
Yes, they have.	No, they haven't.

Yes, No,	+ subject pronoun +	have / has. / haven't / hasn't.

1 We make present perfect *yes / no* questions with *Have / Has* followed by the subject pronoun and the past participle of the verb.
"**Have** you **ridden** a horse?" "**Yes, I have.**"
"**Has** Elena **slept** in a tent?" "**No,** she **hasn't.**"

ever / never

1 *Ever* means "in your life." We use *ever* in *yes / no* questions between the subject pronoun and the past participle.
Have you **ever** visited Canada?

2 *Never* means "not in your life." We use *never* in affirmative sentences between *have / has* and the past participle.
She has **never** visited Mexico.

Present perfect / Simple past

1 We use the simple past to talk about a completed past action. We also usually use the simple past with a past time expression which says when something happened (for example *yesterday, a year ago, last Monday, in 2008*).
I **went** to Miami **last summer**.

2 We use the present perfect to talk about a past action with a present result, or about an experience that happened in our lifetime, but we do not specify when it happened.
Have you **ever been** to Buenos Aires?

(**Student Book** p.57

Word list

Review the Vocabulary. Write your own study notes (or translation) for each word.

Experiences
be in the newspaper _____
climb a mountain _____
do a parachute jump _____
fly in an airplane _____
go whitewater rafting _____
meet a famous person _____
ride a horse _____
sleep in a tent _____
visit a foreign country _____
win a competition _____

Check it out!
at least _____
award _____
caves _____
juggle _____
rocky *(a)* / rocks *(n)* _____
to date _____
unicycle _____
wetsuit _____

Learn it, use it!
Can I help you? _____

I / We'd like to check in. I / We've booked a room for … _____
_____
Could I have your passports or ID cards? _____
Yes, here they are. _____
Can you sign this form, please?
_____
Yes, of course. _____
Here's your key card. It's room …
_____
Thank you. What time do we have to check out? _____

(**Student Book** pp.54, 52, 58, 56

Vocabulary
Experiences

1 Complete the sentences with the words in the box.

airplane   competition   country   ~~horse~~
mountain   newspaper   parachute   person   tent

Last year, I rode a <u>horse</u> on the beach.

1 I climbed Aconcagua last summer – it's the highest _____ in South America.

2 I met a famous _____ at a concert.

3 This weekend, we're going to visit a national park and sleep in a _____.

4 I did a _____ jump last month.

5 My dad travels a lot and he often flies in an _____.

6 My sister won a photography _____.

7 Every summer, we visit a different foreign _____.

8 My mom is often in the _____ because she's the mayor of our town.

Grammar
Present perfect
Affirmative and negative

2 Complete the sentences with the correct present perfect form of the verbs in parentheses. Use short forms when possible.

He <u>'s flown</u> across the Atlantic Ocean three times. (fly)

1 My sister _____ her new cell phone. It fell out of her bag. (lose)

2 I _____ my homework. I'll do it after dinner. (not do)

3 My uncle _____ Mont Blanc twice. He's an experienced climber. (climb)

4 We _____ a lot of American cities, but our favorite is New York. (visit)

5 Carla _____ a horse. She is scared of them. (never ride)

6 I _____ Huckleberry Finn twice. It's my favorite book. (read)

7 I can't go out tonight. The science teacher _____ us a lot of homework. (give)

been / gone

3 Complete the sentences with the correct form of the present perfect and *been* / *gone*.

We <u>'ve been</u> to Mexico a lot of times.

1 I _____ to Europe. I went there last year.

2 My parents aren't here. They _____ to a restaurant.

3 They _____ to Australia three times.

4 "Where's Jacob?" "Umm, I think he _____ to the skatepark."

5 Ricardo _____ to the beach. That's why he is sunburned.

6 Sorry, you can't speak to Alice. She _____ home.

Present perfect
yes / no questions and short answers

4 Complete the dialogue with questions and short answers.

Mom (you / lose / something?)
Ana, <u>have you lost something?</u>

Ana Yes, <u>I have</u> _____.
(you / see / my cell phone?)
¹_____

Mom No, ²_____. (you / try / calling it?) ³_____

Ana Yes, ⁴_____, but I can't hear it anywhere.

Mom (you / look / in your room?)
⁵_____

Ana Yes, ⁶_____, Mom! It isn't there.

Mom (ask / your brother?)
⁷_____

Ana No, ⁸_____.
(he / come / home from school?)
⁹_____

Mom Yes, he ¹⁰_____. He's in his room.

Ana Hey, Mike. (you / take / my cell phone?)
¹¹_____

Mike Um, yes, ¹²_____.
It's here. Sorry, Ana!

Student Book pp.54–55, 57

Extra practice   online

ever / never

5 Complete the dialogue with the present perfect and *ever* or *never*. Use short forms where possible.

Sam Hi. Are you an actor?

Lily No, I'm a stuntwoman. I'm going to run into that fire.

Sam Really? <u>Have you ever run</u> (you / run) into a fire before?

Lily No, I ¹_____ (do) this stunt before.

Sam That's scary! ²_____ (feel) scared before a stunt?

Lily No, I ³_____ (feel) scared because I ⁴_____ (have) an accident.

Sam ⁵_____ (refuse) to do a stunt?

Lily No, I ⁶_____ (refuse) to do a stunt.

Sam Wow! ⁷_____ (you / fall) off a horse?

Lily No, I ⁸_____ (ride) a horse in a movie. I've only ridden motorcycles.

Sam ⁹_____ (swim) with sharks?

Lily No, I ¹⁰_____ (do) that. I hate sharks!

Present perfect / Simple past

6 Complete the dialogues with the correct forms of the present perfect or the simple past. Use short forms where possible.

A <u>Have you ever visited</u> (you / ever / visit) Australia?

B Yes, <u>I have</u>. I <u>went</u> (go) there last year.

1

A Where's Ben? ¹_____ (he / go) to the movies?

B No, he ²_____. I ³_____ (see) him a few minutes ago. He ⁴_____ (go) outside.

2

A ⁵_____ (you / speak) to Andres today?

B No, I ⁶_____. I ⁷_____ (call) him at ten o'clock, but he ⁸_____ (not answer). I don't know where he ⁹_____ (go).

3

A Hey, your sister has a new boyfriend. ¹⁰_____ (you / meet) him?

B Yes, I ¹¹_____. He ¹²_____ (come) to our house last weekend. But my parents ¹³_____ (not like) him.

Round-up

7 Complete the text with the correct forms of the present perfect or simple past. Use short forms where possible.

Martin Harris is a cameraman. He <u>'s traveled</u> (travel) all over the world and he ¹_____ (make) a lot of documentaries. Martin ²_____ (be) born in Canada and he ³_____ (become) interested in wildlife when he ⁴_____ (be) young. As a child, he ⁵_____ (love) taking photographs of animals. Martin ⁶_____ (be) to some extreme places. He ⁷_____ (visit) the freezing Antarctic and he ⁸_____ (camp) in the Amazon Rainforest. He ⁹_____ (do) some exciting things. In February, he ¹⁰_____ (cross) a desert on a camel, and in July, he ¹¹_____ (swim) with sharks. He ¹²_____ (not like) that experience because the sharks ¹³_____ (be) dangerous! Now he is on a safari in South Africa. He ¹⁴_____ (never / be) on a safari before, and he's very excited. Last night, he ¹⁵_____ (sleep) in a tent and he ¹⁶_____ (hear) lions outside.

8 Write questions. Then answer the questions.

Where / be / Martin Harris / born?
<u>Where was Martin Harris born?</u>
<u>He was born in Canada.</u>

1 What / extreme places / he / visit?
_____
_____

2 What / he / do / last February?
_____
_____

3 Martin / ever be / on a safari before?
_____
_____

4 Where / he / sleep / last night?
_____
_____

5 Communication

At the hotel

1 Complete the dialogue with the phrases in the box.

| can you sign do we have to check out |
| Have a nice stay. I'll just check that |
| I've booked ~~We'd like to check in.~~ |
| your key card |

Receptionist Good afternoon. Can I help you?
Man Yes, please. <u>We'd like to check in.</u>
Receptionist Certainly. What's your name, please?
Man It's Steve Roberts. 1_____ a room for two people.
Receptionist OK, 2_____. Yes, ... a double room for three nights. Is that correct?
Mark Yes, that's right.
Receptionist Great. Could I have your passports or ID cards?
Mark Yes, here they are.
Receptionist Thank you. And, 3_____ this form, please?
Mark Yes, of course.
Receptionist Right. Here's 4_____. It's room 305, on the third floor. Breakfast is from 7 a.m. to 10 a.m.
Mark OK, thank you. And what time 5_____?
Receptionist You have to leave the room by 11 a.m.
Mark OK, thank you very much.
Receptionist You're welcome. 6_____

2 Choose the correct answers.

Can I see your passports or ID cards?
a Here I am.
b Yes, please.
c Here they are.

1 Can I help you?
a Yes, please.
b Yes, I can.
c No, you can't.

2 You have to leave the room by 11 a.m.
a OK, thank you.
b OK.
c I know.

3 Can you sign this form, please?
a Yes, I can.
b Thank you.
c Yes, of course.

4 OK, a family room for one night. Is that correct?
a You're right.
b Yes, that's right.
c True.

5 Thank you very much.
a Please.
b It's OK.
c You're welcome.

3 Complete the dialogue.

HOTEL *PARADISE*

Check in:	01/08
Name:	Thomas Lockhart
Number of people:	1 (single room)
Number of nights:	1
Room number:	306

Receptionist Good evening. Can I help you?
You 1_____
Receptionist Certainly. Is that a single or a double room?
You 2_____
Receptionist OK, and what's your name, please?
You 3_____
Receptionist And how many nights are you staying, Mr. Lockhart?
You 4_____
Receptionist OK, Here's your key card. It's room number 306.
You 5_____
Receptionist Breakfast is at seven thirty.
You 6_____
Receptionist Check out is at eleven o'clock.
You 7_____
Receptionist You're welcome. Have a nice stay!

4 You have booked two rooms at the Grand Hotel. Write the dialogue with the receptionist. Use the information on the registration form.

Rooms:	2 single rooms
Nights:	2
Breakfast:	7–9:30 a.m.
Room numbers:	670 and 671
Check out:	10:30 a.m.

Receptionist Hello. Can I help you?
You Yes, I've booked …

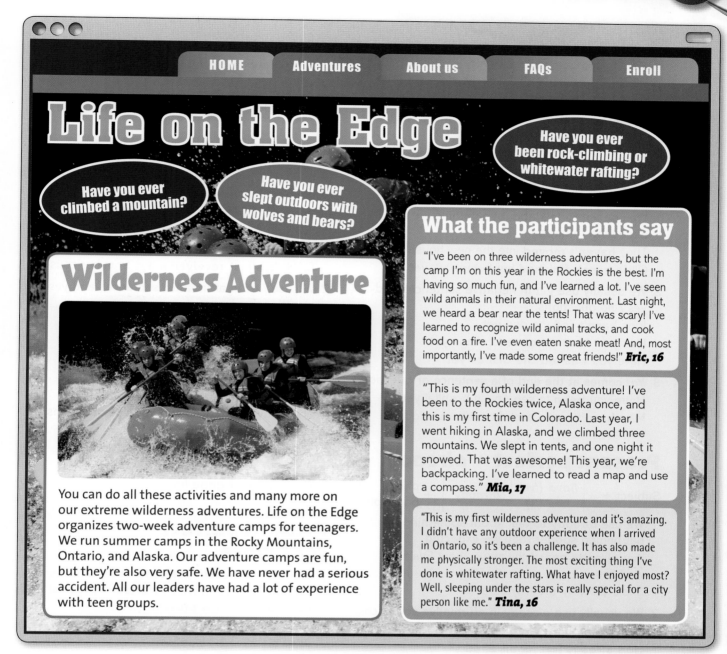

Life on the Edge

HOME | Adventures | About us | FAQs | Enroll

Have you ever climbed a mountain?

Have you ever slept outdoors with wolves and bears?

Have you ever been rock-climbing or whitewater rafting?

Wilderness Adventure

You can do all these activities and many more on our extreme wilderness adventures. Life on the Edge organizes two-week adventure camps for teenagers. We run summer camps in the Rocky Mountains, Ontario, and Alaska. Our adventure camps are fun, but they're also very safe. We have never had a serious accident. All our leaders have had a lot of experience with teen groups.

What the participants say

"I've been on three wilderness adventures, but the camp I'm on this year in the Rockies is the best. I'm having so much fun, and I've learned a lot. I've seen wild animals in their natural environment. Last night, we heard a bear near the tents! That was scary! I've learned to recognize wild animal tracks, and cook food on a fire. I've even eaten snake meat! And, most importantly, I've made some great friends!" *Eric, 16*

"This is my fourth wilderness adventure! I've been to the Rockies twice, Alaska once, and this is my first time in Colorado. Last year, I went hiking in Alaska, and we climbed three mountains. We slept in tents, and one night it snowed. That was awesome! This year, we're backpacking. I've learned to read a map and use a compass." *Mia, 17*

"This is my first wilderness adventure and it's amazing. I didn't have any outdoor experience when I arrived in Ontario, so it's been a challenge. It has also made me physically stronger. The most exciting thing I've done is whitewater rafting. What have I enjoyed most? Well, sleeping under the stars is really special for a city person like me." *Tina, 16*

Reading

1 Read the web page. Then match the teenagers with the camps they are at this year.

1 Eric   a Ontario
2 Mia   b The Rocky Mountains
3 Tina   c Colorado

2 Read the web page again. Correct the mistakes in the sentences.

Life on the Edge has only had a few serious accidents.

Life on the Edge has never had a serious accident.

1 Eric saw a bear near his tent last night.

2 Eric has eaten bear meat.

3 Mia has been on five wilderness adventures.

4 Last year, she camped in snow every night.

5 Tina has found the outdoor experience easy.

Writing

3 Imagine you are on a wilderness adventure. Write a comment to post on the Life on the Edge webpage. Think about the following:

• Which adventure are you doing?
• What activities have you done so far?
• What have you learned?
• Has anything scared you?
• What have you found exciting / challenging?

Present perfect + *yet*

Subject +	have not (*haven't*) has not (*hasn't*)	+ past participle +	yet

Have / Has	+ subject	+ past participle +	yet?

1 We use *yet* to talk about something we are expecting to happen.
They **haven't moved** into the new house **yet**.
Olivia **hasn't finished** her homework **yet**.

2 We usually use *yet* in negative sentences and *yes / no* questions.
John **hasn't fed** the dog **yet**.
Has your brother **started** college **yet**?
Have you **washed the dishes yet**?

3 *Yet* comes at the end of a sentence or question.
Have you **been** to see Ana in hospital **yet**?
Mike **hasn't come** back from his vacation **yet**.

Present perfect + *already*

Subject +	have (*'ve*) has (*'s*)	already	+ past participle

1 We use *already* to talk about something happening sooner than we expected.
I've already heard the news about Eva's wedding.
She's already met my parents.

2 We usually use *already* in affirmative sentences.
We've already invited them to the party.
He's already left for the airport.

3 *Already* comes between the auxiliary verb (*have / has*) and the past participle.
She's already paid for her soda.
We've already ordered the pizzas.

Present perfect + *just*

Subject +	have (*'ve*) has (*'s*)	just	+ past participle

Have / Has	+ subject	just	+ past participle?

1 We use *just* to talk about something that happened a very short time ago.
Our team **has just scored** a goal.
I've just passed my driving test.
We've just had lunch.
Sarah **has just received** a text from her cousin.

2 We use *just* in affirmative sentences and *yes / no* questions.
Emma **has just called**.
My parents **have just bought** a new car.
Has Dave **just left**?
Have you and Liam **just gotten** home?

3 *Just* comes before the past participle in affirmative sentences and *yes / no* questions.
Lily's just finished her exams.
We've just seen a brilliant movie.
Have Simon and Silvia **just had** lunch?
Has Katie **just gone** home?

Present perfect + *for / since*

1 We use the present perfect with *for* or *since* to describe an action which started in the past and continues until the present.
This video **has been** on the Internet **for** six months.
I've known Lucas **for** three years.
I've been a soccer fan **since** I was 15 years old.
They**'ve been** married **for** ten years.
She**'s been** my best friend **since** we started high school.
We've had a tablet **since** 2013.
My grandparents **have lived** in Recife **since** July.

2 We use *for* with a period of time. We use *for* to talk about the length of the period of time.

past	1	2	3	4	now

for four years

They**'ve worked** in St. Louis **for** four years.

3 We can use the following time expressions with *for*:

- *for* + number of minutes
  We've only been here **for five / ten minutes**.
- *for* + number of hours
  The baby's been asleep **for three / four hours.**
- *for* + number of days
  Jan's gone to the mountains **for ten days.**
- *for* + number of weeks
  I've been on vacation **for two / three weeks.**
- *for* + number of months
  We've had a pet dog **for eight / nine months.**
- *for* + number of years
  They've lived in Vancouver **for two / ten years.**
- *for* + expression
  I've been in Miami **for a while.**
  (*A short time, but we don't know exactly how long.*)
  I've been in Miami **for a long time.**
  (*A long time, but we don't know exactly how long.*)

4 We use *since* with a point in time. We use *since* to talk about the beginning of a period of time.

past Monday Tuesday Wednesday (now)

since Tuesday

We've **been** in Sydney **since** Tuesday.

5 We can use the following time expressions with *since*:

- *since* + time
  I've watched TV **since one / two o'clock.**
- *since* + yesterday
  I haven't seen Vilma **since yesterday.**
- *since* + day
  It's rained **since Monday.**
- *since* + month
  We've had a car **since June.**
- *since* + year
  They've studied English **since 2012 / 2013.**
- *since* + specific moment in time
  I've had this computer **since my birthday / Christmas.**
  Nobody has seen Tom **since he left.**

(**Student Book** p.65

Word list

Review the Vocabulary. Write your own study notes (or translation) for each word.

Internet activities
commenting on a picture / post _____
downloading music / videos _____
IMing (instant messaging) _____
playing an online game _____
posting a picture / comment _____
sending an e-mail _____
updating antivirus software / a program _____

_____
using a search engine _____
watching a video _____

Check it out!
cute _____
dragons _____
entertainment _____
fake _____
hilarious _____
(to have) hits _____
keep in touch with _____
mixture _____
no chance _____
playlist _____

Learn it, use it!
I'd like to do a tour of the city. _____
_____
What type of tour are you looking for?
_____
What do you recommend? _____
I think the best way to see the city is on foot / by bike / by bus. _____
_____
How much does the tour cost?
_____
The tickets are ... _____
How long does the tour take?
_____
It takes ... _____
Where does it start? _____
It starts at ... _____
What time does it start? _____
There are three tours. They start at ...
_____

(**Student Book** p.62, 60, 66, 64

Exercises

Vocabulary
Internet activities

1 Reorder the letters in the box to form Internet activities. Then complete the sentences.

> d e v i o s   f o w a r t e s   l a w d o n o d
> MI   ~~m o n c e m t~~   n e d s   n e i g e n
> s e g a m   s t o p

Do you usually _comment_ on your friends' pictures?

1 I _____ music to my MP3 player every week.

2 I don't often use e-mail. I usually _____ my friends.

3 I can only play online _____ on the weekend. It's my parents' rule.

4 We'll _____ our class pictures on the school website.

5 I always use a search _____ to do my homework.

6 It's important to update your antivirus _____ regularly.

7 How often do you _____ e-mails?

8 I love watching funny cat _____ online.

Grammar
Present perfect + *yet* and *already*

2 Complete the dialogues with questions and answers. Use the present perfect and *yet*.

A _Have you commented on Tina's posts yet?_
(you / comment / Tina's posts?)

B _No, I haven't read them yet._
(I / not read / them)

1
A _____
(you / send Alice an e-mail?)

B No, _____.
(I / not turn on / the computer)

2
A _____
(Pablo / have / his test scores?)

B No, _____.
(they / not post / them on the school website)

3
A _____
(Silvia / leave / for Europe?)

B No, _____.
(she / not receive / her passport)

4
A _____
(you / hear / from Joe?)

B No, _____.
(he / not call / us)

3 Answer the questions. Use the present perfect and *already*.

A When are you going to have lunch?

B _I've already had it._

1
A When are you going to make your bed?

B _____

2
A When are you going to take the math test?

B _____

3
A When is Bruno going to send those e-mails?

B _____

4
A When is Ana going to write that letter?

B _____

5
A When are your cousins going to leave?

B _____

6
A When are you and Mark going to see the movie?

B _____

4 Look at Ben's list of things to do and write sentences. Use the present perfect with *already* and *yet*.

> ### Things to do
> download the X-Men movie ✓
> watch Liz's video ✗
> post comments on blogs ✓
> check my e-mails ✗
> post some pictures on Facebook ✓
> play the new online game ✗
> visit my school's website ✓

He's already downloaded the X-Men movie.

1 _____

2 _____

3 _____

4 _____

5 _____

6 _____

W34

Student Book pp.62-63   **Extra practice** online

Present perfect + *just*

5 Complete the sentences with *just* and the present perfect form of the verbs in parentheses.

A Have you done your homework?
B Yes, I _ve just done_ it. (do)

1
A Are you hungry?
B No, I_____ lunch. (have)

2
A Is Belén at home?
B No, she_____ to the park. (go)

3
A Why is your sister so happy?
B She_____ her driving test. (pass)

4
A Why is your brother happy today?
B He_____ a new computer. (buy)

5
A Why are you so tired?
B We_____ a basketball game. (play)

Present perfect + *for / since*

6 Complete the sentences with *for* or *since*.

I've lived in here _for_ fifteen years.
1 She's been there _____ nine o'clock.
2 Juan's played in the team _____ last year.
3 I've had this cell phone _____ two years.
4 I haven't seen him _____ my birthday.
5 We haven't seen Tom _____ a long time.
6 They've worked here _____ 2007.

7 Write sentences with the present perfect and *for* or *since*. Use short forms.

He / live / in Spain / 2009.
He's lived in Spain since 2009.
1 They / be / students / here / September.
_____
2 We / study / Chinese / two years.
_____
3 Oscar / know / Amy / elementary school.
_____
4 You / be / online / three hours.
_____
5 My brother / have / his motorcycle / a month.
_____

Round-up

8 Complete the e-mail with *yet, already, just, for,* or *since*.

Hi, Aunt Lucia,
I'm sorry I haven't written **for** so long, but I've been very busy ¹_____ June doing exams. I've ²_____ finished the last one. Of course, I haven't had any results ³_____. Thanks for your invitation to stay with you. Mom's ⁴_____ found cheap flights online, but she hasn't bought the tickets ⁵_____. I'm excited because I haven't been to L.A. ⁶_____ ages. Jim can't come because he's ⁷_____ made plans for the summer. He's going to work as a lifeguard on the beach!
How about you? Have you done anything interesting ⁸_____ we last spoke? Have you changed your computer ⁹_____? I've ¹⁰_____ posted some new pictures of the family on Facebook. Check them out!
Love,
Donna

9 Read the e-mail again. Then correct the mistakes in the sentences.

Donna writes to Aunt Lucia every week.
Donna hasn't written to Aunt Lucia for a long time.
1 Donna hasn't finished her exams yet.
_____
2 She has already had her exam results.
_____
3 Her mom has just bought the airplane tickets.
_____
4 Donna has been to L.A. recently.
_____
5 Jim hasn't found a summer job yet.
_____
6 Donna is going to post some new pictures on Facebook.
_____

Student Book p.65 **Extra practice** online (W35)

6 Communication

At the visitor center

1 Complete the dialogue with the questions in the box.

> ~~Can I help you?~~   How long does it take?
> How much does it cost?   Where does it start?
> What time does it start?
> What do you recommend?

Assistant	Good morning. _Can I help you?_
Oliver	Yes, please. I'd like to do a tour of the city.
Assistant	There are a lot of different tours. There's a walking tour, a bike tour, and a bus tour.
Oliver	1 _____
Assistant	The walking tour is very good. And I think the best way to see the city is on foot.
Oliver	2 _____
Assistant	The tickets are $10.
Oliver	3 _____
Assistant	It takes three hours.
Oliver	4 _____
Assistant	It starts here at the visitor center.
Oliver	5 _____
Assistant	There are two tours every day – at 10 a.m. and 2 p.m.
Oliver	Thank you. That's great.

2 Match the questions and answers.

1 Can I help you?   _c_
2 How much does it cost?   __
3 Where does it start?   __
4 What do you recommend?   __
5 How long does it take?   __
6 What time does it start?   __

a About two hours.
b It starts from here.
c Yes, please.
d The open-top bus tour is very popular.
e At three o'clock every afternoon.
f Eight dollars for adults and four dollars for children.

3 Write the dialogue in the correct order.

__ You're welcome.
__ It costs $15.
_1_ I'd like to do a tour of the city.
__ $15. OK, and what time does it start?
__ The river tour – great. How much does it cost?
__ Sure. What type of tour would you like to do?
__ OK, thank you.
__ What do you recommend?
__ It starts at 11 a.m. in Canal Street.
__ The river tour is very nice.

4 Imagine that you are at the visitor center in New Orleans and you are asking for information about city tours.

NEW ORLEANS GHOST TOURS!

Discover the city with our ghost tour!
We visit the scariest places in town!

When:
Leaves every evening from Peter Street at 9 p.m.

Duration:
2 hours

Cost:
$20 for adults $10 for children

Assistant	_Good morning. Can I help you?_
Tourist	_Yes, please ..._
Assistant	_____
Tourist	_____
Assistant	_____
Tourist	_____
Assistant	_____
Tourist	_____
Assistant	_____
Tourist	_____
Assistant	_____
Tourist	_____
Assistant	_____
Tourist	_____

Student Book p.64   **Extra practice** online

Brain Power

It's 7 p.m. and 16-year-old Nadine Conner has been online for two hours. She has already read and sent IMs, posted comments on social networking sites, and read an update on a blog she is following. She has researched her science project, and she has just started writing it. Nadine has done all these things since she got home from school.

1 _c_
As Nadine's example shows, the Internet has become an important part of a twenty-first century teenager's life. Today's teens have never known a world without it. They have used the Internet since they were children. But is all this online activity good for their brains? Has it changed the way they read and remember?

2 __
The Internet has certainly changed the way people read. Teenagers find it difficult to concentrate on long texts because they read a lot of short texts online. They click on websites, scan texts quickly, and follow links to different webpages. Their minds follow a lot of different directions. This is a different skill from reading a book.

3 __
Search engines have made it less important for people to use their memories. Why remember something if you can find it in a few seconds on Google? However, even before the Internet, people didn't try to remember everything. There were libraries and reference books to store information. The Internet is just another type of external memory.

4 __
Teenagers are using their brains differently, but this doesn't mean that they are losing their brain power. They can't concentrate on long texts, but they can process small pieces of information extremely fast. They have developed new skills, and their brains are simply adapting to new technology.

Reading

1 Read the article. Then match the paragraphs with the topics.

a Memory
b Adaptation
c Modern Lifestyle
d Reading

2 Read the article again. Answer the questions.

How long has Nadine been on the Internet today?
She's been on the Internet since five o'clock / she got home from school.
1 What is she doing now?
2 What type of texts do teenagers read?

3 What type of texts do they find hard to read?
4 What has replaced reference books?
5 Why are teenagers' brains changing?

Writing

3 Write a paragraph about how you use the Internet. Think about the following:

- How often do you use the Internet each day?
- What do you use to go online – a cell phone, a tablet, etc.?
- What are your favorite online activities?
- What do you read online?
- How many times have you been online today?
- What websites have you visited this week?

7 Grammar rules

Past progressive
Affirmative and negative

Affirmative
I **was sleeping**.
You **were riding** your bike.
He / She **was watching** TV.
It **was raining**.
We **were talking** in class.
You **were waiting** for me.
They **were laughing**.

Subject + | *was / were* | + verb in *-ing* form

Negative	
Full form	**Short form**
I **was not sleeping**.	I **wasn't sleeping**.
You **were not riding** your bike.	You **weren't riding** your bike.
He / She **was not watching** TV.	He / She **wasn't watching** TV.
It **was not raining**.	It **wasn't raining**.
We **were not talking** in class.	We **weren't talking** in class.
You **were not waiting** for me.	You **weren't waiting** for me.
They **were not laughing**.	They **weren't laughing**.

Subject + | *was not (wasn't)* *were not (weren't)* | + verb in *-ing* form

1 We make the affirmative form of the past progressive with the subject + *was / were* + the main verb in the *-ing* form.
She **was riding** her bike on the sidewalk.

2 We make the negative form of the past progressive with the subject + *was / were* + *not* + the main verb in the *-ing* form.
She **was not skateboarding** on the sidewalk.

3 In spoken and written informal English, we usually use the negative short form.
We **weren't watching** videos online.
(= We **were not** watching videos online.)

4 We use the past progressive to talk about actions happening at a specific time in the past.
I **was waiting** for the bus at 4 p.m. this afternoon.

5 We sometimes use time expressions to show the length of time that passed:
  – *from … to …*
  Camila was playing tennis **from** 3 **to** 4 p.m.
  – *between … and …*
  We were reading **between** 7 **and** 7:30 a.m.

6 We often use the past progressive to describe a scene, especially when telling a story.
The sun **was shining** and the birds **were singing**.

yes / no questions and short answers

yes / no questions
Was I **sleeping**?
Were you **riding** your bike?
Was he / she **watching** TV?
Was it **raining**?
Were we **talking** in class?
Were you **waiting** for me?
Were they **laughing**?

Was / Were | + subject + | verb in *-ing* form?

Short answers	
Affirmative	**Negative**
Yes, you **were**.	No, you **weren't**.
Yes, I **was**.	No, I **wasn't**.
Yes, he / she **was**.	No, he / she **wasn't**.
Yes, it **was**.	No, it **wasn't**.
Yes, you **were**.	No, you **weren't**.
Yes, we **were**.	No, we **weren't**.
Yes, they **were**.	No, they **weren't**.

Yes, / *No,* | + subject + | *was / were.* / *wasn't / weren't.*

1 We make *yes / no* questions in the past progressive with *Was / Were* + subject + the main verb in the *-ing* form.
Was she **cooking** dinner?

2 We make affirmative short answers for the past progressive with *Yes,* + subject + *was / were*. We make negative short answers for the past progressive with *No,* + subject + *wasn't / weren't*.
Was she **cooking** dinner?
Yes, she **was**. / **No,** she **wasn't**.

while

1 We also use the past progressive to talk about two longer actions happening at the same time.
Dad **was sleeping** while we **were playing**.
We **were making** pizza while Steve **was doing** the shopping.

2 We use *while* to connect the two actions happening at the same time.
Emily **was listening** to her MP3 player **while** her younger brother **was playing** on his computer.

3 *While* can go between the two actions or at the beginning of the sentence. If *While* is at the beginning of a sentence, there is a comma before the second action / between the two actions.
The teacher was writing on the whiteboard **while** the students were reading.
While the teacher was writing on the whiteboard, the students were reading.

Past progressive and simple past + *when / while*

1 We also use the past progressive to talk about a longer action that happened in the past and that was interrupted by a shorter action.
I **was using** the computer when Dad called me.

Dad called me
↓
Past ─────────────────→ Now
I was using the computer

2 We can connect the short and longer actions with *when* or *while*.
They **were walking** down the street **when** they **saw** an accident.
The teacher **came** into class **while** we **were making** a lot of noise.

3 *When* can come before the shorter action in the simple past or longer action in the past progressive.
Sarah was climbing **when** she fell.
When Sarah was climbing, she fell.

4 *While* must always come before the longer action in the past progressive.
While they were watching a video, someone burglarized the house.
NOT ~~While someone burglarized the house, they were watching a video.~~

(**Student Book** pp.75, 77

Word list

Review the Vocabulary. Write your own study notes (or translation) for each word.

Crime
burglary / burglarize a house _____
kidnapping / kidnap someone _____
mugging / mug someone _____
murder / murder someone _____
pickpocketing / pick someone's pocket _____
robbery / rob a bank _____
shoplifting / shoplift _____
vandalism / vandalize a building _____

Criminals
burglar _____
kidnapper _____
mugger _____
murderer _____
pickpocket _____
robber _____
shoplifter _____
vandal _____

Check it out!
arrested _____
beggar / to beg _____
descendants _____
lock _____
nightmare _____
punishment _____
sentence / to sentence _____
sidewalk _____
suspicious _____
threatening _____

Learn it, use it!
Can I help you? _____
I want to report a crime. _____
What happened? _____
A boy / girl stole my cell phone. _____
Where / When did it happen? _____
It happened in Lincoln Park / this afternoon. _____
_____
What was he / were they wearing? _____
He was wearing … / They were wearing … _____
_____

(**Student Book** pp.74, 72, 78, 76

Vocabulary
Crime

1 Complete the crime verbs.

Take money from someone's jacket or bag in the street. p<u>ickpocket</u>

1 Enter a house and steal things. b_____
2 Attack and steal money from a bank. r_____
3 Push and hit someone in the street and take the person's bag. m_____
4 Steal things from a store. s_____
5 Kill someone. m_____
6 Break public property. v_____
7 Take a person and ask for money in exchange. k_____

2 Change the underlined words for a word from the box.

| burglar kidnapped mugger |
| murderer pickpockets robbers |
| shoplifter stolen vandals |

A <u>person</u> got into our house and stole the TV. <u>burglar</u>

1 Two <u>girls</u> broke the windows of the bus station waiting room. _____
2 The group <u>took</u> the reporter and demanded $1 million in exchange. _____
3 The woman died in hospital. Police identified the <u>man</u> from his fingerprints on the gun. _____
4 A <u>woman</u> took an MP3 player and a tablet from the store. Security guards saw it on a video. _____
5 <u>Street thieves</u> are a serious problem in many tourist areas of big cities. _____
6 Three <u>men</u> ran into the bank and stole $300,000. _____
7 Someone has <u>taken</u> my car! _____
8 A <u>young man</u> hit me and pushed me to the ground. Then he took my cell phone and money. _____

Grammar
Past progressive
Affirmative and negative

3 Complete the past progressive sentences with the affirmative and negative form of the verbs in parentheses.

You <u>weren't using</u> a search engine to do your homework! You <u>were watching</u> an online video. (not use / watch)

1 I _____ a computer game at midnight. I _____. (not play / sleep)
2 Blanca _____ her mom all afternoon. She _____ a video with her friends. (not help / make)
3 That man _____ breakfast at home at 9 a.m. He _____ a bank. (not have / rob)
4 Alan and Ted _____ their grandparents yesterday. They _____ with friends. (not visit / surf)
5 We _____ at 7 p.m. We _____ dinner. (not study / cook)

yes / no questions and short answers

4 Complete the dialogue with the correct past progressive form of the verbs in parentheses.

Officer <u>Were you standing</u> outside Mr. Penn's house at 11:30 last night? (you / stand)
Man Yes, <u>I was</u> _____.
Officer [1]_____ to a young man? (you / talk)
Man Yes, [2]_____ to my brother, Carl. (I / talk)
Officer [3]_____ for someone? (you / wait)
Man Yes, [4]_____ for a friend. (we / wait)
Officer [5]_____ a dark sweater and jeans? (he / wear)
Man Yes, [6]_____.
Officer [7]_____ a house? (he / burglarize)
Man No, [8]_____. [9]_____ a friend. (he / visit)
Officer At eleven thirty at night?

Student Book pp.74-75 **Extra practice** online

while

5 Write sentences with the past progressive and *while*.

Mary / cry / we / watch movie.
Mary was crying while we were watching the movie.

1 We / set the table / my dad / cook dinner.

_____

_____

2 A man / rob the bank / another man / wait in a car.

_____

_____

3 Sara / talk / on her cell phone / I / try to call her.

_____

_____

4 My brother / not do / anything / I / helping with the housework.

_____

_____

5 Tim and Rob / play / loud music / I / try to study.

_____

_____

Past progressive and simple past + when / while

6 Complete the sentences with *when* or *while*.

We were working <u>while</u> you were sleeping.

1 I was having a shower _____ she arrived.
2 _____ you were studying, I was skateboarding.
3 I was walking home _____ I lost my keys.
4 Were you playing soccer _____ Thomas broke the window?
5 Some boys were vandalizing the seats _____ I was riding on the bus!

7 Choose the correct answers.

A Where were you when the man (mugged) / was mugging Dave? ¹Did you see / Were you seeing the accident?
B No ²I wasn't / I didn't. I ³was having / had dinner when it ⁴happened / was happening. I ⁵was going / went to the hospital immediately when I ⁶heard / was hearing the news. Dave ⁷was talking / talked to a doctor when I ⁸arrived / was arriving.
A ⁹Did you speak / Were you speaking to him?
B Yes, ¹⁰I did / I was. Luckily, Dave was fine.

Round-up

8 Read the dialogue. Choose the correct answers.

Paul Have you ever seen a crime, Luke?
Luke Yes, last year. Matt and I left / (were leaving) a store. An old lady ¹walked / was walking in front of us and she ²carried / was carrying a bag. We ³talked / were talking about music ⁴while / when I saw a big, black motorcycle. Two men ⁵rode / were riding it, and they ⁶wore / were wearing black clothes and dark glasses.
Paul What happened?
Luke While the lady ⁷got / was getting something out of her bag, the motorcycle ⁸came / was coming towards her along the street. ⁹While / When it got next to her, the passenger ¹⁰took / was taking her bag and she ¹¹fell / was falling down.
Paul So what did you do?
Luke While Matt ¹²helped / was helping the lady, I ran into the street with my cell phone. ¹³While / When the thieves were riding away, I ¹⁴took / was taking a picture of the motorcycle.
Paul Did you get the registration number?
Luke Yes, I did. The three of us ¹⁵went / were going to the police station and we ¹⁶reported / were reporting the theft.

9 Read the dialogue again. Correct the sentences.

Luke saw a crime when he was walking home.
Luke saw a crime when he was leaving a store.

1 Luke and Matt were listening to music.

_____

2 The lady was talking on her cell phone while the motorcycle was coming towards her.

_____

3 The woman shouted when the motorcyclist took her bag.

_____

4 Luke ran after the thieves while Matt was helping the lady.

_____

At the police station

1 Complete the dialogue with the phrases in the box.

> ~~Can I help you?~~   He was wearing
> It happened at around 8:30   stole
> There was about $25   took my wallet
> walked up to me

Officer	_Can I help you?_
Jim	Yes, I want to report a crime.
Officer	What happened?
Jim	A boy [1]_____ my wallet.
Officer	Where did it happen?
Jim	In West Street. I was going home from basketball practice when a boy [2]_____.
Officer	And then what happened?
Jim	He had a knife and he [3]_____. Then he ran away.
Officer	What time did this happen?
Jim	[4]_____ last night.
Officer	How much money was in your wallet?
Jim	[5]_____ and my bank card.
Officer	What did the boy look like?
Jim	He was about 16 or 17. [6]_____ jeans and a black jacket.

2 Match the questions and answers.

1 Can I help you? ___b___
2 What happened? ___
3 What did he look like? ___
4 What time did this happen? ___
5 Where did it happen? ___

a He was about 18, and he was wearing jeans and a sweater.
b Yes. I want to report a crime.
c At about 4:30.
d In the supermarket parking lot. The woman was getting into her car.
e A man mugged a woman and he stole her bag.

3 Write the questions for the answers.

Officer	_Can I help you?_
Girl	Yes, I want to report a crime.
Officer	_____
Girl	A woman stole my cell phone.
Officer	_____
Girl	On the number 16 bus to the station.
Officer	_____
Girl	She took my cell phone out of my purse and got off the bus in Kent Street.
Officer	_____
Girl	It was about 8:30 this morning.
Officer	_____
Girl	She was about 16. She was wearing black pants and a T-shirt.

4 You saw a crime and you are reporting it. Use the information and the picture to write the dialogue with the police officer.

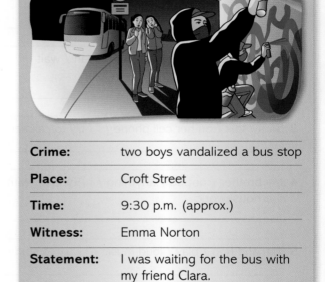

Crime:	two boys vandalized a bus stop
Place:	Croft Street
Time:	9:30 p.m. (approx.)
Witness:	Emma Norton
Statement:	I was waiting for the bus with my friend Clara.

Officer	Can I help you?
You	_Yes, I want to report a crime._
Officer	_____
You	_____
Officer	_____
You	_____
Officer	_____
You	_____
Officer	_____
You	_____

Student Book p.76 **Extra practice** online

HOW TO BE STREET SMART

Stay safe on the streets by following a few simple rules.

Did you know that teenagers are two times more likely than other people to be victims of street crime? Many people are just unlucky, but others take risks. Read two victims' stories. What did Justin and Ava do wrong?

Sixteen-year-old Justin Bolton was walking home in the dark one evening. It was raining and he didn't have a coat, so he decided to take a shorter route across the park. Justin was listening to music on his MP3 player and he didn't hear two boys following him.

Suddenly, the boys attacked him from behind and pushed him to the ground. They stole his wallet, MP3 player, and cell phone, and then they ran away.

Fifteen-year-old Ava Parks was taking the bus home when a girl and boy got on. Ava put her bag on the floor to let the girl sit down. The girl thanked her and they started talking. But while Ava and the girl were chatting, the boy stole Ava's wallet from her bag. The two pickpockets were working together. They both got off at the next stop. When she got home, Ava discovered that her wallet was not in her bag.

Five Streetwise Rules
1 Don't walk alone in quiet places, especially at night. Muggers prefer dark, empty places.
2 Don't put your bag or coat out of your sight.
3 Keep the volume of your MP3 player low, so you can hear cars and people.
4 Don't be paranoid, but be careful of friendly strangers. Some pickpockets work in pairs.
5 If you go to an unfamiliar place, it's better to go with a friend or two.

Reading

1 Read the article. What type of street crimes were Justin and Ava victims of?

2 Read the article again. Answer the questions.

Why did Justin take a shorter route home?

Because it was raining and he didn't have a coat.

1 Why didn't Justin hear the two boys?
2 What did the boys steal?
3 Why did Ava put her bag on the floor?
4 What did the boy steal?
5 What did Ava do wrong?
6 Why should you be careful of friendly strangers?
7 What should you do if you go to an unfamiliar place?

Writing

3 Look at the picture. Answer the questions.

What was the man doing when the picture was taken? Is car theft a problem in your town?

4 Imagine you took the picture. Answer the questions. Then use your answers to write a story. Think about the following:

• Where and when did it happen?
• What were you doing when you took the picture?
• What did the man do?
• What happened in the end?

Relative pronouns:
who / which / that

People
The book is about an astronaut. He travels to Mars. The book is about an astronaut **who / that** travels to Mars.
Einstein was a scientist. He developed the theory of relativity. Einstein was a scientist **who / that** developed the theory of relativity.

Things
We have a cat. It watches TV. We have a cat **which / that** watches TV.
This is the bridge. It connects Manhattan and Brooklyn in New York City. This is the bridge **which / that** connects Manhattan and Brooklyn in New York City.
That is a snake. It can kill you. That is a snake **which / that** can kill you.

1 Relative clauses give important information about a noun. Relative clauses are introduced by relative pronouns. We use the relative pronouns *who / that* to avoid repeating a name or pronoun.

Emma's the new student. She started college last week.
Emma's the new student **who / that** started college last week.

Marie Curie was a scientist. She discovered the element radium.
Marie Curie was the scientist **who / that** discovered the element radium.

This is my new tablet. I bought it from an online store.
This is my new tablet **which / that** I bought from an online store.

Evolution is a theory. Darwin described it.
Evolution is a theory **which / that** Darwin described.

2 We use the relative pronoun *who* for people.

Newton was the scientist **who** described the laws of gravity.
H.G. Wells wrote about a scientist **who** built a time machine.
Mark Twain is the writer **who** created Huckleberry Finn.
We met a man **who** sailed around the world.
Have you met the people **who** live next door?

3 We use the relative pronoun *which* with animals and objects.
The birds **which** you have just seen come from South America.
This is the camera **which** Mo Li used to take pictures on her vacations.
Radium is an element **which** is radioactive.
Is that the book **which** you got from the library?

4 We use the relative pronoun *that* with people, animals, and objects. We usually use *that* in informal spoken and written English.
Harry is the man **that** we met yesterday.
That is the café **that** is open until 10 p.m.
These are the cookies **that** my mom made.
Is Daniel the player **that** scored the most goals last season?

The infinitive of purpose

- We often use an infinitive to talk about a person's purpose – why he or she does something.

I went into the store **to buy** clothes.
NOT ~~I went into the store for buying clothes.~~
NOT ~~I went into the store for to buy clothes.~~

She's studying medicine **to become** a doctor.
NOT ~~She's studying medicine for becoming a doctor.~~
NOT ~~She's studying medicine for to become a doctor.~~

I got up early **to study** for the math test.
NOT ~~I got up early for studying for the math test.~~
NOT ~~I got up early for to study for the math test.~~

She bought some burgers **to cook** on the barbecue.
NOT ~~She bought some burgers for cooking on the barbecue.~~
NOT ~~She bought some burgers for to cook on the barbecue.~~

Which one ...? / Which ones ...?

1 We use *one* instead of a singular noun.
a small bottle → a small **one**
a large orange → a large **one**

2 We use *ones* instead of a plural noun.
small bottles → small **ones**
large oranges → large **ones**

3 We can use *Which one ...? / Which ones ...?* as object pronouns in the question form to refer to people or objects. We use them:
  – when the choice is limited.
    There's some apple juice and some water.
    Which one would you like?

    There are two bags on the chair.
    Which one is yours?

  – to avoid repetition.
    A Can I have some apples?
    B **Which ones?** The red ones or the green ones?

    A I like those jeans.
    B **Which ones?** The black ones or the blue ones?

(**Student Book** p.85

Review the Vocabulary. Write your own study notes (or translation) for each word.

Human achievement – nouns
architect ___
artist ___
composer ___
explorer ___
inventor ___
musician ___
politician ___
scientist ___
writer ___

Human achievement – verbs
build ___
compose music ___
debate ___
design ___
discover ___
draw ___
explore ___
invent ___
negotiate ___
paint ___
play music ___
travel ___
write ___

Check it out!
controversial ___
elements ___
evidence ___
exposure ___
gave up ___
inheritance ___
offspring ___
reveal ___
species ___
treat ___

Learn it, use it!
What's this / are these? ___
It's a / an ... . / They're ... . ___
What's it for? ___
It's for (feeding your dog). / You use it to (feed your dog).
___
___
What are they for? ___
They're for (charging your cell phone). / You use them to (walk on icy roads). ___
___

(**Student Book** pp.74, 72, 78, 76

Vocabulary
Human achievement

1 Complete the names of the professions.

scientist

1 c_____

2 w_____

3 e_____

4 a_____

5 a_____

6 p_____

7 m_____

2 Write the professions.

Roald Amundsen reached the South Pole in 1911. explorer
1 J.K. Rowling created the character Harry Potter. _____
2 Marie Curie discovered polonium and radium. _____
3 Josephine Cochrane created a mechanical dishwasher in 1886. _____
4 Salvador Dali painted in Spain in the 20th century. _____
5 Antonio Vivaldi wrote the violin concertos *The Four Seasons*. _____
6 Franklin Roosevelt was president of the U.S. from 1933 to 1945. _____

Grammar
Relative pronouns: *who / which / that*

3 Rewrite the sentences with *who* or *which*.

Shakespeare was an English writer. He lived in the 16th century.
Shakespeare was an English writer who lived in the 16th century.

1 *Guernica* is a famous painting. It is in the Reina Sofia Museum in Madrid.
_____
_____

2 Zhou Man was a Chinese explorer. He traveled around Asia and Africa in the 13th century.
_____
_____

3 The Ford Model T was a car. It was very popular in the 1920s.
_____
_____

4 Ernest Hemingway was a writer. He came from the U.S.
_____
_____

5 Amelia Earhart was a pilot. She was the first woman to fly solo across the Atlantic Ocean.
_____
_____

4 Match the sentence halves. Then write sentences with *that*.

1 Soccer is a game _____c_____
Soccer is a game that millions of people around the world watch.

2 Uranium is an element ___
_____

3 She's a teacher ___
_____

4 It's a website ___
_____

5 *The Hunger Games* is a movie ___
_____

6 A lawyer is someone ___
_____

a defends people in a court of law.
b has a lot of interesting information.
c millions of people around the world watch.
d is very heavy.
e always gives homework.
f is very exciting.

Student Book pp.82–83 **Extra practice** online

The infinitive of purpose

5 Ella organized a barbecue yesterday. Here is a list of the things she did. Write sentences to explain why she did them.

Things to do:

Get up early – clean the yard ✔

Call Tara and Kim – ask them for help ✔

Go to the store – buy hamburgers and drinks ✔

Buy some candles – put on the tables ✔

Make some ice – put in the drinks ✔

Clean the barbecue – cook the hamburgers ✔

She got up early to clean the yard.

1 _____
2 _____
3 _____
4 _____
5 _____

Which one ...? / Which ones ...?

6 Which word does *one / ones* replace? Read the sentences and circle the correct answers.

There are some (DVDs) on the table.
Which ones are yours?

1 Which of those boys is your cousin?
The one with dark hair.

2 Put those books in the bag over there.
Which ones?

3 The sneakers in this store are cool.
Which ones do you prefer?

4 Which of those men is your tennis coach?
The one with a tattoo on his arm.

5 The songs on this CD are great!
Which one is your favorite?

6 This museum has some cool paintings.
I like the ones in this room best.

Round-up

7 Read the ad. Then complete it with *who*, *which*, or the infinitive form of the verbs in the box.

damage   find   lie   pick
stimulate   stop   turn   work

Welcome to Gizmos.com

Are you a person who _____ likes giving unique and original gifts? If you're looking for great gift ideas [1] _____ are fun and different, then Gizmos.com is the website for you!

The **Bed of Nails** is a perfect gift for someone [2] _____ has a busy life. It's a mat [3] _____ has 6,000 plastic spikes. It's perfect for people [4] _____ suffer from insomnia! It is large enough for an adult [5] _____ on. The spikes are hard enough [6] _____ your circulation, but not pointed enough [7] _____ your skin.

Price: $59
Ideal for: adults [8] _____ suffer from stress or who travel a lot.

Do you know anyone [9] _____ loves working with their hands? **The Magnetic Pick-up Tool** is useful for someone [10] _____ spends their free time repairing or making things. You use it [11] _____ up small metal objects. You don't have to get down on your knees [12] _____ nails or screws; the Magnetic Pick-up Tool will find them for you!

Price: $8.50
Ideal for: adults and teenagers [13] _____ drop things everywhere!

Do you know anyone [14] _____ doesn't exercise? **The Shape Up Alarm Clock** is the ideal gift! It is the perfect way [15] _____ out in the morning! You can't press a button [16] _____ off the alarm. There isn't one! You have to lift the clock thirty times [17] _____ it.

Price: $14.15
Ideal for: lazy adults and teenagers [18] _____ need to get more exercise!

8 Read the ad again. Complete the questions with *one* or *ones*. Then answer the questions or write answers that are true for you.

Which *one* _____ is the most expensive?
The Bed of Nails.

1 Which _____ are for teenagers?
2 Which _____ is only for adults?
3 Which _____ is the most unusual?
4 Which _____ would you like to get as a gift?
5 Which _____ would you choose for a family member or friend? Why?

Discussing what things are for

1 Complete the dialogues with the phrases in the box.

> for telling   They're for   to help
> What are these?   What are they for?
> What's it for?   What's this?   ~~What's this gadget?~~

1
A <u>What's this gadget?</u>
B It's an indoor weather station.
A ¹ _____
B It's ² _____ you the temperature outside. You don't have to go outside to find out how cold it is.

2
A ³ _____
B It's a pedometer.
A What's it for?
B It's for counting your running steps when you go jogging. You attach it to your belt. You use it ⁴ _____ you get fit.

3
A ⁵ _____
B They're microwaveable slippers.
A ⁶ _____
B ⁷ _____ keeping your feet warm. You put them in the microwave for two minutes and then you wear them.

2 Match the questions and answers.

1 What's this?   <u>a</u>
2 What's it for?   ___
3 What are these?   ___
4 What are they for?   ___

a It's a solar charging station.
b They're for making ice cubes.
c They're ice cube bags.
d You use it to charge your cell phone when you're outdoors.

3 Write the dialogues in the correct order.

1
___ It's for making popcorn at home.
___ It's a popcorn machine.
_1_ What's that?
___ I want one of those!
___ What's it for?

2
___ They're reading glasses.
___ What are those?
___ They're for reading in bed.
___ What are they for?
___ They're stupid! I have a lamp by my bed for reading when it's dark!

4 Write dialogues with the information in the product descriptions.

Product description
Name: CD / DVD repair kit
Use: cleans and repairs damaged DVDs and CDs
Price: $19.50

A What's that?
B ¹ _____
A What's it for?
B ² _____
A How much is it?
B ³ _____

Product description
Name: sleep phones
Use: listen to music
Price: $34

A ⁴ _____
B ⁵ _____
A ⁶ _____
B ⁷ _____
A ⁸ _____
B ⁹ _____

Student Book p.84   **Extra practice** online

The Door to Knowledge

Braille is a special writing system for people who cannot see. Its inventor was a Frenchman named Louis Braille, who was blind and became a teacher. His invention made it possible for blind people to read and write, and to communicate independently. Today, nearly every country in the world uses Braille.

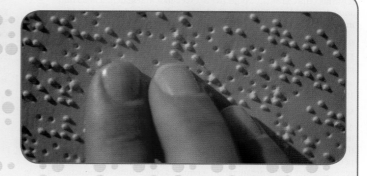

Louis Braille was born in 1809 in a small village near Paris. At the age of 3, he had an accident while he was playing in his father's workshop, and he became blind. In 1819, he went to live and study at the National Institute for Blind People in Paris. But Louis was not happy with his education. He said, "If my eyes won't tell me about men and events and ideas, I must find another way."

At the age of 15, Louis invented the writing system which is named after him. But he didn't stop there! In 1837, he added symbols for math and music. Louis created his code in 1824, but it didn't become popular until after his death. Braille began to spread worldwide in 1868 when a British organization called the Royal Institute for the Blind started using it.

Braille characters are rectangular cells with small dots that blind people can feel with their fingers. Each cell is different and represents a letter, a number, or a punctuation mark. Braille books have very big pages because the cells use a lot of space. These days, there are special braille keyboards which allow blind people to use computers and the Internet.

In his village there is a memorial sign which reads: "His invention opened the door to knowledge for all those who cannot see." Louis Braille was a great and inspirational man who changed the lives of blind people all over the world.

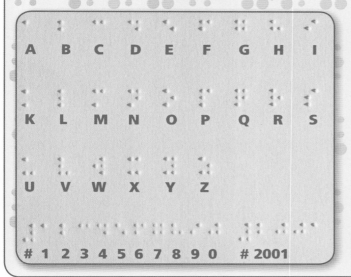

Reading

1 Read the article. What is Braille? Check (✓) the correct answer.

a   a special computer language for blind people

b   a spoken language for people who cannot see

c   a code which people read with their fingers

2 Read the article again. Answer the questions.

Who was Louis Braille?

<u>He was the inventor of a writing system for</u>
<u>blind people.</u>

1   When was he born?

_____

2   Why did he go to a special school in Paris?

_____

3   Why did Louis start to develop his writing system?

_____

4   When did his system become popular?

_____

5   How do people read Braille?

_____

Writing

3 Write a short biography about an important person in the past. Think about the following.

• When and where was he / she born?

• What was his / her profession?

• When and why did he / she become famous?

• What other things was he / she famous for?

OXFORD
UNIVERSITY PRESS

Great Clarendon Street, Oxford, OX2 6DP, United Kingdom

Oxford University Press is a department of the University of Oxford.
It furthers the University's objective of excellence in research, scholarship,
and education by publishing worldwide. Oxford is a registered trade
mark of Oxford University Press in the UK and in certain other countries

ISBN: 978 0 19 446363 8   Student Book and Workbook
ISBN: 978 0 19 446381 2   Student's Access Card
ISBN: 978 0 19 446372 0   Pack
Printed in China

This book is printed on paper from certified and well-managed sources

ACKNOWLEDGEMENTS

Cover images reproduced with permission from: Alamy (cable car/Nikreates); Getty
(mechanics/Echo), (selfie/sturti), (The Colour Run/Peter Muhly); Shutterstock
(the Atlantic road/Igor Plotnikov).

Illustrations by: John Batten/Beehive Illustration Agency pp.4 (all), 5 (ex 16), 12,
14, 27 (all), 46, 78 (map), 82, 89 (all), W6 (all), W12 (ex 1), W24, W42; Paul Daviz
pp.6, 8, 19, 26, 40, 51, 77, 79, W5, W17, W23, W41, W46; Mark Draisey pp.20,
62, 69 (all), 85, W2, W10, W29, W35, W40, W44; Mark Duffin pp.5 (ex 12,
ex 14), 13 (signs), 17, 66 (animal icons), 96 (cells diagrams), W48 (slippers,
glasses); Simon Gurr p.78; Alberto Hoyos pp.35, 54, 65, 74, 105, W12 (ex 4).

*The publisher would like to thank the following for their permission to reproduce
photographs*: Alamy pp.16 (pink Colour Run/Darren Cool), 18 (boy doing
laundry), 24 (plotting course/John Warburton-Lee Photograph), 28 (Nina
and Maggie), 30 (sound engineer/John Kershaw, biologist/Simon Littlejohn,
stuntman), 31 (Asian boy/Ian Shaw, girl, blonde boy), 32 (all), 34 (check-in/
Caro), 36 (hairdressers/Caro, vet), 42 (B Christopher), 43 (Fresh Start Images),
44 (tall son), 48 (Manhattan/Stuwdamdorp), 52 (wakeboarding/Oleksiy
Maksymenko, coasteering/The Photolibrary Wales), 58 (logo/Steven May,
canoeing, girl on unicycle/Aberystwyth), 60 (dog/Jan de Wit), 64 (tourist booth/
Niels van Kampenhout, Duck Tour/Matthew Johnston, helicopter/Radharc
Images), 66 (boy and girl in class), 70 (teens outside, girl on bed/Redsnapper,
teens in classroom), 72 (vandalised bicycle/Julian Money-Kyrle, red bicycle
frame), 76 (Mikael Karlsson), 78 (Kevin Rudd/Justin Qian), 84 (ice grips/Peter
Jordan, charger/David Burton, cat watching tv/Roger Bamber), 87 (e-reader/
Krys Bailey, red case/Hugh Threlfall, tablet in green case/Studiomode),
96 (Campylobacter Jejuni/Medical-on-Line, Clostridium Perfrigens/BSIP SA,
E-Coli, Salmonella, Staphylococcus Aureus/Medical-on-Line), 98 (Cuban
refugees/Everett Collection Historical), 101 (boy writing, basketball team/
B. Leighty/Photri Images, science experiment), W7 (Radharc Images), W11,
W13 (hostel/Archimage), W18 (security/Jim West), W25 (group of teens), W30,
W34, W36 (Mo Peerbacus), W43 mugging/Bubbles Photolibrary, car thief/
Andrew Butterton), W45, W47 (Shakti mat, screwdriver/Eye Ubiquitous),
W48 (pedometer/Bubbles Photolibrary, popcorn machine/Nik Taylor); Corbis
pp.7 (Hitchcock/Cat's Collection), 9 (Chris Trotman/PCN), 10 (girls looking at
phone/Sebastian Pfuetze, Stella, Tom, Sofia), 18 (trash bag), 23, 24 (crew), 33,
48 (voting booths/Steven Clevenger), 52 (kitesurfing/David Pu'u), 56 (Mika),
72 (NYC cycling/Tobbe), 80 (x-ray/Bettmann, Marie Curie/Bettmann),
86 (Charles Darwin/Adoc-photos, tortoise/Tui De Roy/Minden Pictures,
cartoon/The Gallery Collection), 90 (Martin Luther King/Bob Adelman,
Little Rock Nine/Bettmann, march/Flip Schulke, water fountain/Bettmann),
96 (dirty dishes/Foodfolio), 98 (Sitting Bull, slave ship/Heritage Images),
101 (science prize winners/Jon Feingersh), 102 (John Steinbeck/Bettmann,
Mark Twain/Bettmann), 103 (*Little Women*/Bettmann, *Grapes of Wrath*/John
Springer Collection), W23 (vertical farm/David McLain, Professor Folkard
Asch and model of his rice highrise/Bernd Weissbrod), W25 (teen boy/Kevin
Dodge), W28 (HagePhoto/Cultura), W49 (braille alphabet/Stefan Sollfors);
Getty Images pp.22, 24 (yacht/Tim Platt), 34 (security/Education Images/
UIG), 58 (Duke of Edinburgh/Michael Ochs Archives), 66 (girl on sofa, boy on
bus), 84 (man in hat), 102 (Ernest Hemingway/PhotoQuest), W29 (Sue Flood),
W48 (weather station); Kobal p.103 (*Huckleberry Finn*/MGM); Oxford University
Press pp.7 (make-up), 44 (Space Station), 52 (surfing), 60 (microphone), 72 (New
York City/Keith Levit), W18 (check-in), W31, W49 (fingers reading braille);

Rex Features pp.16 (top *Colour Run*/Mark Brake/Newspix), 84 (animal fe
Peter Brooker, alarm clock/Bournemouth News), 102 (Louisa May Alcot
Everett), W47 (yoga class/Markku Ulander); Shutterstock pp.10 (hand h
phone), 10 (Washington DC/Lissandra Melo), 11 (Rocky statue, teen boy),
16 (background), 18 (dishes), 24 (coral background), 28 (wooden background,
stationery items), 30 (pixel people/quinky), 36 (mechanic, chefs, journalist,
garden centre), 38 (all), 44 (x-ray, mosquito), 48 (couple), 52 (background),
58 (background), 60 (teen boy, teen girl, wood background), 63, 66 (binary
code background), 78 (background), 84 (multi-adaptor), 86 (background),
87 (smartphone, old mobile phone, yellow sock), 96 (washing hands, different
types of bacteria, background), 98 (Chinatown, map background), 100 (all),
102 (open book, e-reader, books background, books illustration), 103 (*Farewell
to Arms*/Moviestore Collection), W13 (Melbourne), W17, W19, W37 (both).